Thinking Critically

A Concise Guide

Thinking Critically
A Concise Guide

John Chaffee, Ph.D.

*Director, Center for Critical
Thinking and Language Learning,
LaGuardia College,
City University of New York*

HOUGHTON MIFFLIN COMPANY   BOSTON   NEW YORK

For Jessie and Joshua

Senior sponsoring editor: Suzanne Phelps Weir
Senior development editor: Sarah Helyar Smith
Senior project editor: Carol Newman
Editorial assistant: Marlowe Shaeffer
Senior production/design coordinator: Jill Haber
Senior manufacturing coordinator: Priscilla Bailey
Marketing manager: Cindy Graff Cohen

Cover illustration: © Andy Powell

(Acknowledgments continue on page 321.)

Printed in the U.S.A.

Library of Congress Catalog Card Number: 2003103117
ISBN: 0-618-34882-4

3456789-QWF-10 09 08 07 06

C O N T E N T S

PREFACE

Critical thinking is the cornerstone of higher education, the hallmark of an educated person, and teaching a course in critical thinking is one of the most inspiring and rewarding experiences that a teacher can have. Because the thinking process is such an integral part of who we are as people, the prospect of expanding students' thinking implies expanding who they are as human beings — the perspective from which they view the world, the concepts and values they use to guide their choices, and the impact they have on the world as a result of those choices. Teaching persons to become critical thinkers does not mean simply equipping them with certain intellectual tools; it involves their personal transformation and its commensurate impact on the quality of their lives and those around them. This is truly education at its most inspiring!

Thinking Critically: A Concise Guide is based on *Thinking Critically*, Seventh Edition, and is designed to focus specifically on the core critical thinking abilities needed for academic study and career success. Whereas *Thinking Critically*, Seventh Edition, is a comprehensive introduction to the thinking and language processes and is most often used for a three-credit course devoted mainly to teaching critical thinking, *Thinking Critically: A Concise Guide* is designed to serve as a supplementary text for academic courses in various subject areas that incorporate critical thinking as an integral dimension. This brief text is also intended for critical thinking courses that focus specifically on the skills of critical thinking. In addition to a substantive, in-depth treatment of the core critical thinking abilities, *Thinking Critically: A Concise Guide* retains from its parent book all of the thinking activities associated with these themes, as well as selected readings at the end of each chapter.

Both *Thinking Critically*, Seventh Edition, and *Thinking Critically: A Concise Guide* are based on a nationally recognized interdisciplinary program in critical thinking established in 1979 at LaGuardia College (The City University of New York) and involving more than eighteen hundred students annually. These texts integrate various perspectives on the thinking process drawn from a variety of disciplines such as philosophy, cognitive psychology, linguistics, and the language arts (English, reading, and speech-communication).

Thinking Critically: A Concise Guide addresses a crucial need in higher education by introducing students to the rapidly emerging field of critical thinking and fostering sophisticated intellectual and language abilities. Students apply their evolving thinking abilities to a variety of subjects drawn from academic disciplines, contemporary issues, and their life experiences. This book is based on the assumption, supported by research, that learning to think more effectively is a synthesizing process, knitting critical thinking abilities together with academic content and the fabric of students' experiences. Thinking learned in this way becomes a constitutive part of who students are.

With these considerations in mind, it should be clear that teaching a course in critical thinking involves embarking on high adventure, a journey that is full of unanticipated challenges and unexpected triumphs. I have written this concise edition to serve as an effective guide for this journey. In the final analysis, however, you must embark on the journey with your students, relying on your collective experiences, expertise, and critical thinking abilities to create productive educational experiences.

Features

This book has a number of distinctive characteristics that make it an effective tool for both instructors and students. *Thinking Critically: A Concise Guide*

- **teaches the fundamental thinking, reasoning, and language abilities that students need for academic success.** By focusing on the major thinking and language abilities needed in all disciplines, and by including a wide variety of readings, the text helps students perform more successfully in other courses.

- **stimulates and guides students to think clearly about complex, controversial issues.** The many diverse readings provide in-depth perspectives on significant social issues such as the criminal justice system, racism, euthanasia, AIDS, drug and alcohol abuse, liberty versus security, patriotism, and cloning. More important, the text helps students develop the thinking and language abilities necessary to understand and discuss intelligently these complex issues.

- **presents foundational thinking, reasoning, and language abilities in a developmentally sequenced way**. The text begins with basic abilities and then carefully progresses to more sophisticated thinking and reasoning skills. Cognitive maps open each chapter to help students understand the thinking process as well as the interrelationship of ideas in that chapter.

- **engages students in the active process of thinking.** Interspersed exercises, discussion topics, readings, and writing assignments encourage active participation, stimulating students to critically examine their own and others' thinking and to sharpen and improve their abilities. *Thinking Critically* provides structured opportunities for students to develop their thinking processes in a progressive, reflective way.

- **provides context by continually relating critical thinking abilities to students' daily lives.** Once students learn to apply critical thinking skills to situations in their own experiences, they then apply these skills to more abstract, academic contexts. Additionally, by asking students to think critically about themselves and their experiences, the text fosters their personal development as mature, responsible critical thinkers.

- **integrates the development of thinking abilities with the four language skills so crucial to success in college and careers: reading, writing, speaking, and listening.** The abundant writing assignments (short answer, paragraph, and essay), challenging readings, and discussion exercises serve to improve students' language skills.

- **is accompanied by a provocative critical thinking videotape.** A one-hour critical thinking videotape developed by the author, entitled *Thinking Towards Decisions,* is designed to work in conjunction with Chapter 2, "Thinking Critically." The tape uses a creative interweaving of a dramatic scenario, expert testimony, and a seminar group to develop students' critical thinking abilities.

- **includes a critical thinking test.** The Test of Critical Thinking Abilities, developed by the author and included in the Instructor's Resource Manual for *Thinking Critically,* Seventh Edition, and in interactive form on the Web site, provides for a comprehensive evaluation of student thinking and language abilities. Using a court case format arising from a fatal student drinking incident, the test challenges students to gather and weigh evidence, ask relevant questions, construct informed beliefs, evaluate expert testimony and summation arguments, reach a verdict, and then view the entire case from a problem-solving perspective.

- **uses illustrations and photographs to stimulate thinking.** Numerous photographs and illustrations, many created specifically for this book by the artist Warren Gebert, provoke thoughtful responses, present key concepts, and visually engage the reader.

- **includes substantive treatment of creative thinking.** A concluding Chapter 8, "Thinking Critically, Living Creatively," analyzes the creative process, developing creative thinking abilities, and creating a life philosophy through moral choices. The chapter also explains how "creative thinking" is the natural partner to "critical thinking."

- **includes a capstone section on "The Critical Thinker's Guide to Reasoning"** that provides an illustrated model that integrates the thinking and reasoning abilities explored in the book.

The Influence of Recent Events

September 11, 2001, I was sitting at my desk, working on the seventh edition of *Thinking Critically*. It was a stunningly beautiful day, suddenly pierced by a siren, then a second, quickly swelling into a cacophony of urgent and desperate sounds. I looked out of the window and saw police cars, fire engines, and emergency vehicles screaming down West Side Drive along the Hudson River. Many of the men and women in those first vehicles had only moments left in their lives. I ran to another window facing south, and there, fifteen blocks away, was one of the World Trade Center towers scarred with an obscene gash from which smoke poured. From this spot, I watched with disbelieving eyes the second plane disappear into the second World Trade Center tower, igniting a huge fireball. An hour later, with people streaming up the highway and smoke billowing behind them, the first tower imploded, then the second, extinguishing almost 3,000 souls in a matter of seconds, and changing this nation forever.

This catastrophe has altered each of our lives in profound and lasting ways, and it has informed both the full and concise editions of *Thinking Critically* as well. I have introduced issues and themes related to this event that demand our critical reflection and analysis. I believe it is our unique responsibility as educators to help our students develop the critical thinking abilities required to navigate effectively in this new and perilous world, to help them think clearly and make intelligent choices. And I believe it is our sacred responsibility, as individuals and citizens, to find ways to transform this unimaginable horror into the creation of a more enlightened world. It is by making good come out of evil that we can best ensure that the nearly unbearable loss of those innocent lives will not have been in vain.

The enduring themes surrounding the events of September 11 have been infused throughout the text, encouraging students' (and faculty's) critical reflection and analysis. I urge students to consider not just the World Trade Center attack but larger themes and dilemmas such as patriotism, individual freedom versus national security, and journalists' need to balance security issues against their mission to report breaking news. The text presents a global view by providing news articles and speeches from other countries, allowing students to compare these views with U.S. perspectives.

Ancillaries

Extensive support for users of the *Concise Guide* is available from the Instructor's Resource Manual for *Thinking Critically*, Seventh Edition, designed to help instructors tailor this book to their own courses.

- **Critical thinking courses:** Part 1, "Using *Thinking Critically*," written by John Chaffee, contains an overview of the field of critical thinking as well as suggestions and exercises of interest to teachers using this text. Also included is the Test of Critical Thinking Abilities.
- **Reading and writing courses:** Parts 2 and 3 — "Thinking Critically and Reading" and "Thinking Critically and Writing" — present assignments, useful suggestions, and syllabi for instructors using *Thinking Critically* in reading and writing courses. These materials have been newly revised.
- **Freshman Studies courses and seminars:** Part 4, "Thinking Critically and Freshman Studies," written and revised by Fred Janzow of Southeast Missouri State University, details how to use the text in courses and seminars explicitly devoted to entering freshmen. This section includes a sample syllabus, specific suggestions, and activities designed for the special needs of freshmen students.

The Manual concludes with an extensive bibliography.

The Web site to accompany *Thinking Critically* (both full and concise editions) includes a wealth of links, activities, graphic organizers, quizzes, and video clips to complement the text. Go to *college.hmco.com/english*.

Acknowledgments

Many people from a variety of disciplines have contributed to this book at various stages of its development over the past eighteen years, and I would like to thank my colleagues for their thorough scrutiny of the manuscript and their incisive and creative comments. In addition, I would like to offer my deepest gratitude to the faculty members at LaGuardia who have participated with such dedication and enthusiasm in the Critical Thinking program, and to the countless students whose commitment to learning is the soul of this text.

The following reviewers also provided evaluations that were of great help in preparing either the seventh edition or this concise edition:

Michelle Ballif, University of Georgia

Peter Boltuc, University of Illinois at Springfield

Robert Canter, Virginia Tech University

Maryanne Felter, Cayuga Community College

Ron Fortune, Illinois State University

Dorinda Fox, University of Central Florida

Ann Glauser, University of Georgia

Marguerite Helmers, University of Wisconsin, Oshkosh

Georgina Hill, Western Michigan University

Zhen Huang, Suffolk County Community College

Frank S. Jyszczyk, Western New Mexico University

Marc Kemp, Shasta College

James C. McDonald, University of Louisiana at Lafayette

Sara McLaughlin, Texas Tech University

Lyle W. Morgan, Pittsburgh State University

Ed Moritz, Indiana University — Purdue University, Fort Wayne

Mary Norcliffe and her Critical Thinking students, Atlantic Union College

Jonna Perrillo, New York University

Daniela Ragusa, University of Rhode Island

Althea E. Rhodes, University of Southern Indiana

Jennifer Richardson, Washington State University

Byron T. Robinson, Alamance Community College

Anna Ryan, Western Washington University

Greg Siering, Ball State University

Scott Slawinski, University of South Carolina

Elizabeth A. Wardle, University of Dayton

I have been privileged to work with a stellar team of people at Houghton Mifflin Company who are exemplary professionals and also my friends. Suzanne Phelps Weir continues to provide the kind of wise and imaginative attention that every author hopes for, while displaying an unerring talent for turning obstacles into opportunities. Sarah Helyar Smith guided the creation of this concise edition with an astute and steady hand. Carol Newman is always a special pleasure to work with: passionately exacting, committed to excellence, and with an authentically unique perspective on the world. Jill Haber brought an imaginative and expert perspective to the art design which enriched the entire project. And Cindy Graff Cohen continues to display extraordinary gifts in devising innovative marketing strategies and implementing them with aplomb.

This book also benefited from the talented contributions of Connie Gardner, who displayed her typical excellence in researching photographs, and Warren Gebert, who once again invested his creative genius in developing art for the book. Steve Brauch did a superb job of crafting the new Internet activities for this edition. I would also like to express special appreciation to Edward Heimers, Jr., for his generosity in sharing his expertise on issues explored in the book, and for his friendship during the darkest days following September 11.

Finally, I want to thank my wife, Heide, and my children, Jessie and Joshua, for their complete and ongoing love, support, and inspiration. It is these closest relationships that make life most worth living. And I wish to remember my parents, Charlotte Hess and Hubert Chaffee, who taught me lasting lessons about the most important things in life. They will always be with me.

Although this is a published book, it continues to be a work in progress. In this spirit, I invite you to share your experiences with the text by sending me your comments. I hope that this book serves as an effective vehicle for your own critical thinking explorations in living an examined life. You can contact me on line at jcthink@aol.com, and visit my Web site at *www.thinkingworld.com*. My mailing address is LaGuardia College, City University of New York, Humanities Department, Long Island City, NY 11101.

J.C.

Thinking Critically
A Concise Guide

1 Thinking

Working Toward Goals
How do goals function in my life?
What is the appropriate goal?
What are the steps and strategies?

Thinking
A purposeful, organized, cognitive
process that we use to understand the
world and make informed decisions.

Deciding on a Career
What career should I choose?
What are my interests and abilities?
How do I discover the appropriate
career?

Analyzing Issues
What is the issue?
What is the evidence?
What are the arguments?
What is the conclusion?

Making Decisions
What is the decision?
What are the choices?
What are the pros and cons?
What is the best choice?
What is my plan of action?

Thinking can be developed and improved by becoming
aware of, carefully examining, and practicing the thinking process.

Thinking is the extraordinary process we use every waking moment to make sense of our world and our lives. Successful thinking enables us to solve the problems we are continually confronted with, to make intelligent decisions, and to achieve the goals that give our lives purpose and fulfillment. It is an activity that is crucial for living in a meaningful way.

This book is designed to help you understand the complex, incredible process of thinking. You might think of this text as a map to guide you in exploring the way your mind operates. This book is also founded on the conviction that you can improve your thinking abilities by carefully examining your thinking process and working systematically through challenging activities. Thinking is an active process, and you learn to do it better by becoming aware of and actually using the thought process, not simply by reading about it. By participating in the thinking activities contained in the text and applying these ideas to your own experiences, you will find that your thinking — and language — abilities are becoming sharper and more powerful.

College provides you with a unique opportunity to develop your mind in the fullest sense. Entering college initiates you into a community of people dedicated to learning, and each discipline, or subject area, represents an organized effort to understand some significant dimension of human experience. As you are introduced to various disciplines, you learn new ways to understand the world, and you elevate your consciousness as a result. This book, in conjunction with the other courses in your college experience, will help you become an *educated thinker,* expanding your mind and developing your sensibilities.

Becoming an educated thinker will also help you achieve your career goals. In this rapidly evolving world, it is impossible to predict with precision your exact career (or careers) or the knowledge and skills that this career will require. But as an educated thinker you will possess the essential knowledge and abilities that will enable you to adapt to whatever your career situation demands. In addition, becoming an educated thinker will elevate your understanding of the world you live in and help you develop insight into your self and that of others, qualities that are essential to high achievement in most careers.

In this chapter we will examine three areas of our lives in which we use the thinking process to understand our world and make informed decisions:

- Working toward goals

- Making decisions

- Analyzing issues

VISUAL THINKING

The Mystery of the Mind

● Why is thinking a difficult process to understand? Why does improving our thinking involve sharing ideas with other people? Why does each person think in unique ways?

◎ Living an "Examined" Life

You are an artist, creating your life portrait, and your paints and brush strokes are the choices you make each day of your life. This metaphor provides you with a way to think about your personal development and underscores your responsibility for making the most intelligent decisions possible.

Every day you encounter a series of choices, forks in your life path that have the cumulative effect of defining you as a person. In thinking about these choices, you may discover that there are habitual patterns in your life that rarely change. If you find that your life is composed of a collection of similar activities and routines, don't despair; this is typical, not unusual. However, it may be an indication that you are not living your life in the most thoughtful fashion possible, that your choices have become automatic, and that your experiences are fixed in certain ruts. If this is the case, it may be time to reflect on your life, re-evaluate the choices you are making, and consider living your life in a more reflective and creative fashion.

Our world has become a complex and challenging place to live in. The accelerated pace that many people live at often makes them feel as though they are rushing from deadline to deadline, skating on the surface of life instead of exploring its deeper meanings. What is the purpose of your life? Who are you, and whom do you want to become? These are essential questions that form the core of life, and yet the velocity of our lives discourages us from even posing these questions, much less trying to answer them.

Your efforts to become thoughtful and reflective, to explore the nature of your self and the meaning of your life, is made even more difficult by the unthinking world we live in. Consider all of the foolish opinions, thoughtless decisions, confused communication, destructive behavior, and self-absorbed, thoughtless people that you have to deal with each day. Reflect on the number of times you have scratched your head and wondered, "What was that person thinking?" And how many times have you asked yourself, "What was I thinking?" The disturbing truth is that many people don't think very well; they are not making use of their potential to think clearly and effectively.

Over 2,500 years ago the Greek philosopher Socrates cautioned, "The unexamined life is not worth living," underscoring the insight that when we humans don't make use of our distinctive capacity to think deeply and act intelligently, our lives have diminished meaning. You have the capacity to create a richly fulfilling life, but you must develop and make full use of your thinking potential to do so. By becoming a true educated thinker, you will have the tools to unlock the mysteries of your self and meet the challenges of the world.

VISUAL THINKING

You Are the Artist of Your Life

● In what ways does this metaphor help you understand your personal development? In what ways does it highlight the role of personal responsibility in your life? What choices will you have to make to reach your full potential as a person?

Working Toward Goals

"Ah, but a man's reach should exceed his grasp, / Or what's a heaven for?"

— *Robert Browning*

My future career goal is to become a professional photographer, working for <u>National Geographic Magazine</u> and traveling around the world. I originally had different dreams, but gradually drifted away from them and lost interest. Then I enrolled in a photography course and loved it. I couldn't wait until the weekend was over to attend class on Monday or to begin my next class project — reactions that were really quite unusual for me! Not everyone is certain at my age about what they would like to become, and I think it is important to discover a career you will enjoy because you are going to spend the rest of your life doing it. I have many doubts, as I think everyone does. Am I good enough? The main thing I fear is rejection, people not liking my work, a possibility that is unavoidable in life. There is so much competition in this world that sometimes when you see someone better at what you do, you can feel inadequate. These problems and obstacles that interfere with my goals will have to be overcome. Rejection will have to be accepted and looked at as a learning experience, and competition will have to be used as an incentive for me to work at my highest level. But through it all, if you don't have any fears, then what do you have? Lacking competition and the possibility of rejection, there is no challenge to life.

— Emily Murray (student)

As revealed in this student passage, goals play extremely important functions in your life by organizing your thinking and giving your life order and direction. Whether you are preparing food, preparing for an exam, or preparing for a career, goals suggest courses of action and influence your decisions. By performing these functions, goals contribute meaning to your life. They give you something to aim for and lead to a sense of accomplishment when you reach them, like the satisfaction you may have received when you graduated from high school or entered college. It is your thinking abilities that enable you first to identify what your goals are and then to plan how to reach those goals.

Most of your behavior has a purpose or purposes, a goal or goals, that you are trying to reach. You can begin to discover the goals of your actions by asking yourself why or what you are doing or thinking. For example, answer the following question as specifically as you can:

Why did you come to class today?

This question may have stimulated any number of responses:

- Because I want to pass this course.

- Because I was curious about the topics to be discussed.

- Because I woke up early and couldn't get back to sleep.

Whatever your response, it reveals at least one of your goals in attending class.

Using your response to the question "Why did you come to class today?" as a starting point, try to discover part of your goal patterns by asking a series of *why* questions. After each response, ask why again. (For example: Why did you come to class today? Because I want to pass this course. Why do you want to pass this course? Because . . . .) Try to give thoughtful and specific answers.

As you may have found in completing the activity, this child's game of repeatedly asking why? begins to reveal the network of goals that structure your experience and leads you to progressively more profound questions regarding your basic goals in life, such as "Why do I want to be successful?" or "Why do I want a happy and fulfilling life?" These are complex issues that require thorough and ongoing exploration. A first step in this direction is to examine the way your mind works to achieve your goals, which is the goal of this section. If you can understand the way your mind functions when you think effectively, then you can use this knowledge to improve your thinking abilities. This in turn will enable you to deal more effectively with new situations you encounter. To begin this process, think about an important goal you have achieved in your life, and then complete Thinking Activity 1.1. Thinking Activities are designed to stimulate your thinking process and provide the opportunity to express your ideas about important topics. By sharing these ideas with your teacher and other members of the class, you are not only expanding your own thinking, but also expanding theirs. Each student has a wealth of experiences and insights to offer to the class.

THINKING ACTIVITY 1.1

Analyzing a Goal That You Achieved

1. Describe an important goal that you recently achieved.
2. Identify the steps you had to take to achieve this goal in the order you took them, and estimate the amount of time each step took.
3. Describe how you felt when you achieved your goal.

Achieving Short-Term Goals

By examining your response to Thinking Activity 1.1, you can see that thinking effectively plays a crucial role in helping you to achieve your goals by enabling you to perform two distinct, interrelated activities:

1. Identifying the appropriate goals
2. Devising effective plans and strategies to achieve your goals

You are involved in this goal-seeking process in every aspect of your daily life. Some of the goals you seek to achieve are more immediate (short-term) than others, such as planning your activities for the day or organizing your activities for an upcoming test.

Although achieving these short-term goals seems as if it ought to be a manageable process, the truth is your efforts probably meet with varying degrees of success. You may not always achieve your goals for the day, and you might occasionally find yourself inadequately prepared for a test. By improving your mastery of the goal-seeking process, you should be able to improve the quality of every area of your life. Let's explore how to do this.

Identify five short-term goals you would like to achieve in the next week. Now rank these goals in order of importance, ranging from the goals that are most essential for you to achieve to those that are less significant.

Once this process of identifying and ranking your goals is complete, you can then focus on devising effective plans and strategies to achieve your goals. To complete this stage of the goal-seeking process, select the goal that you ranked 1 or 2, and then *list all of the steps* in the order in which they need to be taken to achieve your goal successfully. After completing this list, estimate how much time each step will take and plan the step in your daily/weekly schedule. For example, if your goal is to prepare for a quiz in biology, your steps might include the following:

Goal: Prepare for biology quiz in 2 days

STEPS TO BE TAKEN	TIME INVOLVED	SCHEDULE
1. Photocopy the notes for the class I missed last week.	20 minutes	after next class
2. Review reading assignments and class notes.	2 hours	tonight
3. Make a review sheet.	1 hour	tomorrow night
4. Study the review sheet.	30 minutes	right before quiz

Method for Achieving Short-Term Goals

Step 1: Identify the goals.
Identify the short-term goals.
Rank the goals in order of importance.
Select the most important goal(s) to focus on.

Step 2: Devise effective plans to achieve your goals.
List all of the steps in the order in which they should be taken.
Estimate how much time each step will take.
Plan the steps in your daily/weekly schedule.

Although this method may seem a little mechanical the first few times you use it, it will soon become integrated into your thinking processes and become a natural and automatic approach to achieving the goals in your daily life. Much of our failure to achieve our short-term goals is due to the fact that we skip one or more of the steps in this process. Common thinking errors in seeking our goals include the following:

- We neglect to explicitly identify important goals.

- We concentrate on less important goals first, leaving insufficient time to work on more important goals.

- We don't identify all of the steps required to achieve our goals, or we approach them in the wrong order.

- We underestimate the time each step will take and/or fail to plan the steps in our schedule.

Achieving Long-Term Goals

Identifying immediate or short-term goals tends to be a fairly simple procedure. Identifying our long-term goals is a much more complex and challenging process: career aims, plans for marriage, paying for children's college, goals for personal development. Think, for example, about the people you know who have full-time jobs. How many of these people get up in the morning excited and looking forward to going to work that day? The unfortunate fact is that many people have not been successful in identifying the most appropriate career goals for themselves, goals that reflect their true interests and talents.

How do you identify the most appropriate long-term goals for yourself? To begin with, you need to develop an in-depth understanding of yourself: your talents, your interests, the things that stimulate you and bring you satisfaction. You also need to discover what your possibilities are, either through research or actual experience. Of course, your goals do not necessarily remain the same throughout your life. It is unlikely that the goals you had as an eight-year-old are the ones you have now. As you grow, change, and mature, it is natural for your goals to change and evolve as well. The key point is that you should keep examining your goals to make sure that they reflect your own thinking and current interests.

Research studies have shown that high-achieving persons are able to envision a detailed, three-dimensional picture of their future in which their goals and aspirations are clearly inscribed. In addition, they are able to construct a mental plan that includes the sequence of steps they will have to take, the amount of time each step will involve, and strategies for overcoming the obstacles they are likely to encounter. Such realistic and compelling concepts of the future enable these persons to make sacrifices in the present to achieve their long-term goals. Of course, they may modify these goals as circumstances change and they acquire more information, but they retain a well-defined, flexible plan that charts their life course.

Research also reveals that people who are low achievers tend to live in the present and the past. Their concepts of the future are vague and ill defined: "I want to be happy," or "I want a high-paying job." This unclear concept of the future makes it difficult for them to identify the most appropriate goals for themselves, to devise effective strategies for achieving these goals, and to make the necessary sacrifices in the present that will ensure that their goals become a reality. For example, imagine that you are faced with the choice of studying for an exam or participating in a social activity. What would you do? If you are focusing mainly on the present rather than the future, then the temptation to go out with your friends may be too strong. But if you see this exam as connected to a future that is real and extremely important to you, then you are better equipped to sacrifice a momentary pleasant time for your future happiness.

THINKING ACTIVITY 1.2

Analyzing an Important Future Goal

Apply some of the insights we have been examining about working toward goals to a situation in your own life.

1. Describe as specifically as possible an important long-term goal that you want to achieve. Your goal can be academic, professional, or personal.

2. Explain the reasons that led you to select the goal you did and why you believe your goal makes sense.

3. Identify both the major and minor steps you will have to take to achieve your goal. List your steps in the order they need to be taken and indicate how much time you think each step will take. Make your responses as specific and precise as possible.

4. Identify some of the sacrifices that you might have to make now to achieve your goal in the future.

THINKING PASSAGE

My American Journey

Colin Powell is the embodiment of the American Dream. Born to immigrant parents from Jamaica, he grew up on the rough streets of Harlem. Though he did not excel as a student, he discovered the military to be an ideal fit for his interests and abilities. With a powerful blend of native intelligence, determination, and bedrock values, he rose to the highest levels of the military and of government, as both a general and a secretary of state. In the following excerpt from his best-selling autobiography *My American Journey*, General Powell provides a glimpse into the challenges he had to face as an African American in 1963 and describes the thinking abilities he used to deal with and triumph over such challenges. These are lessons from which we can all profit.

From MY AMERICAN JOURNEY*
by Colin Powell

I have made clear that I was no great shakes as a scholar. I have joked over the years that the CCNY [City College of New York] faculty handed

---

* From *My American Journey* by Colin Powell with Joseph E. Persico, copyright © 1995 by Colin L. Powell. Used by permission of Random House, Inc.

VISUAL THINKING

Opening Your Mind to New Possibilities

● How can rigid thinking and a lack of imagination prevent you from achieving your goals? How can you open your mind and free your imagination in order to understand all of your future possibilities?

me a diploma, uttering a sigh of relief, and were happy to pass me along to the military. Yet, even this c-average student emerged from CCNY prepared to write, think, and communicate effectively and equipped to compete against students from colleges that I could never have dreamed of attending. If the Statue of Liberty opened the gateway to this country, public education opened the door to attainment here. Schools like my sister's Buffalo State Teachers College and CCNY have served as the Harvards and Princetons of the poor. And they served us well. I am, consequently, a champion of public secondary and higher education. I will speak out for them and support them for as long as I have the good sense to remember where I came from.

Shortly before the commissioning ceremony in Aronowitz Auditorium, Colonel Brookhart called me into his office in the drill hall. "Sit down, Mr. Powell," he said. I did, sitting at attention. "You've done well here (in ROTC). You'll do well in the Army. You're going to Fort Benning soon."

He warned me that I needed to be careful. Georgia was not New York. The South was another world. I had to learn to compromise, to accept a world I had not made and that was beyond my changing. He mentioned the black general Benjamin O. Davis, who had been with him at West Point, where Davis was shunned the whole four years by his classmates, including, I assumed, Brookhart. Davis had gotten himself into trouble in the South, Brookhart said, because he had tried to buck the system. The colonel was telling me, in effect, not to rock the boat, to be a "good Negro.". . .

The Army was becoming more democratic, but I was plunged back into the Old South every time I left the post. I could go into Woolworth's in Columbus, Georgia, and buy anything I wanted, as long as I did not try to eat there. I could go into a department store and they would take my money, as long as I did not try to use the men's room. I could walk along the street, as long as I did not look at a white woman. . . .

One night, exhausted and hungry, I locked up the house and headed back toward the post. As I approached a drive-in hamburger joint on Victory Drive, I thought, okay, I know they won't serve me inside, so I'll just park outside. I pulled in, and after a small eternity, a waitress came to my car window. "A hamburger, please," I said.

She looked at me uneasily. "Are you Puerto Rican?" she asked.

"No," I said.

"Are you an African student?" She seemed genuinely trying to be helpful.

"No," I answered. "I'm a Negro. I'm an American. And I'm an Army officer."

"Look, I'm from New Jersey," the waitress said, "and I don't understand any of this. But they won't let me serve you. Why don't you go behind the restaurant, and I'll pass you a hamburger out the back window."

Something snapped. "I'm not that hungry," I said, burning rubber as I backed out. As I drove away, I could see the faces of the owner and his customers in the restaurant windows enjoying this little exercise in humiliation. . . .

Racism was still relatively new to me, and I had to find a way to cope psychologically. I began by identifying my priorities. I wanted, above all, to succeed at my Army career. I did not intend to give way to self-destructive rage, no matter how provoked. If people in the South insisted on living by crazy rules, then I would play the hand dealt me for now. If I was to be confined to one end of the playing field, then I was going to be a star on that part of the field. Nothing that happened off-post, none of the indignities, none of the injustices, was going to inhibit my performance. I was not going to let myself become emotionally crippled because I could not play on the whole field. I did not feel inferior, and I was not going to let anybody make me believe I was. I was not going to allow someone else's feelings about me to become my feelings about myself. Racism was not just a black problem. It was America's problem. And until the country solved it, I was not going to let bigotry make me a victim instead of a full human being. I occasionally felt hurt; I felt anger; but most of all I felt challenged. I'll show you!

Questions for Analysis

1. Describe an experience in which you were the object of discrimination or prejudice. How did it make you feel? How did you deal with it?
2. Colin Powell was determined to achieve his goals, despite many obstacles. Describe in your own words the thinking approach he used to deal with the pervasive racism that he encountered.
3. Describe a current situation in which you face obstacles that are interfering with your achievement of a personal goal. Apply Colin Powell's approach to the situation, identifying practical thinking strategies that will help you overcome or neutralize these obstacles.
4. Powell concludes his autobiography with an affirmation that seems particularly relevant in these seemingly more perilous times: "Some counted us out, another once great empire in terminal decline. But we came roaring back, while other empires fell instead. We will prevail over our present trials. We will come through because our founders bequeathed us a political system of genius, a system flexible enough for all ages and inspiring noble aspirations for all time. We will continue to flourish because our diverse American society has the strength, hardiness, and resilience of the hybrid plant we are. We will make it because we know we are blessed, and we will not throw away God's gift to us." Discuss the implications of this affirmation.
5. Explain whether you agree with Powell that America's ethnic diversity is a source of strength and resilience, and list the reasons why or why not.

Making Decisions

To reach our goals, we have to learn to make the best decisions for ourselves or our community. Although we all make decisions, we don't always make the most informed or intelligent decisions possible. In fact, most of us regularly have the experience of mentally kicking ourselves because we made a poor decision. For example, think about a decision you made that you would make differently if you had an opportunity to do it over again.

Many of our poor decisions involve relatively minor issues — for example, selecting an unappealing dish in a restaurant, agreeing to go out on a blind date, taking a course that does not meet our expectations. Although these decisions may result in unpleasant consequences, the discomfort is neither life-threatening nor long lasting (although a disappointing course may seem to last forever!). However, there are many more significant decisions in our lives in which poor choices can result in considerably more damaging and far-reaching consequences. For example, one reason that the current divorce rate in the United States stands at 50 percent is the poor decisions people make before or after the vows "till death do us part." Similarly, the fact that many employed adults wake up in the morning unhappy about going to their jobs, anxiously waiting for the end of the day and the conclusion of the week (TGIF!) so they are free to do what they really want to do, suggests that somewhere along the line they made poor career decisions, or they felt trapped by circumstances they couldn't control. Our jobs should be much more than a way to earn a paycheck; they should be vehicles for using our professional skills, opportunities for expressing our creative talents, stimulants to our personal growth and intellectual development, and experiences that provide us with feelings of fulfillment and self-esteem. In the final analysis, our careers are central elements of our lives and important dimensions of our life-portraits. Our career decision is one that we better try to get right!

An important part of becoming an educated thinker is learning to make effective decisions. Let's explore the process of making effective decisions and then apply your knowledge to the challenge of deciding on the most appropriate career for yourself.

 THINKING ACTIVITY 1.3

Analyzing a Previous Decision

1. Think back on an important decision you made that turned out well, and describe the experience as specifically as possible.

2. Reconstruct the reasoning process that you used to make your decision. Did you

- Clearly define the decision to be made and the related issues?

- Consider various choices and anticipate the consequences of these choices?

- Gather additional information to help in your analysis?

- Evaluate the various pros and cons of different courses of action?

- Use a chart or diagram to aid in your deliberations?

- Create a specific plan of action to implement your ideas?

- Periodically review your decision to make necessary adjustments?

An Organized Approach to Making Decisions

As you reflected on the successful decision you were writing about in Thinking Activity 1.3, you probably noticed your mind working in a more or less systematic way as you thought your way through the decision situation. Of course, we often make important decisions with less thoughtful analysis by acting impulsively or relying on our intuition. Sometimes these quick decisions work out well, but often they don't, and we are forced to live with the consequences of these mistaken choices. People who approach decision situations thoughtfully and analytically tend to be more successful decision-makers than people who don't. Naturally, there are no guarantees that a careful analysis will lead to a successful result; often too many unknown elements and factors are beyond our control. But we can certainly improve our success rate as well as our decision-making speed by becoming more knowledgeable about the decision-making process. Expert decision-makers can typically make quick, accurate decisions based on intuitions that are informed, not merely impulsive. However, like most complex abilities in life, we need to learn to walk before we can run, so let's explore a versatile and effective approach for making decisions.

The decision-making approach we will be using consists of five steps. As you gradually master these steps, they will become integrated into your way of thinking, and you will be able to apply them in a natural and flexible way.

Step 1: Define the Decision Clearly. This seems like an obvious step, but a lot of decision-making goes wrong at the starting point. For example, imagine that you decide you want to have a more active social life. The problem with this characterization of your decision is it defines the situation too generally and therefore doesn't give any clear direction for your analysis. Do you want to develop an intimate, romantic relationship? Do you want to cultivate more close friendships? Do you want to engage in more social activities? Do you want to meet new people? In short, there are many ways to define more clearly the decision to have a more active social life. The more specific your definition of the decision to be made, the clearer will be your analysis and the greater the likelihood of success.

Strategy: Write a one-page analysis that articulates your decision-making situation as clearly and specifically as possible.

Step 2: Consider All the Possible Choices. Successful decision-makers explore all of the possible choices in their situation, not simply the obvious ones. In fact, the less obvious choices often turn out to be the more effective ones. For example, a student in a recent class of mine couldn't decide whether he should major in accounting or business management. In discussing his situation with other members of the class, he revealed that his real interest was in the area of graphic design and illustration. Although he was very talented, he considered this area to be only a hobby, not a possible career choice. Class members pointed out to him that this might turn out to be his best career choice, but he needed first to see it as a possibility.

Strategy: List as many possible choices for your situation as you can, both obvious and not obvious. Ask other people for additional suggestions, and don't censor or prejudge any ideas.

Step 3: Gather All Relevant Information and Evaluate the Pros and Cons of Each Possible Choice. In many cases you may lack sufficient information to make an informed choice regarding a challenging, complex decision. Unfortunately, this doesn't prevent people from plunging ahead anyway, making a decision that is often more a gamble than an informed choice. Instead of this questionable approach, it makes a lot more sense to seek out the information you need so you can determine which of the choices you identified has the best chance for success. For example, in the case of the student mentioned in Step 2, there is important information he would need to secure before he could determine whether he should consider a career in graphic design and illustration, including asking: What are the specific careers within this general field? What sort of academic preparation and experience are required for the various careers? What are the prospects for employment in these areas, and how well do they pay?

Strategy: For each possible choice that you identified, create questions regarding information you need to find out, and then locate that information.

In addition to locating all relevant information, each of the possible choices you identified has certain advantages and disadvantages, and it is essential that you analyze these pros and cons in an organized fashion. For example, in the case of the student described earlier, the choice of pursuing a career in accounting might have advantages such as ready employment opportunities, the flexibility of working in many different situations and geographical locations, moderate-to-high income expectations, and job security. Disadvantages, however, might include the fact that accounting may not reflect a deep and abiding interest of the student, he might lose interest over time, or the career might not result in the personal challenge and fulfillment that he seeks.

Strategy: Using a format similar to that outlined in the following worksheet, analyze the pros and cons of each of your possible choices.

Define the decision:

Possible choices	Information needed	Pros	Cons
1.			
2.			
(etc.)			

Step 4: Select the Choice That Seems to Best Meet the Needs of the Situation. The first four steps of this approach are designed to help you analyze your decision situation: to clearly define the decision, generate possible choices, gather relevant information, and evaluate the pros and cons of the choices you identified. In the final step, you must attempt to synthesize all that you have learned, weaving together all of the various threads into a conclusion that you believe is your best choice. How do you do this? There is no one simple way to identify your best choice, but there are some useful strategies for guiding your deliberations.

Strategy: Identify and prioritize the goal(s) of your decision situation and determine which of your choices best meets the goal. This process will probably involve reviewing and perhaps refining your definition of the decision situation. For example, in the case of the student that we have been considering, some goals might include choosing a career that will a. provide financial security, b. provide personal fulfillment, c. make use of special talents, d. offer plentiful opportunities and job security.

Once identified, the goals can be ranked in order of their priority, which will then suggest what the best choice will be. For example, if the student ranks goals *a* and *d* at the top of the list, then a choice of accounting or business administration might make sense. But if the student ranks goals *b* and *c* at the top, then pursuing a career in graphic design and illustration might be the best selection.

Strategy: Anticipate the consequences of each choice by preliving the choices. That is, project yourself into the future, imagining as realistically as you can the consequences of each possible choice. As with previous strategies, this process is aided by writing your thoughts down and discussing them with others.

Step 5: Implement a Plan of Action and Then Monitor the Results, Making Necessary Adjustments. Once you have selected what you consider to be your best choice, you need to develop and implement a specific, concrete plan of action. As was noted in the section on short-term goals, the more specific and concrete your plan of action, the greater the likelihood of success. For example, if the student in the case we have been considering decides to pursue a career in graphic design and illustration, his plan should include reviewing the academic major that best meets his needs, discussing his situation with students and faculty in that department, planning the courses he will be taking, and perhaps speaking to persons in the field.

Strategy: Create a schedule that details the steps you will be taking to implement your decision and a time line for taking these steps.

Of course, your plan is merely a starting point for implementing your decision. As you actually begin taking the steps in your plan, you will likely discover that changes and adjustments need to be made. In some cases, you may find that, based on new information, the choice you selected appears to be the wrong one. For example, as the student we have been discussing takes courses in graphic design and illustration, he may find that his interest in the field is not as serious as he thought and that although he likes this area as a hobby, he does not want it to be his life work. In this case, he should return to considering his other choices and perhaps adding additional choices that he did not consider before.

Strategy: After implementing your choice, evaluate its success by identifying what's working and what isn't, and make the necessary adjustments to improve the situation.

Method for Making Decisions

Step 1: Define the decision clearly.

Step 2: Consider all the possible choices.

Step 3: Gather all relevant information, and evaluate the pros and cons of each possible choice.

Step 4: Select the choice that seems to best meet the needs of the situation.

Step 5: Implement a plan of action and then monitor the results, making necessary adjustments.

THINKING ACTIVITY 1.4

Analyzing a Future Decision

1. Describe an important decision in your academic or personal life that you will have to make in the near future.
2. Using the five-step decision-making approach we just described, analyze your decision and conclude with your best choice.

Share your analysis with other members of the class, and listen carefully to the feedback they give you.

Analyzing Issues

We live in a complex world filled with challenging and often perplexing issues that we are expected to make sense of. For example, the media inform us every day of issues related to abortion, AIDS, terrorism, animal experimentation, budget priorities, child custody, crime and punishment, drugs, environmental pollution, genetic engineering, human rights, individual rights, international conflicts, moral values, pornography, poverty, racism, reproductive technology,

VISUAL THINKING

Weighing Your Decision Carefully

● Why do many people tend to make quick decisions rather than approaching their decisions thoughtfully and analytically? Describe a decision you made that was based on thoughtful analysis. How did it turn out?

the right to die, sex education, and many others. Often these broad social issues intrude into our own personal lives, taking them from the level of abstract discussion into our immediate experience. As effective thinkers, we have an obligation to develop informed, intelligent opinions about these issues so that we can function as responsible citizens and also make appropriate decisions when confronted with these issues in our lives.

Almost everyone has opinions about these and other issues. Some opinions, however, are more informed and well supported than others. To make sense of complex issues, we need to bring to them a certain amount of background knowledge and an integrated set of thinking and language abilities. One of the central goals of this book is to help you develop the knowledge and sophisticated thinking and language abilities needed to analyze a range of complex issues.

What Is the Issue?

Many social issues are explored, analyzed, and evaluated through our judicial system. Imagine that you have been called for jury duty and subsequently impaneled on a jury that is asked to render a verdict on the following situation. (Note: This fictional case is based on an actual case that was tried in May 1990 in Minneapolis, Minnesota.)

> On January 23, the defendant, Mary Barnett, left Chicago to visit her fiancé in San Francisco. She left her six-month-old daughter, Alison, unattended in the apartment. Seven days later, Mary Barnett returned home to discover that her baby had died of dehydration. She called the police and initially told them that she had left the child with a baby sitter. She later stated that she knew she had left the baby behind, that she did not intend to come back, and that she knew Alison would die in a day or two. She has been charged with the crime of second-degree murder: intentional murder without premeditation. If convicted, she could face up to eighteen years in jail.

As a member of the jury, your role is to hear and weigh the evidence, evaluate the credibility of the witnesses, analyze the arguments presented by the prosecution and defense, determine whether the law applies specifically to this situation, and render a verdict on the guilt or innocence of the defendant. To perform these tasks with clarity and fairness, you will have to use a variety of sophisticated thinking and language abilities. To begin with, describe your initial assessment of whether the defendant is innocent or guilty and explain your reasons for thinking so.

As part of the jury selection process, you are asked by the prosecutor and defense attorney whether you will be able to set aside your initial reactions or preconceptions to render an impartial verdict. Identify any ideas or feelings related to this case that might make it difficult for you to view it objectively. Are you a parent? Have you ever had any experiences related to the issues in this case? Do you have any preconceived views concerning individual responsibility in situations like this? Then evaluate whether you will be able to go beyond your initial reactions to see the situation objectively, and explain how you intend to accomplish this.

What Is the Evidence?

The evidence at judicial trials is presented through the testimony of witnesses called by the prosecution and the defense. As a juror, your job is to absorb the information being presented, evaluate its accuracy, and assess the reliability of the individuals giving the testimony. The following are excerpts of testimony from some of the witnesses at the trial. Witnesses for the prosecution are presented first, followed by witnesses for the defense.

CAROLINE HOSPERS: On the evening of January 30, I was in the hallway when Mary Barnett entered the building. She looked distraught and didn't have her baby Alison with her. A little while later the police arrived and I discovered that she had left poor little Alison all alone to die. I'm not surprised this happened. I always thought that Ms. Barnett was a disgrace — I mean, she didn't have a husband. In fact, she didn't even have a steady man after that sailor left for California. She had lots of wild parties in her apartment, and that baby wasn't taken care of properly. Her garbage was always filled with empty whiskey and wine bottles. I'm sure that she went to California just to party and have a good time, and didn't give a damn about little Alison. She was thinking only of herself. It's obvious that she is entirely irresponsible and was not a fit mother.

OFFICER MITCHELL: We were called to the defendant's apartment at 11 P.M. on January 30 by the defendant, Mary Barnett. Upon entering the apartment, we found the defendant holding the deceased child in her arms. She was sobbing and was obviously extremely upset. She stated that she had left the deceased with a baby sitter one week before when she went to California, and had just returned to discover the deceased alone in the apartment. When I asked the defendant to explain in detail what had happened before she left, she stated: "I remember making airline reservations for my trip. Then I tried to find a baby sitter, but I couldn't. I knew that I was leaving Alison alone and that I wouldn't be back for a while, but I had to get to California at all costs. I visited my mother and then left." An autopsy was later performed that determined that the deceased had died of dehydration several days earlier. There were no other marks or bruises on the deceased.

DR. PARKER: I am a professional psychiatrist who has been involved in many judicial hearings on whether a defendant is mentally competent to stand trial, and I am familiar with these legal tests. At the request of the district attorney's office, I interviewed the defendant four times during the last three months. Ms. Barnett is suffering from depression and anxiety, possibly induced by the guilt she feels for what she did. These symptoms can be controlled with proper medication. Based on my interview, I believe that Ms. Barnett is competent to stand trial. She understands the charges against her, and the roles of her attorney, the prosecutor, the judge and jury, and can participate in her own defense. Further, I believe that she was mentally competent on January 23, when she left her child unattended. In my opinion she knew what she was doing and what the consequences of her actions would be. She was aware that she was leaving her child unattended and that the child would be in great danger. I think that she feels guilty for the decisions she made, and that this remorse accounts for her current emotional problems.

To be effective critical thinkers, we should not simply accept information as it is presented. We need to try to determine the accuracy of the information and evaluate the credibility of the people providing the information. Evaluate the credibility of the prosecution witnesses by identifying those factors that led you to believe their testimony and those factors that raised questions in your mind about the accuracy of the information presented. You can use these questions to guide your evaluation:

- What information is the witness providing?

- Is the information relevant to the charges?

- Is the witness credible? What biases might influence the witness's testimony?

- To what extent is the testimony accurate?

On a jury, performing these activities effectively involves using many of the higher-order thinking and language abilities explored in the chapters ahead, including Chapter 4, "Perceiving, Believing, and Knowing"; and Chapter 5, "Reporting, Inferring, and Judging." Based on the testimony you have heard up to this point, do you think the defendant is innocent or guilty of intentional murder without premeditation? Explain the reasons for your conclusion.

Now let's review testimony from the witnesses for the defense.

ALICE JONES: I have known the defendant, Mary Barnett, for over eight years. She is a very sweet and decent woman, and a wonderful mother. Being a single parent isn't easy, and Mary has done as good a job as she could. But shortly after Alison's birth, Mary got depressed. Then her fiancé, Tim Stewart, was transferred to California. He's a navy engine mechanic. She started drinking to overcome her depression, but this just made things worse. She began to feel trapped in her apartment with little help raising the baby and few contacts with her family or friends. As her depression deepened, she clung more closely to Tim, who as a result became more distant and put off their wedding, which caused her to feel increasingly anxious and desperate. She felt that she had to go to California to get things straightened out, and by the time she reached that point I think she had lost touch with reality. I honestly don't think she realized that she was leaving Alison unattended. She loved her so much.

DR. BLOOM: Although I have not been involved in judicial hearings of this type, Mary Barnett has been my patient, twice a week for the last four months, beginning two months after she returned from California and was arrested. In my professional opinion, she is mentally ill and not capable of standing trial. Further, she was clearly not aware of what she was doing when she left Alison unattended and should not be held responsible for her action. Ms. Barnett's problems began after the birth of Alison. She became caught in the grip of the medical condition known as postpartum depression, a syndrome that affects many women after the birth of their children, some more severely than others. Women feel a loss of purpose, a sense of hopelessness, and a deep depression. The extreme pressures of caring for an infant create additional anxiety. When Ms. Barnett's fiancé left for California, she felt completely overwhelmed by her circumstances. She turned to alcohol to raise her spirits, but this just exacerbated her condition. Depressed, desperate, anxious, and alcoholic, she lapsed into a serious neurotic state and became obsessed with the idea of reaching her fiancé in California. This single hope was the only thing she could focus on, and when she acted on it she was completely unaware that she was putting her daughter in danger. Since the trial has begun, she has suffered two anxiety attacks, the more severe resulting in a near-catatonic state necessitating her hospitalization for several days. This woman is emotionally disturbed. She needs professional help, not punishment.

MARY BARNETT: I don't remember leaving Alison alone. I would never have done that if I had realized what I was doing. I don't remember saying any of the things that they said I said, about knowing I was leaving her. I have tried to put the pieces together through the entire investigation, and I just can't do it. I was anxious, and I was real frightened. I didn't feel like I was in control, and it felt like it was getting worse. The world was closing in on me, and I had nowhere to turn. I knew that I had to get to Tim, in California, and that he would be able to fix everything. He was always the one I went to, because I trusted him. I must have assumed that someone was taking care of Alison, my sweet baby. When I was in California, I knew something wasn't right. I just didn't know what it was.

Based on this new testimony, do you think that the defendant is innocent or guilty of intentional murder without premeditation? Have your views changed? Explain the reasons for your current conclusion. Evaluate the credibility of the defense witnesses by identifying those factors that led you to believe their testimony and those factors that raised questions in your mind about the accuracy of the information being presented. Use the questions on page 24 as a guide.

What Are the Arguments?

After the various witnesses present their testimony through examination and cross-examination questioning, the prosecution and defense then present their final arguments and summations. The purpose of this phase of the trial is to tie together — or raise doubts about — the evidence that has been presented in order to persuade the jury that the defendant is guilty or innocent. Included here are excerpts from these final arguments.

PROSECUTION ARGUMENTS: Child abuse and neglect are a national tragedy. Every day thousands of innocent children are neglected, abused, and even killed. The parents responsible for these crimes are rarely brought to justice because their victims are usually not able to speak in their own behalf. In some sense, all of these abusers are emotionally disturbed, because it takes emotionally disturbed people to torture, maim, and kill innocent children. But these people are also responsible for their actions and they should be punished accordingly. They don't have to hurt these children. No one is forcing them to hurt these children. They can choose not to hurt these children. If they have emotional problems, they can choose to seek professional help. Saying you hurt a child because you have "emotional problems" is the worst kind of excuse.

The defendant, Mary Barnett, claims that she left her child unattended, to die, because she has "emotional problems" and that she is not responsible for what she did. This is absurd. Mary Barnett is a self-centered, irresponsible, manipulative, deceitful mother who abandoned her six-month-old daughter to die so that she could fly to San Francisco to party all week with her fiancé. She was conscious, she was thinking, she knew exactly what she was doing, and that's exactly what she told the police when she returned from her little pleasure trip. Now she claims that she can't remember making these admissions to the police, nor can she remember leaving little Alison alone to die. How convenient!

You have heard testimony from her neighbor, Caroline Hospers, that she was considerably less than an ideal mother: a chronic drinker who liked to party rather than devoting herself to her child. You have also heard the testimony of Dr. Parker, who stated that Mary Barnett was aware of what she was doing on the fateful day in January and that any emotional disturbance is the result of her feelings of guilt over the terrible thing she did, and her fear of being punished for it.

Mary Barnett is guilty of murder, pure and simple, and it is imperative that you find her so. We need to let society know that it is no longer open season on our children.

After reviewing these arguments, describe those points you find most persuasive and those you find least persuasive, and then review the defense arguments that follow.

DEFENSE ARGUMENTS: The district attorney is certainly correct — child abuse is a national tragedy. Mary Barnett, however, is not a child abuser. You heard the police testify that the hospital found no marks, bruises, or other indications of an abused child. You also heard her friend, Alice Jones, testify that Mary was a kind and loving mother who adored her child. But if Mary Barnett was not a child abuser, then how could she have left her child unattended? Because she had snapped psychologically. The combination of postpartum depression, alcoholism, the pressures of being a single parent, and the loss of her fiancé were too much for her to bear. She simply broke under the weight of all that despair and took off blindly for California, hoping to find a way out of her personal hell. How could she leave Alison unattended? Because she was completely unaware that she was doing so. She had lost touch with reality and had no idea what was happening around her.

You have heard the in-depth testimony of Dr. Bloom, who has explained to you the medical condition of postpartum depression and how this led to Mary's emotional breakdown. You are aware that Mary has had two severe anxiety attacks while this trial has taken place, one resulting in her hospitalization. And you have seen her desperate sobbing whenever her daughter Alison has been mentioned in testimony.

Alison Barnett is a victim. But she is not a victim of intentional malice from the mother who loves her. She is the victim of Mary's mental illness, of her emotional breakdown. And in this sense Mary is a victim also. In this enlightened society we should not punish someone who has fallen victim to mental illness. To do so would make us no better than those societies who used to torture and burn mentally ill people whom they thought were possessed by the devil. Mary needs treatment, not blind vengeance.

After reviewing the arguments presented by the defense, identify those points you find most persuasive and those you find least persuasive.

The process of analyzing and evaluating complex arguments like those presented by the prosecution and defense involves using a number of sophisticated thinking and language abilities we will be exploring in the chapters ahead, including Chapter 2, "Thinking Critically"; Chapter 6, "Constructing Arguments"; and Chapter 7, "Reasoning Critically."

What Is the Verdict?

Following the final arguments and summations, the judge will sometimes give specific instructions to clarify the issues to be considered. In this case the judge reminds the jury that they must focus on the boundaries of the law and determine whether the case falls within these boundaries or outside them. The jury then retires to deliberate the case and render a verdict.

For a defendant to be found guilty of second-degree murder, the prosecution must prove that he or she intended to kill someone, made a conscious decision to do so at that moment (without premeditation), and was aware of the consequences of his or her actions. In your discussion with the other jurors, you must determine whether the evidence indicates, beyond a reasonable doubt, that the defendant's conduct in this case meets these conditions. What does the qualification "beyond a reasonable doubt" mean? A principle like this is always difficult to define in specific terms, but in general the principle means that it would not make good sense for thoughtful men and women to conclude otherwise.

Based on your analysis of the evidence and arguments presented in this case, describe what you think the verdict ought to be and explain your reasons for thinking so.

Verdict: Guilty_____   Not Guilty_____

THINKING ACTIVITY 1.5

Analyzing Your Verdict

Exploring this activity has given you the opportunity to analyze the key dimensions of a complex court case. Now synthesize your thoughts regarding this case by composing a two-page paper in which you explain the reasons and evidence that influenced your verdict. Be sure to discuss the important testimony and your evaluation of the credibility of the various witnesses.

Final Thoughts

The first line of this chapter stated, "Thinking is the extraordinary process we use every waking moment to make sense of our world and our lives." Throughout this chapter we have explored the different ways our thinking enables us to make sense of the world by working toward goals, making decisions, and analyzing issues. Of course, our thinking helps us make sense of the world in other ways as well. When we attend a concert, listen to a lecture, or try to understand someone's behavior, it is our thinking that enables us to figure out what is happening. In fact, these attempts to make sense of what is happening are going on all the time in our lives, and they represent the heart of the thinking process.

If we review the different ways of thinking we have explored in this chapter, we can reach several conclusions about thinking:

- Thinking is directed toward a purpose. When we think, it is usually for a purpose — to reach a goal, make a decision, or analyze an issue.

- Thinking is an organized process. When we think effectively, there is usually an order or organization to our thinking. For each of the thinking activities we explored, we saw that there are certain steps or approaches to take that help us reach goals, make decisions, and analyze issues.

We can put together these conclusions about thinking to form a working definition of the term.

thinking *A purposeful, organized cognitive process that we use to understand the world and make informed decisions.*

VISUAL THINKING

"Members of the Jury, Don't Be Deceived . . ."

- Courtroom dramas, like that depicted in this photo, provide rich contexts for sophisticated critical thinking. What crime do you think the defendant (in the witness chair) might have been charged with? Do you have any positive or negative bias toward him based on his appearance and facial expression? Do you think the woman addressing the jury is the prosecutor or defense attorney? Why?

Thinking develops with use over a lifetime, and we can improve our thinking in an organized and systematic way by following these steps:

- Carefully examining our thinking process and the thinking process of others. In this chapter we have explored various ways in which our thinking works. By focusing our attention on these (and other) thinking approaches and strategies, we can learn to think more effectively.

- Practicing our thinking abilities. To improve our thinking, we actually have to think for ourselves, to explore and make sense of thinking situations by using our thinking abilities. Although it is important to read about thinking and learn how other people think, there is no substitute for actually doing it ourselves.

The ability to think for ourselves by carefully examining the way that we make sense of the world is one of the most satisfying aspects of being a mature human being. We will refer to this ability to think carefully about our thinking as the ability to think critically.

thinking critically *Carefully exploring the thinking process to clarify our understanding and make more intelligent decisions.*

We are able to think critically because of our natural human ability to reflect — to think back on what we are thinking, doing, or feeling. By carefully thinking back on our thinking, we are able to figure out the way our thinking operates and thus learn to do it more effectively. In the following chapters we will be systematically exploring many dimensions of the way our minds work, providing the opportunity to deepen our understanding of the thinking process and stimulating us to become more effective thinkers.

Of course, carefully examining the ideas produced by the thinking process assumes that there are ideas that are worth examining. We produce such ideas by thinking creatively, an activity we can define as follows.

thinking creatively *Using our thinking process to develop ideas that are unique, useful, and worthy of further elaboration.*

Examining the creative thinking process is a rich and complex enterprise. Although it is not the primary focus of this book, we will nevertheless be addressing important aspects of the creative thinking process as we explore in depth the critical thinking process. In fact, these two dimensions of the thinking process are so tightly interwoven that both must be addressed together in order to understand them individually. Creative thinking and critical thinking work as partners to produce productive and effective thinking, enabling us to make informed decisions and lead successful lives. As this text unfolds, you will be given the opportunity to become familiar with both of these powerful forms of thought as you develop your abilities to think both critically and creatively.

THINKING PASSAGE

Jurors' Reasoning Processes

The following article, "Jurors Hear Evidence and Turn It into Stories," by Daniel Goleman, author of the best-selling book Emotional Intelligence, describes recent research that gives us insight into the way jurors think and reason during the process of reaching a verdict. As you read this article, reflect on the reasoning process you engaged in while thinking about the Mary Barnett case, and then answer the questions found at the end of the article.

JURORS HEAR EVIDENCE AND TURN IT INTO STORIES*
by Daniel Goleman

Studies Show They Arrange Details to Reflect Their Beliefs

Despite the furor over the verdict in the Rodney G. King beating case, scientists who study juries say the system is by and large sound. Many also believe that it is susceptible to manipulation and bias, and could be improved in various specific ways suggested by their research findings.

If there is any lesson to be learned from the research findings, it is that juries are susceptible to influence at virtually every point, from the moment members are selected to final deliberation.

Much of the newest research on the mind of the juror focuses on the stories that jurors tell themselves to understand the mounds of disconnected evidence, often presented in a confusing order. The research suggests that jurors' unspoken assumptions about human nature play a powerful role in their verdicts.

"People don't listen to all the evidence and then weigh it at the end," said Dr. Nancy Pennington, a psychologist at the University of Colorado. "They process it as they go along, composing a continuing story throughout the trial that makes sense of what they're hearing."

That task is made difficult by the way evidence is presented in most trials, in an order dictated for legal reasons rather than logical ones. Thus, in a murder trial, the first witness is often a coroner, who establishes that a death occurred.

"Jurors have little or nothing to tie such facts to, unless an attorney suggested an interpretation in the opening statement," in the form of a story line to follow, Dr. Pennington said.

---

* "Jurors Hear Evidence and Turn It into Stories," by Daniel Goleman, The *New York Times*, May 12, 1992. Copyright © 1992 by The New York Times Co. Reprinted by permission.

In an article in the November 1991 issue of *Cardozo Law Review,* Dr. Pennington, with Dr. Reid Hastie, also a psychologist at the University of Colorado, reported a series of experiments that show just how important jurors' stories are in determining the verdict they come to. In the studies, people called for jury duty but not involved in a trial were recruited for a simulation in which they were to act as jurors for a murder trial realistically reenacted on film.

In the case, the defendant, Frank Johnson, had quarreled in a bar with the victim, Alan Caldwell, who threatened him with a razor. Later that evening they went outside, got into a fight, and Johnson knifed Caldwell, who died. Disputed points included whether or not Caldwell was a bully who had started the first quarrel when his girlfriend had asked Johnson for a ride to the racetrack, whether Johnson had stabbed Caldwell or merely held his knife out to protect himself, and whether Johnson had gone home to get a knife.

In detailed interviews of the jurors, Dr. Pennington found that in explaining how they had reached their verdicts, 45 percent of the references they made were to events that had not been included in the courtroom testimony. These included inferences about the men's motives and psychological states, and assumptions the jurors themselves brought to the story from their own experience.

The stories that jurors told themselves pieced together the evidence in ways that could lead to opposite verdicts. One common story among the jurors, which led to a verdict of first-degree murder, was that the threat with the razor by Caldwell had so enraged Johnson that he went home to get his knife — a point that was in dispute — with the intention of picking a fight, during which he stabbed him to death.

By contrast, just as many jurors told themselves a story that led them to a verdict of not guilty: Caldwell started the fight with Johnson and threatened him with a razor, and Caldwell ran into the knife that Johnson was using to protect himself.

Role of Jurors' Backgrounds

The study found that jurors' backgrounds could lead to crucial differences in the assumptions they brought to their explanatory stories. Middle-class jurors were more likely to find the defendant guilty than were working-class jurors. The difference mainly hinged on how they interpreted the fact that Johnson had a knife with him during the struggle.

Middle-class jurors constructed stories that saw Johnson's having a knife as strong evidence that he planned a murderous assault on Caldwell in their second confrontation. But working-class jurors said it was likely that a man like Johnson would be in the habit of carrying a knife with him for protection, and so they saw nothing incriminating about his having the knife.

"Winning the battle of stories in the opening statements may help determine what evidence is attended to, how it is interpreted, and what is recalled both during and after the trial," Dr. Richard Lempert, a psychologist at the University of Michigan Law School, wrote in commenting on Dr. Pennington's article.

Verdicts that do not correspond to one's own "story" of a case are shocking. In the King case, "We didn't hear the defense story of what was going on, but only saw the strongest piece of the prosecution's evidence, the videotape," said Dr. Stephen Penrod, a psychologist at the University of Minnesota Law School. "If we had heard the defense theory, we may not have been so astonished by the verdict."

In the contest among jurors to recruit fellow members to one or another version of what happened, strong voices play a disproportionate role. Most juries include some people who virtually never speak up, and a small number who dominate the discussion, typically jurors of higher social status, according to studies reviewed in *Judging the Jury* (Plenum Press, 1986) by two psychologists, Dr. Valerie Hans of the University of Delaware and Dr. Neil Vidmar of Duke University.

The research also reveals that "juries are more often merciful to criminal defendants" than judges in the same cases would be, said Dr. Hans.

Blaming the Victim

In recent research, Dr. Hans interviewed 269 jurors in civil cases and found that many tended to focus on the ability of victims to have avoided being injured. "You see the same kind of blaming the victim in rape cases, too, especially among female jurors," Dr. Hans said. "Blaming the victim is reassuring to jurors because if victims are responsible for the harm that befell them, then you don't have to worry about becoming a victim yourself because you know what to do to avoid it."

That tendency may have been at work among the King jurors, Dr. Hans said, "when the jurors said King was in control and that if he stopped moving the police would have stopped beating him."

"Of course, the more they saw King as responsible for what happened, the less the officers were to blame in their minds," Dr. Hans said.

Perhaps the most intensive research has focused on the selection of a jury. Since lawyers can reject a certain number of prospective jurors during jury selection without having to give a specific reason, the contest to win the mind of the jury begins with the battle to determine who is and is not on the jury.

The scientific selection of juries began in the early 1970s when social scientists volunteered their services for the defense in a series of political trials, including proceedings arising from the 1971 Attica prison uprising in upstate New York. One method used was to poll the community where the trial was to be held to search for clues to attitudes that might work against the defendant, which the defense lawyers could then use to eliminate jurors.

For example, several studies have shown that people who favor the death penalty are generally pro-prosecution in criminal cases, and so more likely to convict a defendant. Defense lawyers can ask prospective jurors their views on the death penalty, and eliminate those who favor it.

On the basis of such a community survey for a trial in Miami, Dr. Elizabeth Loftus, a psychologist at the University of Washington, found that as a group, whites trust the honesty and fairness of the police far more than blacks. "If you knew nothing else, you'd use that demographic variable in picking a jury in the King case," she said. "But in Ventura County, there's a jury pool with almost no blacks. It was a gift to the defense, in retrospect."

Over the last two decades, such methods have been refined to the point that 300 or more consulting groups now advise lawyers on jury selection.

Questions for Analysis

1. Reflect back on your own deliberations of the Mary Barnett case and describe the reasoning process you used to reach a verdict. Did you find that you were composing a continuing story to explain the testimony you were reading? If so, was this story changed or modified as you learned more information or discussed the case with your classmates?

2. Explain how factors from your own personal experience (age, gender, experience with children, etc.) may have influenced your verdict and the reasoning process that led up to it.

3. Explain how your beliefs about human nature and free will may have influenced your analysis of Mary Barnett's motives and behavior.

4. Explain whether you believe that the research strategies lawyers are using to select the "right" jury for their cases are undermining the fairness of the justice system.

2 Thinking Critically

Carefully Exploring Situations with Questions

Thinking Independently

Viewing Situations from Different Perspectives

Supporting Diverse Perspectives with Reasons and Evidence

Thinking Critically
Carefully exploring the thinking process to clarify our understanding and make more intelligent decisions.

Thinking Actively

Discussing Ideas in an Organized Way

Becoming a Critical Thinker

A college education is the road that can lead you to your life's work, a career that will enable you to use your unique talents to bring you professional fulfillment. However, there are many other benefits to a college education, among them the opportunity to become what we have called an "educated thinker." Becoming an educated thinker is essential for achieving the greatest possible success in your chosen career, and it enriches your life in many other ways as well.

Traditionally, when people refer to an "educated thinker," they mean someone who has developed a knowledgeable understanding of our complex world, a thoughtful perspective on important ideas and timely issues, the capacity for penetrating insight and intelligent judgment, and sophisticated thinking and language abilities. These goals of advanced education have remained remarkably similar for several thousand years. In ancient Greece, most advanced students studied philosophy in order to achieve "wisdom." (The term *philosophy* in Greek means "lover of wisdom.") In today's world, many college students are hoping through their studies to become the modern-day equivalent: informed, *critical thinkers*.

The word *critical* comes from the Greek word for "critic" (*kritikos*), which means "to question, to make sense of, to be able to analyze." It is by questioning, making sense of situations, and analyzing issues that we examine our thinking and the thinking of others. These critical activities aid us in reaching the best possible conclusions and decisions. The word *critical* is also related to the word *criticize*, which means "to question and evaluate." Unfortunately, the ability to criticize is often only used destructively, to tear down someone else's thinking. Criticism, however, can also be *constructive* — analyzing for the purpose of developing a better understanding of what is going on. We will engage in constructive criticism as we develop our ability to think critically.

Thinking is the way you make sense of the world; thinking critically is thinking about your thinking so that you can clarify and improve it. If you can understand the way your mind works when you work toward your goals, make informed decisions, and analyze complex issues, then you can learn to think more effectively in these situations. In this chapter you will explore ways to examine your thinking so that you can develop it to the fullest extent possible. That is, you will discover how to *think critically*.

thinking critically *Carefully exploring the thinking process to clarify our understanding and make more intelligent decisions.*

Becoming a critical thinker transforms you in positive ways by enabling you to become an expert learner, view the world clearly, and make productive choices as you shape your life. Critical thinking is not simply one way of thinking; it is a total approach to understanding how you make sense of a world that includes many parts.

The best way to develop a clear and concrete idea of the critical thinker you want to become is to think about people you have known who can serve as critical thinking models. In my personal life, I had a number of teachers who taught me what it means to be a critical thinker through the example of their lives. I considered them to be brilliant critical thinkers because of the power of their minds and the commitment of their souls. They had a *vision:* a perspective on life that they were always trying to enhance through relentless curiosity and open-minded exploration. They also modeled a generosity of spirit as they sought to inspire thinking in others.

But you don't have to look only in college classrooms to find critical thinkers. They appear throughout humanity. The Greek philosopher Socrates was in many ways the original critical thinker for whom we have a historical record, and the depth and clarity of his thinking is immortalized in the *Dialogues* recorded by Plato, his student. As a renowned teacher in his native city of Athens, Socrates had created his own school and spent decades teaching young people how to analyze important issues through dialectical questioning — an approach that became known as the Socratic Method. At the age of seventy, he was deemed a dangerous troublemaker by the ruling politicians. Based on his teachings, students were asking embarrassing questions; in particular, they were questioning the politicians' authority and threatening their political careers. The politicians gave Socrates an ultimatum: Either leave the city where he had spent his entire life, never to return, or be put to death. Rather than leave his beloved Athens and the life he had created, Socrates chose death. Surrounded by his family and friends, he calmly drank a cup of hemlock-laced tea. He reasoned that leaving Athens would violate the intellectual integrity upon which he had built his life and had taught his students to uphold. Instead of sacrificing his beliefs, he ended his life, concluding with the words: *"Now it is time for us to part, I to die and you to live. Whether life or death is better is known to God, and to God only."*

Today especially, we all need to become philosophers, to develop a philosophical framework. Critical thinking is a modern reworking of a philosophical perspective.

Who would *you* identify as expert critical thinkers? To qualify, the people you identify should have lively, energetic minds. Specifically, they should be:

VISUAL THINKING

"Now It Is Time for Us to Part, I to Die and You to Live . . ."

● What can you tell about Socrates' reaction to his impending death based on this painting by Jean Louis David? What is the reaction of his family and friends? If you were a close friend of Socrates, what would be your reaction? Why?

● *Open-minded:* In discussions they listen carefully to every viewpoint, evaluating each perspective carefully and fairly.

● *Knowledgeable:* When they offer an opinion, it's always based on facts or evidence. On the other hand, if they lack knowledge of the subject, they acknowledge this.

● *Mentally active:* They take initiative and actively use their intelligence to confront problems and meet challenges, instead of simply responding passively to events.

● *Curious:* They explore situations with probing questions that penetrate beneath the surface of issues, instead of being satisfied with superficial explanations.

- *Independent thinkers:* They are not afraid to disagree with the group opinion. They develop well-supported beliefs through thoughtful analysis, instead of uncritically "borrowing" the beliefs of others or simply going along with the crowd.

- *Skilled discussants:* They are able to discuss ideas in an organized and intelligent way. Even when the issues are controversial, they listen carefully to opposing viewpoints and respond thoughtfully.

- *Insightful:* They are able to get to the heart of the issue or problem. While others may be distracted by details, they are able to zero in on the essence, seeing the "forest" as well as the "trees."

- *Self-aware:* They are aware of their own biases and are quick to point them out and take them into consideration when analyzing a situation.

- *Creative:* They can break out of established patterns of thinking and approach situations from innovative directions.

- *Passionate:* They have a passion for understanding and are always striving to see issues and problems with more clarity.

 THINKING ACTIVITY 2.1

WHO IS A CRITICAL THINKER?

Think about people you know whom you admire as expert thinkers and list some of the qualities these people exhibit that you believe qualify them as "critical thinkers." For each critical thinking quality, write down a brief example involving the person. Identifying such people will help you visualize the kind of people you'd like to emulate. As you think your way through this book, you will be creating a portrait of the kind of critical thinker you are striving to become, a blueprint you can use to direct your development and chart your progress.

This chapter explores some of the cognitive abilities and attitudes that characterize critical thinkers, including the following:

- Thinking actively

- Carefully exploring situations with questions

- Thinking independently

- Viewing situations from different perspectives

- Supporting diverse perspectives with reasons and evidence

- Discussing ideas in an organized way

The remaining chapters in the book examine additional thinking abilities that you will need to develop in order to become a fully mature critical thinker.

⊚ Thinking Actively

When you think critically, you are actively using your intelligence, knowledge, and abilities to deal effectively with life's situations. When you think actively, you are

- Getting involved in potentially useful projects and activities instead of remaining disengaged

- Taking initiative in making decisions on your own instead of waiting passively to be told what to think or do

- Following through on your commitments instead of giving up when you encounter difficulties

- Taking responsibility for the consequences of your decisions rather than unjustifiably blaming others or events "beyond your control"

When you think actively, you are not just waiting for something to happen. You are engaged in the process of achieving goals, making decisions, and solving problems. When you react passively, you let events control you or permit others to do your thinking for you. To make an intelligent decision about your future career, for example, you have to work actively to secure more information, try out various possibilities, speak with people who are experienced in your area of interest, and then critically reflect on all these factors. Thinking critically requires that you think actively — not react passively — to deal effectively with life's situations.

Influences on Your Thinking

As our minds grow and develop, we are exposed to influences that encourage us to think actively. We also, however, have many experiences that encourage us to think passively. For example, some analysts believe that when people, especially children, spend much of their time watching television, they are being influenced to think passively, thus inhibiting their intellectual growth. Listed here are some of the influences we experience in our lives. As you read through the list, place an *A* next to those items you believe in general influence you to think *actively*, and a *P* next to those you consider to be generally *passive* influences.

Activities: *People:*

Reading books   Family members
Writing   Friends
Watching television   Employers
Dancing   Advertisers
Drawing/painting   School/college teachers
Playing video games   Police officers
Playing sports   Religious leaders
Listening to music   Politicians

THINKING ACTIVITY 2.2

Influences on Our Thinking

All of us are subject to powerful influences on our thinking, influences that we are often unaware of. For example, advertisers spend billions of dollars to manipulate our thinking in ways that are complex and subtle. For this exercise, choose one of the following tasks:

1. Watch some typical commercials, with several other class members if possible, and discuss with other watchers the techniques each advertiser is using to shape your thinking. Analyze with the other viewers how each of the elements in a commercial — images, language, music — affects an audience. Pay particular attention to the symbolic associations of various images and words, and identify the powerful emotions that these associations elicit. Why are the commercials effective? What influential roles do commercials play in our culture as a whole? For instance, think about how the impact of Nike commercials extends far beyond merely selling athletic shoes and sportswear to creating idealized images that people strive to emulate.

2. Select a web site that uses advertisements and do an in-depth analysis of it. Explain how each of the site's elements — design, content, use of advertisements, links — works to influence our thinking. Pay particular

VISUAL THINKING

"Now About That Skin Cancer and Those Premature Wrinkles . . ."

● The advertisers in this photo are trying to influence your thinking: what's their message? What strategies and techniques are they using to accomplish their goal? If you were encouraging someone to think critically about this ad, what would you say? What approaches can we use to make ourselves less susceptible to these types of mental manipulation?

attention to the advertisements: Are they static or flashing (in the same place, but changing every few minutes)? If you are observing a changing advertisement, monitor it for an hour or two and see how often it changes and who the advertisers are. What does this tell you about the site and the creators of the site?

Of course, in many cases people and activities can act as both active and passive influences, depending on the specifics of situations and our individual responses. For example, consider employers. If we are performing a routine, repetitive job, as I did during the summer I spent in a peanut butter cracker factory hand-scooping 2,000 pounds of peanut butter a day, the very nature of the work tends to encourage passive, uncreative thinking (although it might also lead to creative daydreaming!). We are also influenced to think passively if our employer gives us detailed instructions for performing every task, instructions that permit no exception or deviation. On the other hand, when our employer gives us general areas of responsibility within which we are expected to make thoughtful and creative decisions, then we are being stimulated to think actively and independently.

These contrasting styles of supervision are mirrored in different approaches to raising children. Some parents encourage children to be active thinkers by teaching them to express themselves clearly, make independent decisions, look at different points of view, and choose what they think is right for themselves. Other parents influence their children to be passive thinkers by not letting them do things on their own. These parents give the children detailed instructions they are expected to follow without question and make the important decisions for them. They are reluctant to give their children significant responsibilities, creating, unintentionally, dependent thinkers who are not well adapted to making independent decisions and assuming responsibility for their lives.

Becoming an Active Learner

Critical thinkers actively use their intelligence, knowledge, and abilities to deal with life's situations. Similarly, active thinking is one of the keys to effective learning. Each of us has our own knowledge framework that we use to make sense of the world, a framework that incorporates all that we have learned in our lives. When we learn something new, we have to find ways to integrate this new information or skill into our existing knowledge framework. For example, if one of your professors is presenting material on Sigmund Freud's concept of the unconscious or the role of Heisenberg's uncertainty principle in the theory of quantum mechanics, you need to find ways to relate these new ideas to things you already know in order to make this new information "your own." How do you do this? By actively using your mind to integrate new information into your existing knowledge framework, thereby expanding the framework to include this new information.

For example, when your professor provides a detailed analysis of Freud's concept of the unconscious, you use your mind to call up what you know about Freud's theory of personality and what you know of the concept of the unconscious. You then try to connect this new information to what you already know, integrating it into your expanding knowledge framework. In a way, learning is analogous to the activity of eating: You ingest food (*information*) in one form, actively transform it through digestion (*mental processing*), and then integrate the result into the ongoing functioning of your body.

◎ Carefully Exploring Situations with Questions

As you have just seen, thinking critically involves actively using your thinking abilities to attack problems, meet challenges, and analyze issues. An important dimension of thinking actively is carefully exploring the situations in which you are involved with relevant questions. In fact, the ability to ask appropriate and penetrating questions is one of the most powerful thinking tools you possess, although many people do not make full use of it. Active learners explore the learning situations they are involved in with questions that enable them to understand the material or task at hand, and then integrate this new understanding into their knowledge framework. In contrast, passive learners rarely ask questions. Instead, they try to absorb information like sponges, memorizing what is expected and then regurgitating what they memorized on tests and quizzes.

Questions come in many different forms and are used for a variety of purposes. For instance, questions can be classified in terms of the ways that people organize and interpret information. We can identify six such categories of questions, a schema that was first suggested and elaborated by the educator Benjamin Bloom:

1. Fact   **4.** Synthesis

2. Interpretation   **5.** Valuation

3. Analysis   **6.** Application

Active learners are able to ask appropriate questions from all of these categories in a very natural and flexible way. These various types of questions are closely interrelated, and an effective thinker is able to use them in a productive relation to one another. Also, these categories of questions are very general and at times overlap with one another. This means that a given question may fall into more than one of the six categories of questions. Following is a summary of the six categories of questions along with sample forms of questions from each category.

1. *Questions of Fact:* Questions of fact seek to determine the basic information of a situation: who, what, when, where, how. These questions seek information that is relatively straightforward and objective.

Who, what, when, where, how ————————————————————?

Describe ————————————————————————.

2. ***Questions of Interpretation:*** Questions of interpretation seek to select and organize facts and ideas, discovering the relationships between them. Examples of such relationships include the following:
   - *Chronological relationships:* relating things in time sequence
   - *Process relationships:* relating aspects of growth, development, or change
   - *Comparison/contrast relationships:* relating things in terms of their similar/different features
   - *Causal relationships:* relating events in terms of the way some events are responsible for bringing about other events

Retell ——————————————————— in your own words.

What is the *main idea* of ————————————————?

What is the *time sequence* relating the following events: ——————?

What are the steps in the *process of growth* or *development* in ————?

How would you *compare and contrast* ————— and ————?

What was the *cause* of —————? The *effect* of —————?

3. ***Questions of Analysis:*** Questions of analysis seek to separate an entire process or situation into its component parts and to understand the relation of these parts to the whole. These questions attempt to classify various elements, outline component structures, articulate various possibilities, and clarify the reasoning being presented.

What are the *parts or features* of ————————————————?

Classify ————— according to ————————————.

Outline/diagram/web ————————————————————.

What *evidence* can you present to support ————————?

What are the *possible alternatives* for _____?

Explain the *reasons why* you think _____.

4. **Questions of Synthesis:** Questions of synthesis have as their goal combining ideas to form a new whole or come to a conclusion, making inferences about future events, creating solutions, and designing plans of action.

    What would you *predict/infer* from _____?

    What ideas can you *add to* _____?

    How would you *create/design* a new _____?

    What might happen if you *combined* _____ with _____?

    What *solutions/decisions* would you suggest for _____?

5. **Questions of Evaluation:** The aim of evaluation questions is to help us make informed judgments and decisions by determining the relative value, truth, or reliability of things. The process of evaluation involves identifying the criteria or standards we are using and then determining to what extent the things in common meet those standards.

    How would you *evaluate* _____, and what standards would you use?

    Do you agree with _____? Why or why not?

    How would you *decide* about _____?

    What *criteria* would you use to assess _____?

6. **Questions of Application:** The aim of application questions is to help us take the knowledge or concepts we have gained in one situation and apply them to other situations.

    How is _____ *an example of* _____?

    How would you *apply* this rule/principle to _____?

Mastering these forms of questions and using them appropriately will serve as powerful tools in your learning process.

Becoming an expert questioner is an ongoing project, and you can practice it throughout the day. When you are talking to people about even everyday topics, get in the habit of asking questions from all of the different categories. Similarly, when you are attending class, taking notes, or reading assignments, make a practice of asking — and trying to answer — appropriate questions. You will find that by actively exploring the world in this way you are discovering a great deal and learning what you have discovered in a meaningful and lasting fashion.

As children, we were natural questioners, but this questioning attitude was often discouraged when we entered the school system. Often we were given the message, in subtle and not so subtle ways, that "schools have the questions; your job is to learn the answers." The educator Neil Postman has said: "Children enter schools as question marks and they leave as periods." In order for us to become critical thinkers and effective learners, we have to become question marks again.

THINKING ACTIVITY 2.3

Analyzing a Complex Issue

Review the following decision-making situation (based on an incident that happened in Springfield, Missouri), and then critically examine it by posing questions from each of the six categories we have considered in this section:

1. Fact   **4.** Synthesis

2. Interpretation   **5.** Evaluation

3. Analysis   **6.** Application

Imagine that you are a member of a student group at your college that has decided to stage the controversial play *The Normal Heart* by Larry Kramer. The play is based on the lives of real people and dramatizes their experiences in the early stages of the AIDS epidemic. It focuses on their efforts to publicize the horrific nature of this disease and to secure funding from a reluctant federal government to find a cure. The play is considered controversial because of its exclusive focus on the subject of AIDS, its explicit homosexual themes, and the large amount of profanity contained in the script. After lengthy discussion, however, your student group has decided that the educational and moral benefits of the play render it a valuable contribution to the life of the college.

While the play is in rehearsal, a local politician seizes upon it as an issue and mounts a political and public relations campaign against it. She distributes selected excerpts of the play to newspapers, religious groups, and civic organizations. She also introduces a bill in the state legislature to withdraw state funding for the college if the play is performed. The play creates a firestorm of controversy, replete with local and national news reports, editorials, and impassioned speeches for and against it. Everyone associated with the play is subjected to verbal harassment, threats, crank phone calls, and hate mail. The firestorm explodes when the house of one of the key spokespersons for the play is burned to the ground. The director and actors go into hiding for their safety, rehearsing in secret and moving from hotel to hotel.

Your student group has just convened to decide what course of action to take. Analyze the situation using the six types of questions listed previously and then conclude with your decision and the reasons that support your decision.

ⓔ Thinking Independently

Answer the following questions, based on what you believe to be true.

	Yes	*No*	*Not Sure*
1. Is the earth flat?			
2. Is there a God?			
3. Is abortion wrong?			
4. Have alien life forms visited the earth?			
5. Should men be the breadwinners and women the homemakers?			

Your responses to these questions reveal aspects of the way your mind works. How did you arrive at these conclusions? Your views on these and many other issues probably had their beginnings with your family, especially your parents. When we are young, we are very dependent on our parents, and we are influenced by the way they see the world. As we grow up, we learn how to think, feel, and behave in various situations. In addition to our parents, our "teachers" include our brothers and sisters, friends, religious leaders, schoolteachers, books, television, and so on. Most of what we learn we absorb without even being aware of the process. Many of your ideas about the issues raised in the preceding questions were most likely shaped by the experiences you had growing up.

As a result of our ongoing experiences, however, our minds — and our thinking — continue to mature. Instead of simply accepting the views of others, we gradually develop the ability to examine this thinking and to decide whether it makes sense to us and whether we should accept it. As we think through such ideas, we use this standard to make our decisions: Are there good reasons or evidence that support this thinking? If there are good reasons, we can actively decide to adopt these ideas. If they do not make sense, we can modify or reject them.

Of course, we do not *always* examine our own thinking or the thinking of others so carefully. In fact, we very often continue to believe the same ideas we were brought up with, without ever examining and deciding for ourselves what to think. Or we often blindly reject the beliefs we have been brought up with, without really examining them.

How do you know when you have examined and adopted ideas yourself instead of simply borrowing them from others? One indication of having thought through your ideas is being able to explain *why* you believe them, explaining the reasons that led you to these conclusions.

For each of the views you expressed at the beginning of this section, explain how you arrived at it and give the reasons and evidence that you believe support it.

1. *Example:* Is the earth flat?

   Explanation: I was taught by my parents and in school that the earth was round.

   Reasons/Evidence:

   a. *Authorities:* My parents and teachers taught me this.

   b. *References:* I read about this in science textbooks.

   c. *Factual evidence:* I have seen a sequence of photographs taken from outer space that show the earth as a globe.

   d. *Personal experience:* When I flew across the country, I could see the horizon line changing.

2. Is there a God?

3. Is abortion wrong?

4. Have alien life forms visited the earth?

5. Should men be the breadwinners and women the homemakers?

Of course, not all reasons and evidence are equally strong or accurate. For example, before the fifteenth century the common belief that the earth was flat was supported by the following reasons and evidence:

- *Authorities:* Educational and religious authorities taught people the earth was flat.

- *References:* The written opinions of scientific experts supported belief in a flat earth.

- *Factual evidence:* No person had ever circumnavigated the earth.

- *Personal experience:* From a normal vantage point, the earth looks flat.

Many considerations go into evaluating the strengths and accuracy of reasons and evidence, and we will be exploring these areas in this and future chapters. Let's examine some basic questions that critical thinkers automatically consider when evaluating reasons and evidence by completing Thinking Activity 2.4.

 THINKING ACTIVITY 2.4

Evaluating Your Beliefs

Evaluate the strengths and accuracy of the reasons and evidence you identified to support your beliefs on the five issues by addressing questions such as the following:

- *Authorities:* Are the authorities knowledgeable in this area? Are they reliable? Have they ever given inaccurate information? Do other authorities disagree with them?

- *References:* What are the credentials of the authors? Are there other authors who disagree with their opinions? On what reasons and evidence do the authors base their opinions?

- *Factual evidence:* What are the source and foundation of the evidence? Can the evidence be interpreted differently? Does the evidence support the conclusion?

- *Personal experience:* What were the circumstances under which the experiences took place? Were distortions or mistakes in perception possible? Have other people had either similar or conflicting experiences? Are there other explanations for the experience?

Thinking independently doesn't mean automatically rejecting all traditional beliefs and conventional wisdom. In critically evaluating beliefs, it makes sense to accept traditional beliefs insofar as they enrich and sharpen our thinking. If they don't stand up to critical scrutiny, then we need to have the courage to think for ourselves, even if it means rejecting "conventional wisdom."

Analogously, thinking for yourself doesn't always mean doing exactly what you want to; it may mean becoming aware of the social guidelines and expectations of a given situation and then making an informed decision about what is in your best interests. For example, even though you may have a legal right to choose whatever clothes you want to wear at your workplace, if your choice doesn't conform to your employer's guidelines or "norms," then you may suffer unpleasant consequences as a result. In other words, thinking for yourself often involves balancing your view of things against those of others, integrating yourself into social structures without sacrificing your independence or personal autonomy.

Learning to become an independent, critical thinker is a complex, ongoing process that involves all the abilities we have been examining in this chapter up to this point:

- Thinking actively

- Carefully exploring situations with questions

- Thinking independently

As you confront the many decisions you have to make in your life, you should try to gather all the relevant information, review your priorities, and then carefully weigh all the factors before arriving at a final decision. One helpful strategy for exploring thinking situations is the one we have been practicing: *Identify* the important questions that need to be answered and then try to *answer* these questions.

Viewing Situations from Different Perspectives

Although it is important to think for yourself, others may have good ideas from which you can learn and benefit. A critical thinker is a person who is willing to listen to and examine carefully other views and new ideas. In addition to your viewpoint, there may be other viewpoints that are equally important and need to be taken into consideration if you are to develop a more complete understanding of a situation.

VISUAL THINKING

Thinking Independently

● What are the reasons that people too often get locked into passive, dependent ways of thinking? What strategies can we use to overcome these forces and think independently? Describe a time when you took an independent, and unpopular, stand on an issue. What was the experience like?

As children we understand the world from only our own point of view. As we grow, we come into contact with people who have different viewpoints and begin to realize that our viewpoint is often inadequate, we are frequently mistaken, and our perspective is only one of many. If we are going to learn and develop, we must try to understand and appreciate the viewpoints of others. For example, consider the following situation:

> Imagine that you have been employed at a new job for the past six months. Although you enjoy the challenge of your responsibilities and you are performing well, you find that you simply cannot complete all your work during office hours. To keep up, you have to work late, take work home, and even occasionally work on weekends. When you explain this to your employer, she says that although she is sorry that the job interferes with your personal life, it has to be done. She suggests that you view these sacrifices as an investment in your future and that you should try to work more efficiently. She reminds you that there are many people who would be happy to have your position.

1. Describe this situation from your employer's standpoint, identifying reasons that might support her views.
2. Describe some different approaches that you and your employer might take to help resolve this situation.
3. We are a society that in general expects people to work with great dedication in order to achieve meaningful success. This typically means working long hours and encroaching on personal time outside of the work environment. Do you think that people who are prepared to make a greater commitment to their careers should enjoy more success? Why or why not?

For most of the important issues and problems in your life, one viewpoint is simply not adequate to provide a full and satisfactory understanding. To increase and deepen your knowledge, you must seek *other perspectives* on the situations you are trying to understand. You can sometimes accomplish this by using your imagination to visualize other viewpoints. Usually, however, you need to seek actively (and *listen* to) the viewpoints of others. It is often very difficult for people to see things from points of view other than their own, and if you are not careful, you can make the mistake of thinking that the way you see things is the way things really are. In addition to identifying with perspectives other than your own, you also have to work to understand the *reasons* that support these alternate viewpoints. This approach deepens your understanding of the issues and also stimulates you to evaluate critically your beliefs.

THINKING ACTIVITY 2.5

Analyzing a Belief from Different Perspectives

Describe a belief of yours about which you feel very strongly. Then explain the reasons or experiences that led you to this belief.

Next, describe a point of view that conflicts with your belief. Identify some of the reasons why someone might hold this belief. A student example follows.

A BELIEF THAT I FEEL STRONGLY ABOUT

I used to think that we should always try everything in our power to keep a person alive. But now I strongly believe that a person has a right to die in peace and with dignity. The reason why I believe this now is because of my father's illness and death.

It all started on Christmas Day, December 25, when my father was admitted to the hospital. The doctors diagnosed his condition as a heart attack. Following this episode, he was readmitted and discharged from several different hospitals. On June 18, he was hospitalized for what was initially thought to be pneumonia but which turned out to be lung cancer. He began chemotherapy treatments. When complications occurred, he had to be placed on a respirator. At first he couldn't speak or eat. But then they operated on him and placed the tube from the machine in his throat instead of his mouth. He was then able to eat and move his mouth. He underwent radiation therapy when they discovered he had three tumors in his head and that the cancer had spread all over his body. We had to sign a paper which asked us to indicate, if he should stop breathing, whether we would want the hospital to try to revive him or just let him go. We decided to let him go because the doctors couldn't guarantee that he wouldn't become brain-dead. At first they said that there was a forty percent chance that he would get off the machine. But instead of that happening, the percentage went down.

It was hard seeing him like that since I was so close to him. But it was even harder when he didn't want to see me. He said that by seeing me suffer, his suffering was greater. So I had to cut down on seeing him. Everybody that visited him said that he had changed dramatically. They couldn't even recognize him.

The last two days of his life were the worst. I prayed that God would relieve him of his misery. I had come very close to taking him off the machine in order for him not to suffer, but I didn't. Finally he passed away on November 22, with not the least bit of peace or dignity. The loss was great then and still is, but at least he's not suffering. That's why I believe that when people have terminal diseases with no hope of recovery, they shouldn't place them on machines to prolong their lives of suffering, but instead they should be permitted to die with as much peace and dignity as possible.

Somebody else might believe very strongly that we should try everything in our power to keep people alive. It doesn't matter what kind of illness or disease the people have. What's important is that they are kept alive, especially if they are loved ones. Some people want to keep their loved ones alive with them as long as they can, even if it's by a machine. They also believe it is up to God and medical science to determine whether people should live or die. Sometimes doctors give them hope that their loved ones will recover, and many people wish for a miracle to happen. With these hopes and wishes in mind, they wait and try everything in order to prolong a life, even if the doctors tell them that there is nothing that can be done.

Being open to new ideas and different viewpoints means being *flexible* enough to change or modify your ideas in the light of new information or better insight. Each of us has a tendency to cling to the beliefs we have been brought up with and the conclusions we have arrived at. If we are going to continue to grow and develop as thinkers, however, we have to be willing to change or modify our beliefs when evidence suggests that we should. For example, imagine that you have been brought up with certain views concerning an ethnic group — African American, Caucasian, Hispanic, Asian, Native American, or any other. As you mature and your experience increases, you may find that the evidence of your experience conflicts with the views you have been raised with. As critical thinkers, we have to be *open* to receiving this new evidence and *flexible* enough to change and modify our ideas on the basis of it.

In contrast to open and flexible thinking, *un*critical thinking tends to be one-sided and close-minded. People who think this way are convinced that they alone see things as they really are and that everyone who disagrees with them is wrong. The words we use to describe this type of person include "dogmatic," "subjective," and "egocentric." It is very difficult for such people to step outside their own viewpoints in order to see things from other people's perspectives. Part of being an educated person is being able to think in an open-minded and flexible way.

THINKING ACTIVITY 2.6

Writing from Interactive Perspectives

Think of a well-known person, either historical (e.g., Socrates) or contemporary (e.g., Oprah Winfrey), and identify different perspectives from which that person can be viewed. For example, consider viewing Oprah Winfrey as

- pop culture icon
- a black activist
- a cult leader
- a feminist

- a wealthy celebrity
- a self-help guru
- an actress
- a political liberal

Next, select two perspectives from the ones you identified and, using research, provide an explanatory background for each perspective. Then, through investigative analysis, describe the interactive relationship between the two perspectives, the basis on which they interact, and the ways in which each supports the other. Finally, in a summary conclusion to your findings, assess the significance of the two perspectives for contemporary thought.*

Supporting Diverse Perspectives with Reasons and Evidence

When you are thinking critically, what you think makes sense, and you can give good reasons to back up your ideas. As we have seen and will continue to see throughout this book, it is not enough simply to take a position on an issue or make a claim; we have to *back up our views* with other information that we feel supports our position. In other words, there is an important distinction as well as relationship between *what* you believe and *why* you believe it.

If someone questions why you see an issue the way you do, you probably respond by giving reasons or arguments you feel support your belief. For example, take the question of what sort of college to attend: two-year or four-year, residential or commuting. What are some of the reasons you might offer to support your decision to attend the kind of college in which you enrolled?

---

*This activity was developed by Frank Juszcyk.

VISUAL THINKING

"You Leave — I Was Here First!"

- Critical thinkers actively try to view issues from different perspectives. Why would someone take the position, "Let's get rid of illegal immigrants in America?" How would native Americans view the person making that statement? What is your perspective on illegal immigrants in this country? Why?

Although all the reasons you just gave for attending your sort of college support your decision, some are obviously more important to you than others. In any case, even though going to your college may be the right thing for you to do, this decision does not mean that it is the right thing for everyone to do. In order for you to fully appreciate this fact, to see both sides of the issue, you have to put yourself in the position of others and try to see things from their points of view. What are some of the reasons or arguments someone might give for attending a different kind of college?

The responses you just gave demonstrate that, if you are interested in seeing all sides of an issue, you have to be able to give supporting reasons and evidence not just for *your* views but for the views of *others* as well. Seeing all sides of an issue thus combines these two critical thinking abilities:

- Viewing issues from different perspectives

- Supporting diverse viewpoints with reasons and evidence

Combining these two abilities enables you not only to understand other views about an issue but also to understand *why* these views are held. Consider the issue of whether using a cell phone while driving should be prohibited. As you try to make sense of this issue, you should attempt to identify not just the reasons that support your view but also the reasons that support other views. The following are reasons that support each view of this issue.

Issue:

Cell phone use while driving should be prohibited.	Cell phone use while driving should be permitted.
SUPPORTING REASONS:	SUPPORTING REASONS:
1. Studies show that using cell phones while driving increases accidents.	1. Many people feel that cell phones are no more distracting than other common activities in cars.

Now see if you can identify additional supporting reasons for each of these views on cell phone use while driving.

SUPPORTING REASONS:	SUPPORTING REASONS:
2.	2.
3.	3.
4.	4.

THINKING ACTIVITY 2.7

Analyzing Different Sides of an Issue

For each of the following issues, identify reasons that support each side of the issue.

Issue:

1. Multiple-choice and true/false exams should be given in college-level courses.

   Multiple-choice and true/false exams should not be given in college-level courses.

Issue:

2. Immigration quotas should be reduced.

   Immigration quotas should be increased.

Issue:

3. The best way to deal with crime is to give long prison sentences.

   Long prison sentences will not reduce crime.

Issue:

4. When a couple divorces, the children should choose the parent with whom they wish to live.

   When a couple divorces, the court should decide all custody issues regarding the children.

THINKING ACTIVITY 2.8

Analyzing Different Perspectives

Working to see different perspectives is crucial in helping you get a more complete understanding of the ideas being expressed in the passages you are reading. Read each of the following passages and then do the following:

1. Identify the main idea of the passage.
2. List the reasons that support the main idea.
3. Develop another view of the main issue.
4. List the reasons that support the other view.

- In a letter that has stunned many leading fertility specialists, the acting head of their professional society's ethics committee says it is sometimes acceptable for couples to choose the sex of their children by selecting either male or female embryos and discarding the rest. The group, the American Society of Reproductive Medicine, establishes positions on ethical issues, and most clinics say they abide by them. One fertility specialist, Dr. Norbet Gleicher, whose group has nine centers and who had asked for the opinion, was quick to act on it. "We will offer it immediately," Dr. Gleicher said of the sex-selection method. "Frankly, we have a list of patients who asked for it." Couples would have to undergo in vitro fertilization, and then their embryos would be examined in the first few days when they consisted of just eight cells. Leading fertility specialists said they were taken aback by the new letter and could hardly believe its message. "What's the next step?" asked Dr. William Schoolcraft. "As we learn more about genetics, do we reject kids who do not have superior intelligence or who don't have the right color hair or eyes?" (*New York Times*, September 28, 2001).

- When Dr. Hassan Abbass, a Veterans Affairs Department surgeon, and his wife arrived at the airport to leave for vacation last May 24, they were pulled aside and forced to submit to a careful search before boarding the plane. They became one of thousands of Americans of Middle Eastern heritage who have complained that a secretive and side-scale "profiling" system sponsored by the government and aimed at preventing air terrorism has caused them to be unfairly selected for extra scrutiny at airports. "Profiling" of this type is being used more frequently in many areas of law-enforcement, raising fundamental questions of how a free society balances security fears with civil liberties and the desire to avoid offensive stereotyping (*New York Times*, August 11, 1997).

- Most wicked deeds are done because the doer proposes some good to himself. The liar lies to gain some end; the swindler and thief want things which, if honestly got, might be good in themselves. Even the murderer may be removing an impediment to normal desires or gaining possession of something which his victim keeps from him. None of these people usually does evil for evil's sake. They are selfish or unscrupulous, but their deeds are not gratuitously evil. The killer for sport has no such comprehensible motive. He prefers death to life, darkness to light. He gets nothing except the satisfaction of saying,

"Something which wanted to live is dead. There is that much less vitality, consciousness, and, perhaps, joy in the universe. I am the Spirit that Denies." When a human wantonly destroys one of humankind's own works we call him Vandal. When he wantonly destroys one of the works of God we call him Sportsman.

- More than at any other time in history, America is plagued by the influence of cults, exclusive groups that present themselves as religions devoted to the worship of a single individual. Initially, most Americans were not terribly concerned with the growth of cults, but then in 1979, more than nine hundred cult members were senselessly slaughtered in the steamy jungles of a small South American country called Guyana. The reason for the slaughter was little more than the wild, paranoid fear of the leader, the Reverend Jim Jones, who called himself father and savior. Since that time, evidence has increased that another cult leader, the Reverend Sun Myung Moon, has amassed a large personal fortune from the purses of his followers, male and female "Moonies," who talk of bliss while peddling pins and emblems preaching the gospel of Moon. Cults, with their hypnotic rituals and their promises of ecstasy, are a threat to American youth, and it is time to implement laws that would allow for a thorough restriction of their movements.

Discussing Ideas in an Organized Way

Thinking critically often takes place in a social context, not in isolation. Although it is natural for every person to have his or her own perspective on the world, no single viewpoint is adequate for making sense of complex issues, situations, or even people. As we will see in the chapters ahead, we each have our own "lenses" through which we view the world — filters that shape, influence, and often distort the way we see things. The best way to expand our thinking and compensate for the bias that we all have is to discuss our experiences with other people.

This is the way in which thinking develops: being open to the viewpoints of others and being willing to listen and to exchange ideas with them. This process of give-and-take, of advancing our views and considering those of others, is known as discussion. When we participate in a discussion, we are not simply talking; we are exchanging and exploring our ideas in an organized way.

Unfortunately, our conversations with other people about important topics are too often not productive exchanges. They often degenerate into name calling, shouting matches, or worse. Consider the following dialogue:

PERSON A: A friend of mine sent a humorous email in which he wrote about "killing the president." He wasn't serious, of course, but two days later the FBI showed up on his doorstep! This is no longer a free society — it's a fascist regime!

PERSON B: Your friend's an idiot, and unpatriotic as well. You don't kid about killing the president. Your friend is lucky he didn't wind up in jail, where he deserves to be!

PERSON A: Since when is kidding around treason? With the way our freedoms are being stolen, we might as well be living in a dictatorship!

PERSON B: You're friend isn't the only idiot — you're an idiot, too! You don't deserve to live in America. It's attitudes like yours that make terrorist attacks possible, like those against the World Trade Center and the Pentagon.

PERSON A: You're calling me a terrorist? I can't talk to a fascist like you!

PERSON B: And I can't talk to an unpatriotic traitor like you. America: Love it or leave it! Good-bye and good riddance!

If we examine the dynamics of this dialogue, we can see that the two people here are not really

- Listening to each other

- Supporting their views with reasons and evidence

- Responding to the points being made

- Asking — and trying to answer — important questions

- Trying to increase their understanding rather than simply winning the argument

In short, the people in this exchange are not *discussing* their views; they are simply *expressing* them, and each is trying to influence the other person into agreeing. Contrast this first dialogue with the following one. Although it begins the same way, it quickly takes a much different direction.

PERSON A: A friend of mine sent a humorous email in which he wrote about "killing the president." He wasn't serious, of course, but two days later the FBI showed up on his doorstep! This is no longer a free society — it's a fascist regime!

PERSON B: Your friend's an idiot, and unpatriotic as well. You don't kid about killing the president. Your friend is lucky he didn't wind up in jail, where he deserves to be!

PERSON A: Since when is kidding around treason? With the way our freedoms are being stolen, we're living in a repressive dictatorship!

PERSON B: Don't you think it's inappropriate to be talking about killing the president, even if you are kidding? And why do you think we're living in a repressive dictatorship?

PERSON A: Well, you're probably right that emailing a message like this isn't very intelligent, particularly considering the leaders who have been assassinated — John F. Kennedy and Martin Luther King, for example — and the terrorist attacks that we have suffered. But the only way FBI agents could have known about the email is if they are monitoring our private emails on an ongoing basis. Doesn't that concern you? It's like "Big Brother" is watching our every move, and pouncing when we do something they think is wrong.

PERSON B: You're making a good point. It is a little unnerving to realize that our private conversations on the Internet may be monitored by the government. But doesn't it have to take measures like this in order to ensure we're safe? After all, remember the catastrophic attacks that destroyed the World Trade towers and part of the Pentagon, and the Oklahoma City bombing. If the government has to play the role of "Big Brother" to make sure we're safe, I think it's worth it.

PERSON A: I see what you're saying. But I think that the government has a tendency to go overboard if it's not held in check. Just consider the gigantic file the FBI compiled on Martin Luther King and other peaceful leaders, based on illegal wiretaps and covert surveillance.

PERSON B: I certainly don't agree with those types of activities against peaceful citizens. But what about people who are genuine threats? Don't we have to let the government do whatever's necessary to identify and arrest them? After all, threatening to kill the president is like telling airport personnel that you have a bomb in your suitcase — it's not funny, even if you're not serious.

PERSON A: You're right: It's important for the government to do what's necessary to make sure we're as safe as possible from terrorist threats. But we can't give it a blank check to read our email, tap our phones, and infringe on our personal freedoms in other ways. After all, it's those freedoms that make America what it is.

PERSON B: Yes, I guess the goal is to strike the right balance between security and personal freedoms. How do we do that?

PERSON A: That's a very complicated question we're going to have to explore with many other discussions. Right now, though, I better get to class before my professor sends Big Brother to look for me!

How would you contrast the level of communication taking place in this dialogue with that in the first dialogue? What are the reasons for your conclusion?

Naturally, discussions are not always quite this organized and direct. Nevertheless, this second dialogue does provide a good model for what can take place in our everyday lives when we carefully explore an issue or a situation with someone else. Let us take a closer look at this discussion process.

Listening Carefully

Review the second dialogue and notice how each person in the discussion listens carefully to what the other person is saying and then tries to comment directly on what has just been said. When you are working hard at listening to others, you are trying to understand the point they are making and the reasons for it. This enables you to imagine yourself in their position and see things as they see them. Listening in this way often brings new ideas and different ways of viewing the situation to your attention that might never have occurred to you. An effective dialogue in this sense is like a game of tennis — you hit the ball to me, I return the ball to you, you return my return, and so on. The "ball" the discussants keep hitting back and forth is the subject they are gradually analyzing and exploring.

Supporting Views with Reasons and Evidence

Critical thinkers support their points of view with evidence and reasons and also develop an in-depth understanding of the evidence and reasons that support other viewpoints. Review the second dialogue and identify some of the reasons used by the participants to support their points of view. For example, Person B expresses the view that the government may have to be proactive in terms of identifying terrorists and ensuring our security, citing as evidence the horrific consequences of terrorist attacks. Person A responds with the concern that the government sometimes goes overboard in situations like this, citing as evidence the FBI's extensive surveillance of Martin Luther King.

Responding to the Points Being Made

When people engage in effective dialogue, they listen carefully to the people speaking and then respond directly to the points being made instead of simply trying to make their own points. In the second dialogue, Person B responds to Person A's concern that "'Big Brother' is watching our every move" with the acknowledgment that "It is a little unnerving to realize that our private conversations on the Internet may be monitored by the government" and also with the question "But doesn't it have to take measures like this in order to ensure we're safe?" When you respond directly to other people's views, and they to yours, you extend and deepen the explorations into the issues being discussed. Although people involved in the discussion may not ultimately agree, they should develop a more insightful understanding of the important issues and a greater appreciation of other viewpoints. Examine the second sample dialogue and notice how each person keeps responding to what the other is saying, creating an ongoing, interactive discussion.

Asking Questions

Asking questions is one of the driving forces in your discussions with others. You can explore a subject first by raising important questions and then by trying to answer them together. This questioning process gradually reveals the various reasons and evidence that support each of the different viewpoints involved. For example, although the two dialogues begin the same way, the second dialogue moves in a completely different direction from that of the first when Person A poses the question: "Since when is kidding around treason?" Asking this question directs the discussion toward a mutual exploration of the issues and away from angry confrontation. Identify some of the other key questions that are posed in the dialogue.

A guide to the various types of questions that can be posed in exploring issues and situations begins on page 45 of this chapter.

Increasing Understanding

When we discuss subjects with others, we often begin by disagreeing with them. In fact, this is one of the chief reasons that we have discussions. In an effective discussion, however, our main purpose should be to develop our understanding — not to prove ourselves right at any cost. If we are determined to prove that we are right, then we are likely not to be open to the ideas of others and to viewpoints that differ from our own.

Imagine that instead of ending, the second dialogue had continued for a while. Create responses that expand the exploration of the ideas being examined, and be sure to keep the following discussion guidelines in mind as you continue the dialogue.

- When we discuss, we have to listen to each other.

- When we discuss, we keep asking — and trying to answer — important questions.

- When we discuss, our main purpose is to develop a further understanding of the subject we are discussing, not to prove that we are right and the other person is wrong.

PERSON B: Yes, I guess the goal is to strike the right balance between security and personal freedoms. But how do we do that? (etc.)

THINKING ACTIVITY 2.9

Creating a Dialogue

Select an important social issue and write a dialogue that analyzes the issue from two different perspectives. As you write your dialogue, keep in mind the qualities of effective discussion: listening carefully to the other person and trying to comment directly on what has been said, asking and trying to answer important questions about the subject, and trying to develop a fuller understanding of the subject instead of simply trying to prove yourself right.

After completing your dialogue, read it to the class (with a classmate as a partner). Analyze the class's dialogues by using the criteria for effective discussions that we have examined.

LOOKING CRITICALLY @ Evaluating Internet Information

The information "superhighway" of the Internet is an incredibly rich source of information on virtually every subject that exists. But it's important to remember that information is not knowledge. Information doesn't become *knowledge* until we think critically about it. As a critical thinker, you

VISUAL THINKING

"I Used Q-tips, But Do I Hear You?"

- What does this illustration mean to you? Does it imply that *hearing* is not the same as *listening*? Does it indicate how language styles may cause two people to express a similar idea in two different ways? Or might it suggest that we can't count on what we say being interpreted in the way we meant it? Provide your own interpretation.

should never accept information at face value without first establishing its accuracy, evaluating the credibility of the source, and determining the point of view or bias of the source. These are issues that we will explore throughout this book, but for now you can use the checklist on page 70 to evaluate the information on the Internet — and other sources as well.

After you have read through the checklist, log onto any web site — either one you're already familiar with or one you've never visited before — and evaluate it by answering the questions in the checklist. Record your answers and then discuss your evaluation with other class members.

Keep in mind, however, that the first stage of evaluating web sources should happen even *before* you search the Internet!

Before You Search

The first stage of evaluating web sources should happen even *before* you search the Internet!

Ask yourself what you are looking for. If you don't know what you're looking for, you probably won't find it!

You might want

- narratives
- facts
- opinions
- photographs or graphics
- arguments
- statistics
- eyewitness reports

Do you want new ideas, support for a position you already hold, or something entirely different? Once you decide, you will be better able to evaluate what you find on the web.

Choose Sources Likely to Be Reliable

Ask yourself, "What sources (or what kinds of sources) would be most likely to give me the kind of reliable information I'm looking for?"

Some sources are more likely than others to

- be fair
- be objective
- lack hidden motives
- show quality control

Sometimes a site's "address" (URL, or "uniform resource locator") suggests its reliability or its purpose. Sites ending in

- .edu indicate educational or research material
- .gov indicate government resources
- .com indicate commercial products or commercially sponsored sites

"~NAME" in a URL may indicate a "personal" home page without recognized affiliation.

Keep these considerations in mind; don't just accept the opinion of the first sources you locate.

✔ CHECKLIST   **Evaluating the Quality of Internet Resources**

Criterion 1: Authority

☑ Is it clear who sponsors the page and what the sponsor's purpose in maintaining the page is? Is there a respected, well-known organizational affiliation?

☑ Is it clear who wrote the material and what the author's qualifications for writing on this topic are?

☑ Is there a way of verifying the legitimacy of the page's sponsor? In particular, is there a phone number or postal address to contact for more information? (An email address alone is not enough.)

☑ If the material is protected by copyright, is the name of the copyright holder given? Is there a date of page creation or version?

☑ *Beware!* Avoid anonymous sites and affiliations that you've never heard of or that can't be easily checked.

Criterion 2: Accuracy

☑ Are the sources for any factual information clearly listed so they can be verified in another source?

☑ Has the sponsor provided a link to outside sources (such as product reviews or reports filed with the SEC) that can be used to verify the sponsor's claims?

☑ Is the information free of grammatical, spelling, and other typographical errors? (These kinds of errors not only indicate a lack of quality control but can actually produce inaccuracies in information.)

☑ Are statistical data in graphs and charts clearly labeled and easy to read?

☑ Does anyone monitor the accuracy of the information being published?

☑ *Beware!* Avoid unverifiable statistics and claims not supported by reasons and evidence.

Criterion 3: Objectivity

☑ For any given piece of information, is it clear what the sponsor's motivation is for providing it?

☑ Is the information content clearly separated from any advertising or opinion content?

☑ Is the point of view of the sponsor presented in a clear manner, with its arguments well supported?

☑ *Beware!* Avoid sites offering "information" in an effort to sell a product or service as well as sites containing conflicts of interest, bias and one-sidedness, emotional language, and slanted tone.

Criterion 4: Currentness

☑ Are there dates on the page to indicate when the page was written, first placed on the Web, and last revised?

☑ Are there any other indications that the material is kept current?

☑ If material is presented in graphs or charts, is there a clear statement as to when the data were gathered?

☑ Is there an indication that the page has been completed and is not still in the process of being developed?

☑ *Beware!* Avoid sites that lack any dates, sources, or references.

Becoming a Critical Thinker

In this chapter we have discovered that critical thinking is not just one way of thinking — it is a total approach to the way we make sense of the world, and it involves an integrated set of thinking abilities and attitudes that include the following:

- *Thinking actively* by using our intelligence, knowledge, and skills to question, explore, and deal effectively with ourselves, others, and life's situations

- *Carefully exploring situations* by asking — and trying to answer — relevant questions

- *Thinking independently* by carefully examining various ideas and arriving at our own thoughtful conclusions

- *Viewing situations from different perspectives* to develop an in-depth, comprehensive understanding and *supporting viewpoints with reasons and evidence* to arrive at thoughtful, well-substantiated conclusions

- *Discussing ideas in an organized way* in order to exchange and explore ideas with others

These critical thinking qualities are a combination of cognitive abilities, basic attitudes, and thinking strategies that enable you to clarify and improve your understanding of the world. By carefully examining the process and products of your thinking — and the thinking of others — you develop insight into the thinking process and learn to do it better. Becoming a critical thinker does not simply involve mastering certain thinking abilities, however; it affects the entire way that you view the world and live your life. For example, the process of striving to understand other points of view in a situation changes the way you think, feel, and behave. It catapults you out of your own limited way of viewing things, helps you understand others' viewpoints, and broadens your understanding. All of these factors contribute to your becoming a sophisticated thinker and mature human being.

Becoming a critical thinker is a lifelong process. Developing the thinking abilities needed to understand the complex world you live in and to make informed decisions requires ongoing analysis, reflection, and practice. The qualities of critical thinking that you have explored in this chapter represent signposts in your journey to become a critical thinker.

Critical thinkers are better equipped to deal with the difficult challenges that life poses: to solve problems, to establish and achieve goals, and to make sense of complex issues. The foundation of thinking abilities and critical attitudes introduced in these first two chapters will be reinforced and elaborated upon in the chapters ahead, helping to provide you with the resources to be successful at college, in your chosen career, and throughout the other areas of your life as well.

 THINKING PASSAGE

Liberty Versus Security

The catastrophic terrorist attacks of September 11, 2001, underscored the issue of how people living in a free and democratic society can best ensure their security without sacrificing the liberties that they most cherish. The following reading explores the tension between liberty and security. "Liberty v Security" argues that free societies like the United States and England must find a way to strike a balance between these sometimes conflicting impulses. After completing the reading, answer the questions that follow the article.

LIBERTY V SECURITY
by *The Economist*

The Current Emergency Justifies a Shifting of the Balance — But Under Clear Democratic Controls

George Bush correctly called the attack on America "an attack on freedom." It was also, to some extent, an "attack through freedom." The terrorists were able to strike at the world's most open society partly by exploiting its openness. Now, as western governments rush to block these loopholes, many fear that they will inadvertently finish what the terrorists began — and curtail the very freedoms which they are fighting to protect.

In America, Mr. Bush, who came to power hoping to reduce the reach of government, is overseeing an increase in its powers. Some of that is planned through new programmes and activities, but some has reflected immediate action by the FBI and police: More than 350 people have

VISUAL THINKING

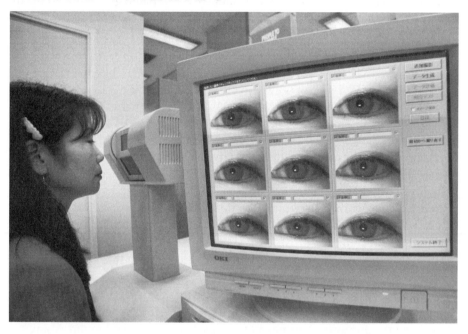

"You Have Beautiful Eyes . . . Let Me Read You Your Rights."

• A democratic society needs to balance personal liberties with the need for security. What do you think about security systems, like the one depicted in this photo, that can identify you instantly? Do you think these kinds of security procedures should be increased to make us safer? Or do you think they should be restricted in order to protect personal privacy? If you were in charge of national security, what policies would you advocate?

already been arrested under emergency rules. In Britain, the debate about introducing national identity cards has gained new vigour. In many countries, leaders are looking at tougher "anti-terrorism" laws ranging from surveillance and powers of arrest to financial disclosure and racial profiling. As one headline has it, "thousands dead, millions deprived of civil liberties." Politicians acidly reply that theoretical liberties were not of much use to the dead in the World Trade Centre.

Amid all this sound and fury, both sides need to consider the fundamental question: In light of the attack, where must the balancing point between security and liberty be set? Civil libertarians should begin by admitting that, contrary to much of their rhetoric, some sort of a balance has always had to be struck. Even fundamental freedoms — for instance, that of speech — are not absolute. People who shout fire in a crowded theatre can expect to be arrested. Defence is the area in which freedoms are most often restricted. Most democracies already grant some discretion to their policemen over whom they investigate, and offer broad protections for secrecy. Many require their citizens to carry identity cards.

Next, libertarians need to accept that, from a security point of view, September 11th was genuinely a day when the world changed. To be sure, that change was most dramatic in America, a country which has had relatively few terrorist attacks of any sort. But even for western countries that have been exposed to bombs and bullets for longer, the bombings of the World Trade Centre and the Pentagon unveiled a new level of threat. The scale of the outrage (the death toll was ten times larger than any comparable tragedy), the use of suicide bombers, the lack of warning, the conversion of aircraft into flying missiles, all should serve as prompts to re-examine old procedures and question established liberties — be they "the freedom" to carry and buy knives at airports or "the freedom" to stash your money in a numbered account in Liechtenstein.

However, if libertarians must accept that something changed on September 11th, authoritarians need to accept that not everything did. Many of the failures of security were not connected to unrestrained liberty, and some measures currently being floated are only tangentially linked to the disaster. Most Britons would not worry too much about carrying identity cards, since they already carry many bits of plastic that serve to identify them; the main objection would be to being charged with a crime, or held on suspicion, simply if they have left their card at home. Nevertheless, supporters of identity cards have overlooked the fact that the hijackers did produce identity papers of one sort or another at the airport. Several were travelling under stolen passports. Identity theft is a growing crime in America — and presumably would be even worse in Britain, where records are appalling.

On the whole, the security lapses in America had less to do with liberty than inefficiency. Security was found wanting, partly because it had to deal with what once seemed an unimaginable threat and partly because, on the evidence available, it did not work well. In particular, America's lavishly funded intelligence services failed to spot that dozens of cohorts of the country's "public enemy number one" had entered the United States, were taking flying lessons and loitering around airports.

Much of the failure can be ascribed to an old-fashioned lack of inform-
ants and poor collation of existing information, though restrictive laws
on wiretapping and other surveillance methods cannot have helped.

The Emergency v the Longer Term

The most important distinction that will need to be drawn is between
those measures that are necessary because of a current emergency and
those that are desirable for the longer term. With military action likely to
prompt further atrocities from terrorist groups, the case for greater emergency powers of surveillance and arrest is strong in any country in which
retaliation could occur. Such powers should, however, be granted only
with sunset clauses attached so that they need to be reconsidered in a
democratic forum before they can be reinstated. Such powers should also
remain subject to case-by-case judicial approval — when practical, in
advance, but if necessary, in retrospect — in order both to avoid their
misuse and to maintain public confidence.

The longer term will pose tougher issues, for even then the security
will be needed not against a visible enemy such as another country but
against an invisible, potential enemy which September 11th showed
could come from many quarters. Efficient security, whether at airports or
in any other public place, is itself a challenge to liberty for it steals away
time, involves intrusive searches, and restricts freedoms of movement
and behaviour. The likelihood must be that, as long as it is done in a way
that is non-discriminatory and subject to legal controls, people in democratic countries will choose to accept such security in their own interests.
But as this campaign proceeds and as the debate develops, they will have
to be given that choice, either directly or through their elected represen-
tatives. Democracy is, after all, another of the values that the terrorists
have sought to challenge.

Questions for Analysis

1. Explain the meaning of the heading "The Current Emergency Justifies a
   Shifting of the Balance — But Under Clear Democratic Controls."
2. Identify the arguments for and against having a national I.D. card. Would
   such a card make you feel more secure? What personal concerns might you
   have about such a system?

3. The government routinely reviews email in general for threats to national security. Do you believe that this surveillance should be increased and extended to phone calls, in order to better identify terrorist threats?

4. Imagine that you have been appointed by the president to be director of Security Initiatives. Create a plan involving the issues discussed in these articles that *you* believe strikes the appropriate balance between liberty and security.

3

Solving Problems

An Organized Approach to Analyzing Difficult Problems

Step 1: What Is the Problem?

What do I know about the situation?
What results am I aiming for?
How can I define the problem?

Step 5: How Well Is the Solution Working?

What is my evaluation?
What adjustments are necessary?

Step 2: What Are the Alternatives?

What are the boundaries?
What are possible alternatives?

Step 4: What Is the Solution?

Which alternatives will I pursue?
What steps can I take?

Step 3: What Are the Advantages and/or Disadvantages of Each Alternative?

What are the advantages?
What are the disadvantages?
What additional information do I need?

ⓖ Thinking Critically About Problems

Throughout your life, you are continually solving problems, including the many minor problems that you solve each day: negotiating a construction delay on the road, working through an unexpected difficulty at your job, help-ing an upset child deal with a disappointment. As a student, you are faced with a steady stream of academic assignments, quizzes, exams, and papers. Relatively simple problems like these do not require a systematic or complex analysis. You can solve them with just a little effort and concentration. For example, in order to do well on an exam, you need to *define* the problem (what areas will the exam cover, and what will be the format?), identify and evaluate various *alternatives* (what are possible study approaches?), and then put all these factors together to reach a *solution* (what will be your study plan and schedule?). But the difficult and complicated problems in life require more attention.

The idea of "having a problem" certainly conjures up unpleasant associa-tions for most people, but the truth is that solving problems is an integral and natural part of the process of living. It is the human ability to solve problems that accounts for our successful longevity on this planet. At the same time, it is our *inability* to solve problems that has resulted in senseless wars, unnecessary famine, and irrational persecution. You can undoubtedly discern this same duality in your own life: Your most satisfying accomplishments are likely to be the consequence of successful problem-solving, while your greatest disap-pointments probably resulted at least in part from your failure to solve some crucial problems. For example, think about some of the very difficult problems you have solved through dedication and intelligent action. How did your suc-cess make you feel? What were some of the positive results of your success? On the other hand, review some of the significant problems that you were not able to solve. What were some of the negative consequences of your failed efforts? The psychiatrist and author M. Scott Peck sums up the centrality of problems in our lives:

> Problems call forth our courage and our wisdom; indeed, they create our courage and our wisdom. It is only because of problems that we grow men-tally and spiritually. When we desire to encourage the growth of the human spirit, we challenge and encourage the human capacity to solve problems, just as in school we deliberately set problems for our children to solve.

> Problems are the crucible that forges the strength of our characters. When you are tested by life, forced to overcome adversity and think your way

through the most challenging situations — you will emerge a more intelligent, resourceful, and resilient person. However, if you lead a sheltered existence that insulates you from life's trials, or if you flee from situations at the first sign of trouble — then you will be weak and unable to cope with the eruptions and explosions that are bound to occur in your carefully protected world. Adversity reveals for all to see the person you have become, the character you have created. As the Roman philosopher and poet Lucretius explained, "So it is more useful to watch a man in times of peril, and in adversity to discern what kind of man he is; for then, at last, words of truth are drawn from the depths of his heart, and the mask is torn off, reality remains."

The quality of your life can be traced in large measure to your competency as a problem-solver. The fact that some people are consistently superior problem-solvers is largely due to their ability to approach problems in an informed and organized way. Less competent problem-solvers just muddle through when it comes to confronting adversity, using hit-or-miss strategies that rarely provide the best results. How would you rate yourself as a problem-solver? Do you generally approach difficulties confidently, analyze them clearly, and reach productive solutions? Or do you find that you often get "lost" and confused in such situations, unable to understand the problem clearly and to break out of mental ruts? Of course, you may find that you are very adept at solving problems in one area of your life — such as your job — and miserable at solving problems in other areas, such as your love life or your relationships with your children.

If you are less able to solve complex and challenging problems than you would like to be, don't despair! Becoming an expert problem-solver is not a genetic award; it is, for the most part, a learned skill that you can develop by practicing and applying the principles described in this chapter. You can learn to view problems as *challenges,* opportunities for growth instead of obstacles or burdens. You can become a person who attacks adversity with confidence and enthusiasm. This possibility may seem unlikely to you at this point, but I can assure you that, based on my experience teaching thousands of people for the past twenty years, becoming an expert problem-solver is well within your grasp.

Introduction to Solving Problems

Consider the following problem:

My best friend is addicted to drugs, but he won't admit it. Jack always liked to drink, but I never thought too much about it. After all, a lot of people like to drink socially, get relaxed, and have a good time. But over the last few years he's started using other drugs as well as alcohol, and it's ruining his life. He's stopped taking classes at the college and will soon lose his job if he doesn't change. Last week I told him that I was really worried about him, but he told me that he has no drug problem and that in any case it really isn't any of my business. I just don't know what to do. I've known Jack since we were in grammar school together and he's a wonderful person. It's as if he's in the grip of some terrible force and I'm powerless to help him.

In working through this problem, the student who wrote this description will have to think carefully and systematically in order to reach a solution. When we think effectively in situations like this, we usually ask ourselves a series of questions, although we may not be aware of the process that our minds are going through.

1. What is the *problem?*
2. What are the *alternatives?*
3. What are the *advantages* and/or *disadvantages* of each alternative?
4. What is the *solution?*
5. How well is the solution *working?*

Let's explore these questions further — and the thinking process that they represent — by applying them to the problem described here. Put yourself in the position of the student whose friend seems to have a serious drug problem.

What Is the Problem?   There are a variety of ways to define the problem facing this student. Describe as specifically as possible what *you* think the problem is.

What Are the Alternatives?   In dealing with this problem, you have a wide variety of possible actions to consider before selecting the best choices. Identify some of the alternatives you might consider.

1. Speak to my friend in a candid and forceful way to convince him that he has a serious problem.
2.
etc.

What Are the Advantages and/or Disadvantages of Each Alternative?
Evaluate the strengths and weaknesses of each of the problems you identified
so you can weigh your choices and decide on the best course of action.

1. Speak to my friend in a candid and forceful way to convince him that he has
a serious problem.

Advantage: He may respond to my direct emotional appeal, acknowledge
that he has a problem, and seek help.

Disadvantage: He may react angrily, further alienating me from him and
making it more difficult for me to have any influence on him.

2.

Advantage:

Disadvantage:

etc.

What Is the Solution?   After evaluating the various alternatives, select what
you think is the most effective alternative for solving the problem and describe
the sequence of steps you would take to act on the alternative.

How Well Is the Solution Working?   The final step in the process is to
review the solution and decide whether it is working well. If it is not, you must
be able to modify your solution or perhaps choose an alternate solution that
you had disregarded earlier. Describe what results would inform you that the
alternative you had selected to pursue was working well or poorly. If you concluded that your alternative was working poorly, describe what your next
action would be.

In this situation, trying to figure out the best way to help your friend recognize his problem and seek treatment, leads to a series of decisions. This is what
the thinking process is all about — trying to make sense of what is going on in
our world and acting appropriately in response. When we solve problems
effectively, our thinking process exhibits a coherent organization. It follows the
general approach we have just explored.

If we can understand the way our minds operate when we are thinking
effectively, then we can apply this understanding to improve our thinking in
new, challenging situations. In the remainder of this chapter, we will explore a
more sophisticated version of this problem-solving approach and apply it to a
variety of complex, difficult problems.

Problem-Solving Method (Basic)

1. What is the *problem*?
2. What are the *alternatives* available to me?
3. What are the *advantages* and/or *disadvantages* of each alternative?
4. What is the *solution*?
5. How well is the solution *working*?

THINKING ACTIVITY 3.1

Analyzing a Problem You Solved

1. Describe in specific detail an important problem you have solved recently.
2. Explain how you went about solving the problem. What were the steps, strategies, and approaches you used to understand the problem and make an informed decision?
3. Analyze the organization exhibited by your thinking process by completing the five-step problem-solving method we have been exploring.
4. Share your problem with other members of the class and have them try to analyze and solve it. Then explain the solution you arrived at.

Solving Complex Problems

Imagine yourself in the following situations. What would your next move be, and what are your reasons for it?

Procrastination   I am a procrastinator. Whenever I have something important to do, especially if it's difficult or unpleasant, I tend to put it off. Though this chronic delaying bothers me, I try to suppress my concern and instead work on more trivial things. It doesn't matter how much time I allow for certain responsibilities, I always end up waiting until the last minute to really focus and get things done, or I overschedule too many things for the time available. I usually meet my deadlines, but not always, and I don't enjoy working under this kind of pressure. In many cases I know that I'm not producing my best work. To make matters worse, the feeling that I'm always behind is causing me to feel really stressed out and is undermining my confidence. I've tried every kind of schedule and technique, but my best intentions simply don't last, and I end up slipping into my old habits. I must learn to get my priorities in order and act on them in an organized way so that I can lead a well-balanced and happier life.

Losing Weight My problem is the unwelcome weight that has attached itself to me. I was always in pretty good physical shape when I was younger, and if I gained a few extra pounds, they were easy to lose if I adjusted my diet slightly or exercised a little more. As I've gotten older, however, it seems easier to add the weight and more difficult to take it off. I'm eating healthier than I ever have before and getting just as much exercise, but the pounds just keep on coming. My clothes are tight, I'm feeling slow and heavy, and my self-esteem is suffering. How can I lose this excess poundage?

Smoking One problem in my life that has remained unsolved for about twelve years is my inability to stop smoking. I know it is dangerous for my health, and I tell my children that they should not smoke. They then tell me that *I* should stop, and I explain to them that it is very hard to do. I have tried to stop many times without success. The only times I previously was able to stop were during my two pregnancies, because I didn't want to endanger my children's health. But after their births, I went back to smoking, although I realize that second-hand smoke can also pose a health hazard. I want to stop smoking because it's dangerous, but I also enjoy it. Why do I continue, knowing it can only damage me and my children?

Loss of Financial Aid I'm just about to begin my second year of college, following a very successful first year. To this point, I have financed my education through a combination of savings, financial aid, and a part-time job (sixteen hours per week) at a local store. However, I just received a letter from my college stating that it was reducing my financial aid package by half due to budgetary problems. The letter concludes, "We hope this aid reduction will not prove to be too great an inconvenience." From my perspective, this reduction in aid isn't an inconvenience — it's a disaster! My budget last year was already tight, and with my job, I had barely enough time to study, participate in a few college activities, and have a modest (but essential) social life. To make matters worse, my mother has been ill, a condition which has reduced her income and created financial problems at home. I'm feeling panicked! What in the world am I going to do?

VISUAL THINKING

"Eureka! I Found the Needle!"

● Why is this person's solution to finding the needle "creative"? Why do people usually settle for conventional alternatives when trying to solve problems, rather than pushing for truly innovative ideas? Describe a time when you were able to solve a difficult problem with a flash of creative insight that no one else was able to think of.

When we first approach a difficult problem, it often seems a confused tangle of information, feelings, alternatives, opinions, considerations, and risks. The problem of the college student just described is a complicated situation that does not seem to offer a single simple solution. Let's imagine ourselves in the student's predicament. Without the benefit of a systematic approach, our thoughts might wander through the tangle of issues like this:

> I want to stay in school . . . but I'm not going to have enough money. . . . I could work more hours at my job . . . but I might not have enough time to study and get top grades . . . and if all I'm doing is working and studying, what about my social life? . . . And what about mom and the kids? . . . They might need my help. . . . I could drop out of school for a while . . . but if I don't stay in school, what kind of future do I have? . . .

Very often when we are faced with difficult problems like this, we simply do not know where to begin in trying to solve them. Every issue is connected to many others. Frustrated by not knowing where to take the first step, we often give up trying to understand the problem. Instead, we may

1. *Act impulsively* without thought or consideration (e.g., "I'll just quit school").
2. *Do what someone else suggests* without seriously evaluating the suggestion (e.g., "Tell me what I should do — I'm tired of thinking about this").
3. *Do nothing* as we wait for events to make the decision for us (e.g., "I'll just wait and see what happens before doing anything").

None of these approaches is likely to succeed in the long run, and they can gradually reduce our confidence in dealing with complex problems. An alternative to these reactions is to *think critically* about the problem, analyzing it with an organized approach based on the five-step method described earlier.

Although we will be using an organized method for working through difficult problems and arriving at thoughtful conclusions, the fact is that our minds do not always work in such a logical, step-by-step fashion. Effective problem-solvers typically pass through all the steps we will be examining, but they don't always do so in the sequence we will be describing. Instead, the best problem-solvers have an integrated and flexible approach to the process in which they deploy a repertoire of problem-solving strategies as needed. Sometimes exploring the various alternatives helps them go back and redefine the original problem; similarly, seeking to implement the solution can often suggest new alternatives.

The key point is that although the problem-solving steps are presented in a logical sequence here, you are not locked into following these steps in a mechanical and unimaginative way. At the same time, in learning a problem-solving method like this it is generally not wise to skip steps, because each step deals with an important aspect of the problem. As you become more proficient in using the method, you will find that you can apply its concepts and strategies to problem-solving in an increasingly flexible and natural fashion, just as learning the basics of an activity like driving a car gradually gives way to a more organic and integrated performance of the skills involved.

Before applying a method like the one just outlined above to your problem, however, you need first to ready yourself by *accepting* the problem.

Accepting the Problem

To solve a problem, you must first be willing to *accept* the problem by *acknowledging* that the problem exists and *committing* yourself to trying to solve it.

Problem-Solving Method (Advanced)

1. Step 1: What is the problem?
   a. What do I know about the situation?
   b. What results am I aiming for in this situation?
   c. How can I define the problem?

2. Step 2: What are the alternatives?
   a. What are the boundaries of the problem situation?
   b. What alternatives are possible within these boundaries?

3. Step 3: What are the advantages and/or disadvantages of each alternative?
   a. What are the advantages of each alternative?
   b. What are the disadvantages of each alternative?
   c. What additional information do I need to evaluate each alternative?

4. Step 4: What is the solution?
   a. Which alternative(s) will I pursue?
   b. What steps can I take to act on the alternative(s) chosen?

5. Step 5: How well is the solution working?
   a. What is my evaluation?
   b. What adjustments are necessary?

Sometimes you may have difficulty recognizing there *is* a problem unless it is pointed out to you. Other times you may actively resist acknowledging a problem, even when it is pointed out to you. The person who confidently states, "I don't really have any problems," sometimes has very serious problems — but is simply unwilling to acknowledge them.

On the other hand, mere acknowledgment is not enough to solve a problem. Once you have identified a problem, you must commit yourself to trying to solve it. Successful problem-solvers are highly motivated and willing to persevere through the many challenges and frustrations of the problem-solving process. How do you find the motivation and commitment that prepare you to enter the problem-solving process? There are no simple answers, but a number of strategies may be useful to you.

1. *List the benefits.* Making a detailed list of the benefits you will derive from successfully dealing with the problem is a good place to begin. Such a

process helps you clarify why you might want to tackle the problem, motivates you to get started, and serves as a source of encouragement when you encounter difficulties or lose momentum.

2. *Formalize your acceptance.* When you formalize your acceptance of a problem, you are "going on record," either by preparing a signed declaration or by signing a "contract" with someone else. This formal commitment serves as an explicit statement of your original intentions that you can refer to if your resolve weakens.

3. *Accept responsibility for your life.* Each one of us has the potential to control the direction of our lives, but to do so we must accept our freedom to choose and the responsibility that goes with it. As you saw in the last chapter, critical thinkers actively work to take charge of their lives rather than letting themselves be passively controlled by external forces.

4. *Create a "worst-case" scenario.* Some problems persist because you are able to ignore their possible implications. When you use this strategy, you remind yourself, as graphically as possible, of the potentially disastrous consequences of your actions. For example, using vivid color photographs and research conclusions, you can remind yourself that excessive smoking, drinking, or eating can lead to myriad health problems and social and psychological difficulties as well as an early and untimely demise.

5. *Identify what's holding you back.* If you are having difficulty accepting a problem, it is usually because something is holding you back. For example, you might be concerned about the amount of time and effort involved, you might be reluctant to confront the underlying issues that the problem represents, you might be worried about finding out unpleasant things about yourself or others, or you might be inhibited by other problems in your life, such as a tendency to procrastinate. Whatever the constraints, using this strategy involves identifying and describing all of the factors that are preventing you from attacking the problem and then addressing these factors one at a time.

Step 1: What Is the Problem?

The first step in solving problems is to determine exactly what the central issues of the problem are. If you do not clearly understand what the problem really is, then your chances of solving it are considerably reduced. You may spend your time trying to solve the wrong problem. For example, consider the different formulations of the following problems. How might these formulations lead you in different directions in trying to solve the problems?

"School is boring." vs. "I feel bored in school."

"I'm a failure." vs. "I just failed an exam."

In each of these cases, a very general conclusion (left column) has been replaced by a more specific characterization of the problem (right column).

The general conclusions ("I'm a failure") do not suggest productive ways of resolving the difficulties. They are too absolute, too all encompassing. On the other hand, the more specific descriptions of the problem situation ("I just failed an exam") *do* permit us to attack the problem with useful strategies. In short, the way you define a problem determines not only *how* you will go about solving it, but also whether you feel that the problem can be solved at all. Correct identification of a problem is essential if you are going to be able to perform a successful analysis and reach an appropriate conclusion. If you misidentify the problem, you can find yourself pursuing an unproductive and even destructive course of action.

Let us return to the problem of the college finances we encountered on page 83 and analyze it using our problem-solving method. *(Note:* As you work through this problem-solving approach, apply the steps and strategies to an unsolved problem in your own life. You will have an opportunity to write up your analysis when you complete Thinking Activity 3.2 on page 101.) In order to complete the first major step of this problem-solving approach — "What is the problem?" — you need to address three component questions:

1. What do I know about the situation?
2. What results am I aiming for in this situation?
3. How can I define the problem?

Step 1A: What Do I Know About the Situation?   Solving a problem begins with determining what information you *know* to be the case and what information you *think* might be the case. Your need to have a clear idea of the details of your beginning circumstances to explore the problem successfully. Sometimes a situation may appear to be a problem when it really isn't simply because your information isn't accurate. For example, you might be convinced that someone you are attracted to doesn't reciprocate your interest. If this belief is inaccurate, however, then your "problem" doesn't really exist.

You can identify and organize what you know about the problem situation by using *key questions.* In Chapter 2, we examined six types of questions that can be used to explore situations and issues systematically: *fact, interpretation, analysis, synthesis, evaluation,* and *application.* By asking — and trying to answer — questions of fact, you are establishing a sound foundation for the exploration of your problem. Answer the following questions of fact — who, what, where, when, how, why — about the problem described at the beginning of the chapter.

1. *Who* are the people involved in this situation?
   Who will benefit from solving this problem?
   Who can help me solve this problem?
2. *What* are the various parts or dimensions of the problem?
   What are my strengths and resources for solving this problem?
   What additional information do I need to solve this problem?
3. *Where* can I find people or additional information to help me solve the problem?
4. *When* did the problem begin?
   When should the problem be resolved?
5. *How* did the problem develop or come into being?
6. *Why* is solving this problem important to me?
   Why is this problem difficult to solve?
7. *Additional questions:*

Step 1B: What Results Am I Aiming for in This Situation?   The second part of answering the question "What is the problem?" consists of identifying the specific *results* or objectives you are trying to achieve. The results are those goals that will eliminate the problem if you are able to attain them. Whereas the first part of Step 1 oriented you in terms of the history of the problem and the current situation, this part encourages you to look ahead to the future. In this respect, it is similar to the process of establishing and working toward your goals that you examined in Chapter 1. To identify your results, you need to ask yourself this question: "What are the objectives that, once achieved, will solve this problem?" For instance, one of the results or objectives in the sample problem might be having enough money to pay for college. Describe additional results you might be trying to achieve in this situation.

Step 1C: How Can I Define the Problem?   After exploring what you know about the problem and the results you are aiming to achieve, you need to conclude Step 1 by defining the problem as clearly and specifically as possible. Defining the problem is a crucial task in the entire problem-solving process because this definition will determine the direction of the analysis. To define the problem, you need to identify its central issue(s). Sometimes defining the problem is relatively straightforward, such as: "Trying to find enough time to exercise." Often, however, identifying the central issue of a problem is a much more complex process. For example, the statement "My problem is relating to other people" suggests a complicated situation with many interacting variables that resists simple definition. In fact, you may only begin to develop a clear idea of the problem as you engage in the process of trying to solve it. You might begin by believing that your problem is, say, not having the *ability* to succeed and end by concluding that the problem is really a *fear* of success. As you will see, the same insights apply to nonpersonal problems as well. For example, the problem of high school dropouts might initially be defined in terms of problems in the school system, whereas later formulations may identify drug use or social pressure as the core of the problem.

Although there are no simple formulas for defining challenging problems, you can pursue several strategies in identifying the central issue most effectively:

1. *View the problem from different perspectives.* As you saw in Chapter 2, perspective-taking is a key ingredient of thinking critically, and it can help you zero in on many problems as well. For example, when you describe how various individuals might view a given problem — such as the high school dropout rate — the essential ingredients of the problem begin to emerge. In the college finances problem, how would you describe the following perspectives?

   Your perspective:

   The college's perspective:

   Your mother's perspective:

2. *Identify component problems.* Larger problems are often composed of component problems. To define the larger problem, it is often necessary to identify and describe the subproblems that comprise it. For example, poor performance at school might be the result of a number of factors, such as ineffective study habits, inefficient time management, and preoccupation with a personal problem. Defining, and dealing effectively with, the larger problem means defining and dealing with the subproblems first. Identify possible subproblems in the sample problem:

   Subproblem a:

   Subproblem b:

3. *State the problem clearly and specifically.* A third defining strategy is to state the problem as clearly and specifically as possible, based on an exam-

ination of the results that need to be achieved to solve the problem. This sort of clear and specific description of the problem is an important step in solving it. For if you state the problem in very general terms, you won't have a clear idea of how best to proceed in dealing with it. But if you can describe your problem in more specific terms, then your description will begin to suggest actions you can take to solve the problem. Examine the differences between the statements of the following problem:

General: "My problem is money."

More specific: "My problem is budgeting my money so that I won't always run out near the end of the month."

Most specific: "My problem is developing the habit and the discipline to budget my money so that I won't always run out near the end of the month."

Review your analysis of the sample problem and then state the problem as clearly and specifically as possible.

Step 2: What Are the Alternatives?

Once you have identified your problem clearly and specifically, your next move is to examine each of the possible actions that might help you solve the problem. Before you list the alternatives, however, it makes sense to determine first which actions are possible and which are impossible. You can do this by exploring the *boundaries* of the problem situation.

Step 2A: What Are the Boundaries of the Problem Situation?   Boundaries are the limits in the problem situation that you cannot change. They are a part of the problem, and they must be accepted and dealt with. For example, in the sample situation, the fact that a day has only twenty-four hours must be accepted as part of the problem situation. There is no point in developing alternatives that ignore this fact. At the same time, you must be careful not to identify as boundaries circumstances that can actually be changed. For instance, you might assume that your problem must be solved in your current location without realizing that relocating to another, less expensive college is one of your options. Identify additional boundaries that might be a part of the sample situation and some of the questions you would want to answer regarding the boundary. For example:

Time limitations: How much time do I need for each of my basic activities — work, school, social life, travel, and sleep? What is the best way to budget this time?

Step 2B: What Alternatives Are Possible Within These Boundaries?   After you have established a general idea of the boundaries of the problem situation, you can proceed to identify the possible courses of action that can take place within these boundaries. Of course, identifying all the possible alternatives is not always easy; in fact, it may be part of your problem. Often we do not see a way out of a problem because our thinking is set in certain ruts, fixed in certain perspectives. We may be blind to other approaches, either because we reject them before seriously considering them ("That will never work!") or because they simply do not occur to us. You can use several strategies to overcome these obstacles:

1. *Discuss the problem with other people.* Discussing possible alternatives with others uses a number of the aspects of critical thinking you explored in Chapter 2. As you saw then, thinking critically involves being open to seeing situations from different viewpoints and discussing your ideas with others in an organized way. Both of these abilities are important in solving problems. As critical thinkers we live — and solve problems — in a community, not simply by ourselves. Other people can often suggest possible alternatives that we haven't thought of, in part because they are outside the situation and thus have a more objective perspective, and in part because they naturally view the world differently than we do, based on their past experiences and their personalities. In addition, discussions are often creative experiences that generate ideas the participants would not have come up with on their own. The dynamics of these interactions often lead to products that are greater than the individual "sum" of those involved.

2. *Brainstorm ideas.* Brainstorming, a method introduced by Alex Osborn, builds on the strengths of working with other people to generate ideas and solve problems. In a typical brainstorming session, a group of people work together to generate as many ideas as possible in a specific period of time. As ideas are produced, they are not judged or evaluated, as this tends to inhibit the free flow of ideas and discourages people from making suggestions. Evaluation is deferred until a later stage. People are encouraged to build on the ideas of others since the most creative ideas are often generated through the constructive interplay of various minds.

3. *Change your location.* Your perspective on a problem is often tied into the circumstances in which the problem exists. For example, a problem you

VISUAL THINKING

"I Have a Creative Idea!"

● Most problems have more than one possible solution, and to discover the most creative ideas we need to go beyond the obvious. Imagine that you are faced with the challenge depicted in the illustration; then describe your own creative solution for getting the ball out of the glass cannister without damaging either. Where did your creative idea come from? How does it compare to the solutions of other students in your class?

may be having in school is tied into your daily experiences and habitual reactions to these experiences. Sometimes what you need is a fresh perspective, getting away from the problem situation so that you can view it with more clarity and in a different light. Using these strategies, as well as your own reflections, identify as many alternatives as you can think of to help solve the sample problem.

Step 3: What Are the Advantages and/or Disadvantages of Each Alternative?

Once you have identified the various alternatives, your next step is to *evaluate* them by using the kinds of evaluation questions described in Chapter 2. Each possible course of action has certain advantages in the sense that if you select that alternative, there will be some positive results. At the same time, each of the possible courses of action likely has disadvantages as well in the sense that if you select that alternative, there may be a cost involved or a risk of some negative results. It is important to examine the potential advantages and/or disadvantages in order to determine how helpful each course of action would be in solving the problem.

Step 3A: What Are the Advantages of Each Alternative?   The alternative you listed in Step 2 for the sample problem ("Attend college part-time") might include the following advantages:

Alternatives:	*Advantages:*
Attend college part-time	This would remove some of the immediate time and money pressures I am experiencing while still allowing me to prepare for the future. I would have more time to focus on the courses that I am taking and to work additional hours.

Identify the advantages of each of the alternatives that you listed in Step 2. Be sure that your responses are thoughtful and specific.

Step 3B: What Are the Disadvantages of Each Alternative?   You also need to consider the disadvantages of each alternative. The alternative you listed for the sample problem might include the following disadvantages:

Alternatives:	*Disadvantages:*
Attend college part-time	It would take me much longer to complete my schooling, thus delaying my progress toward my goals. Also, I might lose motivation and drop out before completing school because the process was taking so long. Being a part-time student might even threaten my eligibility for financial aid.

Now identify the disadvantages of each of the alternatives that you listed. Be sure that your responses are thoughtful and specific.

Step 3C: What Additional Information Do I Need to Evaluate Each Alternative?

The next part of Step 3 consists of determining what you must know *(information needed)* to best evaluate and compare the alternatives. For each alternative there are questions that must be answered if you are to establish which alternatives make sense and which do not. In addition, you need to figure out where best to get this information *(sources)*.

One useful way to identify the information you need is to ask yourself the question *"What if* I select this alternative?" For instance, one alternative in the sample problem was "Attend college part-time." When you ask yourself the question *"What if* I attend college part-time?" you are trying to predict what will occur if you select this course of action. To make these predictions, you must answer certain questions and find the information to answer them.

- How long will it take me to complete my schooling?

- How long can I continue in school without losing interest and dropping out?

- Will I threaten my eligibility for financial aid if I become a part-time student?

The information — and the sources for it — that must be located for the first alternative in the sample problem might include the following:

Alternative:	*Information Needed and Sources:*
Attend college part-time	*Information:* How long will it take me to complete my schooling? How long can I continue in school without losing interest and dropping out? Will I threaten my eligibility for financial aid if I become a part-time student? *Sources:* Myself, other part-time students, school counselors, the financial aid office.

Identify the information needed and the sources of this information for each of the alternatives that you identified. Be sure that your responses are thoughtful and specific.

Step 4: What Is the Solution?

The purpose of Steps 1 through 3 is to analyze your problem in a systematic and detailed fashion — to work through the problem in order to become thoroughly familiar with it and the possible solutions to it. After breaking down the problem in this way, the final step should be to try to put the pieces back together — that is, to decide on a thoughtful course of action based on your increased understanding. Even though this sort of problem analysis does not guarantee finding a specific solution to the problem, it should *deepen your understanding* of exactly what the problem is about. And in locating and evaluating your alternatives, it should give you some very good ideas about the general direction you should move in and the immediate steps you should take.

Step 4A: Which Alternative(s) Will I Pursue?   There is no simple formula or recipe to tell you which alternatives to select. As you work through the different courses of action that are possible, you may find that you can immediately rule some out. For example, in the sample problem you may know with certainty that you do not want to attend college part-time (alternative 1) because you will forfeit your remaining financial aid. However, it may not be so simple to select which of the other alternatives you wish to pursue. How do you decide?

The decisions we make usually depend on what we believe to be most important to us. These beliefs regarding what is most important to us are known as *values*. Our values are the starting points of our actions and strongly influence our decisions. For example, if we value staying alive (as most of us do), then we will make many decisions each day that express this value — eating proper meals, not walking in front of moving traffic, and so on.

Our values help us *set priorities* in life — that is, decide what aspects of our lives are most important to us. We might decide that, for the present, going to school is more important than having an active social life. In this case, going to school is a higher priority than having an active social life. Unfortunately, our values are not always consistent with each other — we may have to choose *either* to go to school or to have an active social life. Both activities may be important to us; they are simply not compatible with each other. Very often the *conflicts* between our values constitute the problem. Let's examine some strategies for selecting alternatives that might help us solve the problem.

1. *Evaluate and compare alternatives.* Although each alternative may have certain advantages and disadvantages, not all advantages are equally desirable or potentially effective. For example, giving up on college entirely

VISUAL THINKING

"Why Didn't I Think of That!"

● The figure on the right was able to solve this problem when the others weren't. Why? Recall a time in your life when you were able to use a similar thinking process to come up with a creative solution to a problem involving "time" or "money," and share your creative solution with your classmates.

would certainly solve some aspects of the sample problem, but its obvious disadvantages would rule out this solution for most people. Thus it makes sense to try to evaluate and rank the various alternatives based on how effective they are likely to be and how they match up with your value system. A good place to begin is the "Results" stage, Step 1B. Examine each of the alternatives and evaluate how well it will contribute to achieving the results you are aiming for in the situation. You may want to rank the alternatives or develop your own rating system to assess their relative effectiveness.

After evaluating the alternatives in terms of their anticipated *effectiveness*, the next step is to evaluate them in terms of their *desirability*, based on your needs, interests, and value system. Again, you can use either a ranking or a rating system to assess their relative desirability. After completing these two separate evaluations, you can then select the alternative(s) that seem most appropriate. Review the alternatives you identified in the sample problem and then rank or rate them according to their potential effectiveness and desirability, assuming this problem was your own.

2. *Combine alternatives.* After reviewing and evaluating the alternatives you generated, you may develop a new alternative that combines the best qualities of several options while avoiding the disadvantages some of them would have if chosen exclusively. In the sample problem, you might combine attending college part-time during the academic year with attending school during the summer session so that progress toward your degree won't be impeded. Examine the alternatives you identified and develop a new option that combines the best elements of several of them.

3. *Try out each alternative in your imagination.* Focus on each alternative and try to imagine, as concretely as possible, what it would be like if you actually selected it. Visualize what impact your choice would have on your problem and what the implications would be for your life as a whole. By trying out the alternative in your imagination, you can sometimes avoid unpleasant results or unexpected consequences. As a variation of this strategy, you can sometimes test alternatives on a very limited basis in a practice situation. For example, if you are trying to overcome your fear of speaking in groups, you can practice various speaking techniques with your friends or family until you find an approach you are comfortable with.

After trying out these strategies on the sample problem, select the alternative(s) you think would be most effective and desirable from your standpoint.

Step 4B: What Steps Can I Take to Act on the Alternative(s) Chosen? Once you have decided on the correct alternative(s) to pursue, your next move is to plan the steps you will have to take to put it into action. This is the same process of working toward your goals that we explored in Chapter 1. Planning the specific steps you will take is extremely important. Although thinking carefully about your problem is necessary, it is not enough if you hope to solve the problem. You have to take action, and planning specific steps is where you begin. In the sample problem, for example, imagine that one of the alternatives you have selected is "Find additional sources of income that will enable me to work part-time and go to school full-time." The specific steps you would want to take might include the following:

1. Contact the financial aid office at the school to see what other forms of financial aid are available and what you have to do to apply for them.
2. Contact some of the local banks to see what sort of student loans are available.
3. Look for a higher-paying job so that you can earn more money without working additional hours.
4. Discuss the problem with students in similar circumstances in order to generate new ideas.

Identify the steps you would have to take in pursuing the alternative(s) you identified on page 98.

Of course, plans do not implement themselves. Once you know what actions you have to take, you need to commit yourself to taking the necessary steps. This is where many people stumble in the problem-solving process, paralyzed by inertia or fear. Sometimes, to overcome these blocks and inhibitions, you need to reexamine your original acceptance of the problem, perhaps making use of some of the strategies you explored on pages 85–87. Once you get started, the rewards of actively attacking your problem are often enough incentive to keep you focused and motivated.

Step 5: How Well Is the Solution Working?

As you work toward reaching a reasonable and informed conclusion, you should not fall into the trap of thinking that there is only one "right" decision and that all is lost if you do not figure out what it is and carry it out. You should remind yourself that any analysis of a problem situation, no matter how careful and systematic, is ultimately limited. You simply cannot anticipate or predict everything that is going to happen in the future. As a result, every decision you make is provisional in the sense that your ongoing experience will inform you if your decisions are working out or if they need to be changed and modified. As you saw in Chapter 2, this is precisely the attitude of the critical thinker — someone who is *receptive* to new ideas and experiences and *flexible* enough to change or modify beliefs based on new information. Critical thinking is not a compulsion to find the "right" answer or make the "correct" decision; it is an ongoing process of exploration and discovery.

Step 5A: What Is My Evaluation?   In many cases the relative effectiveness of your efforts will be apparent. In other cases it will be helpful to pursue a more systematic evaluation along the lines suggested in the following strategies:

1. *Compare the results with the goals.* The essence of evaluation is comparing the results of your efforts with the initial goals you were trying to achieve. For example, the goals of the sample problem are embodied in the results you specified on page 89. Compare the anticipated results of the alternative(s) you selected. To what extent will your choice meet these goals? Are there goals that are not likely to be met by your alternative(s)? Which ones? Could they be addressed by other alternatives? Asking these and other questions will help you clarify the success of your efforts and provide a foundation for future decisions.

2. *Get other perspectives.* As you have seen throughout the problem-solving process, getting the opinions of others is a productive strategy at virtually every stage, and this is certainly true for evaluation. Other people can often provide perspectives that are both different and more objective than yours. Naturally, the evaluations of others are not always better or more accurate than your own, but even when they are not, reflecting on these different views usually deepens your understanding of the situation. It is not always easy to receive the evaluations of others, but open-mindedness toward outside opinions is a very valuable attitude to cultivate, for it will stimulate and guide you to produce your best efforts.

    To receive specific, practical feedback from others, you need to ask specific, practical questions that will elicit this information. General questions ("What do you think of this?") typically result in overly general, unhelpful responses ("It sounds okay to me"). Be focused in soliciting feedback, and remember: You do have the right to ask people to be *constructive* in their comments, providing suggestions for improvement rather than flatly expressing what they think is wrong.

Step 5B: What Adjustments Are Necessary?   As a result of your review, you may discover that the alternative you selected is not feasible or is not leading to satisfactory results. For example, in the sample problem, you may find that it is impossible to find additional sources of income so that you can work part-time instead of full-time. In that case, you simply have to go back and review the other alternatives to identify another possible course of action. At other times you may find that the alternative you selected is working out fairly well but still requires some adjustments as you continue to work toward your desired outcomes. In fact, this is a typical situation that you should expect to occur. Even when things initially appear to be working reasonably well, an active thinker continues to ask questions such as "What might I have over-looked?" and "How could I have done this differently?" Of course, asking — and trying to answer — questions like these is even more essential if solutions are hard to come by (as they usually are in real-world problems) and if you are to retain the flexibility and optimism you will need to tackle a new option.

THINKING ACTIVITY 3.2

Analyzing an Unsolved Problem

Select a problem from your own life. It should be one that you are currently grappling with and have not yet been able to solve. After selecting the problem you want to work on, strengthen your acceptance of the problem by using one or more of the strategies described on pages 86–87 and describing your efforts. Then analyze your problem using the problem-solving method described in this chapter. Discuss your problem with other class members to generate fresh perspectives and unusual alternatives that might not have occurred to you. Using your own paper, write your analysis in outline style, giving specific responses to the questions in each step of the problem-solving method. Although you might not reach a "guaranteed" solution to your problem, you should deepen your understanding of the problem and develop a concrete plan of action that will help you move in the right direction. Implement your plan of action and then monitor the results.

THINKING ACTIVITY 3.3

Analyzing College Problems

Analyze the following problems using the problem-solving approach presented in this chapter.

Problem 1: Background Information

The most important unsolved problem that exists for me is my inability to make that crucial decision of what to major in. I want to be secure with respect to both money and happiness when I make a career for myself, and I don't want to make a mistake in choosing a field of study. I want to make this decision before beginning the next semester so that I can start immediately in my career. I've been thinking about managerial studies. However, I often wonder if I have the capacity to make executive decisions when I can't even decide on what I want to do with my life.

Problem 2: Background Information

One of my problems is my difficulty in taking tests. It's not that I don't study. What happens is that when I get the test, I become nervous and my mind goes blank. For example, in my social science class, the teacher told the class on Tuesday that there would be a test on Thursday. That afternoon I went home and began studying for the test. By Thursday I knew most of the material, but when the test was handed out, I got nervous and my mind went blank. For a long time I just stared at the test, and I ended up failing it.

Problem 3: Background Information

One of the serious problems in my life is learning English as a second language. It is not so easy to learn a second language, especially when you live in an environment where only your native language is spoken. When I came to this country three years ago, I could speak almost no English. I have learned a lot, but my lack of fluency is getting in the way of my studies and my social relationships.

Problem 4: Background Information

This is my first year of college, and in general I'm enjoying it a great deal. The one disturbing thing I have encountered is the amount of drinking that students engage in when they socialize. Although I enjoy drinking in moderation, most students drink much more than "in moderation" at parties. They want to "get drunk," "lose control," "get wasted." And the parties aren't just on weekends — they're every night of the week! The problem is that there is a lot of pressure for me to join in the drinking and partying. Most of the people I enjoy being with are joining in, and I don't want to be left out of the social life of the college. But it's impossible to party so much and still keep up to date with my course work. And all that drinking certainly isn't good for me physically. But on the other hand, I don't want to be excluded from the social life, and when I try to explain that I don't enjoy heavy drinking, my friends make me feel immature and a little silly. What should I do?

Effective problem-solvers are masters of information: They know what questions to ask, where to get those questions answered, and what to do with the information once they secure it. The Internet is an extraordinary source of information that is relevant to virtually any problem (or question) that you will explore. However, extracting the "right" information from the web in a timely and efficient way is a challenge in itself. In addition to web search engines such as Google and Yahoo!, you can also use web subject directories such as Librarians' Index to the Internet (lii.org) and WWW virtual library (vlib.org).

As you become familiar with these and other rsources, you will find that you are able to zero in quickly on the questions you want answered while discovering new ideas and information that you may not have been aware of. Used properly, the Internet can be a powerful extension of your own cognitive functioning.

Solving Nonpersonal Problems

The problems we have analyzed up to this point have been "personal" problems in the sense that they represent individual challenges encountered by us as we live our lives. Problems are not only of a personal nature, however. We also face problems as members of a community, a society, and the world. As with personal problems, we need to approach these kinds of problems in an organized and thoughtful way in order to explore the issues, develop a clear understanding, and decide on an informed plan of action. For example, racism and prejudice directed toward African Americans, Hispanics, Asians, Jews, homosexuals, and other minority groups seem to be on the rise at many college campuses. There has been an increase of overt racial incidents at colleges and universities during the past several years, a particularly disturbing situation given the lofty egalitarian ideals of higher education. Experts from different fields have offered a variety of explanations to account for this behavior.

Describe why you believe these racial and ethnic incidents are occurring with increasing frequency.

Making sense of a complex, challenging situation like this is not a simple process. Although the problem-solving method we have been using in this chapter is a powerful approach, its successful application depends on having sufficient information about the situation we are trying to solve. As a result, it is often necessary for us to research articles and other sources of information to develop informed opinions about the problem we are investigating.

The famous newspaperman H. L. Mencken once said, "To every complex question there is a simple answer — and it's wrong!" We have seen in this chapter that complex problems do not admit simple solutions, whether they concern personal problems in our lives or larger social problems like racial prejudice or world hunger. We have also seen, however, that by working through these complex problems thoughtfully and systematically, we can achieve a deeper understanding of their many interacting elements, as well as develop strategies for solving them.

Becoming an effective problem-solver does not merely involve applying a problem-solving method in a mechanical fashion any more than becoming a mature critical thinker involves mastering a set of thinking skills. Rather, solving problems, like thinking critically, reflects a total approach to making sense of experience. When we think like problem-solvers, we approach the world in a distinctive way. Instead of avoiding difficult problems, we have the courage to meet them head-on and the determination to work through them. Instead of acting impulsively or relying exclusively on the advice of others, we are able to make sense of complex problems in an organized way and develop practical solutions and initiatives.

A sophisticated problem-solver employs all of the critical-thinking abilities that we have examined so far and those we will explore in the chapters ahead. And while we might agree with H. L. Mencken's evaluation of simple answers to complex questions, we might endorse a rephrased version: "To many complex questions there are complex answers — and these are worth pursuing!"

THINKING ACTIVITY 3.4

Analyzing Social Problems

Identify an important local, national, or international problem that needs to be solved. Locate two or more articles that provide background information and analysis of the problem. Using these articles as a resource, analyze the problem using the problem-solving method developed in this chapter.

THINKING PASSAGE

Living with Diversity

Living in diverse communities is a challenge facing not just college students but Americans in general. One of America's great strengths is its extraordinary diversity of people: different ages, sexes, races, religions, cultures, geographical origins, languages, and countless other contrasts as well. These differences are a source of great cultural richness and synergistic creativity. But they also pose significant difficulties that call on our critical thinking and problem-solving abilities. People often distrust and reject cultures and religions that are different from their own. Racial discrimination and hatred have been staples of human culture since recorded history right up through the present, in every society. Common also on campuses and in society at large is prejudice based on sexual orientation, dress and appearance, physical disabilities, and even age, as many returning older students discover. That's what makes the United States so distinctive: it is a nation composed of diverse groups, founded on the principles of freedom, equality, and tolerance. Of course, ideals and realities are often two very different things when people are involved.

The following reading explores some of the problems facing diverse groups of individuals living together, such as those likely to comprise your college campus. The article, "Racism Creeps into Campus Lives," examines some of the subtle and not-so-subtle forms of discrimination based on race and sexual orientation.

After reading the article, select an important problem facing your campus related to the theme of diversity and prejudice. Analyze the problem you have identified by using the problem-solving method developed in this chapter. Then share your thoughts and conclusions with other class members. Working together, you can begin to implement your strategies for making your campus — and the world — a more enlightened place in which to live.

RACISM CREEPS INTO CAMPUS LIVES
by Lisa Haarlander

Writer Kevin Allison, assistant professor of psychology, and a white colleague walked into a Dairy Queen in a small town outside of State College one day. Allison, who is black, ordered a sundae. Even though he held his hand out for the change, the white cashier put it on the counter. When his white co-worker went up to the counter and did not put his hand out for the change, the cashier insisted on handing it to him. This is just one example of what many researchers call subtle racism. A recent University study conducted by several professors in the psychology department asked 51 black students to keep a daily diary of subtler forms of what happened to them. During a two-week period, about two-thirds said they experienced an incident that was definitely racially motivated. The other third was uncertain about the cause of the incident or said it was not racially motivated. Incidents the students reported included being overlooked at a bar or restaurant in favor of a white person, having change put on a counter instead of handed to them, having food slammed on a counter or being stared at. Although this number may surprise many white students, many minority students said those incidents are just a fact of life for them. . . .

Many Asian students are also treated differently because of their ethnicity. One night, Binglai Chen went with some friends to Denny's Restaurant. As they sat at their table, an Asian employee went to another table to give a group of white men their bill. After the employee left, the men in the booth started making fun of the employee and mimicking his accent. "I got so mad," said Chen, who is Chinese. "I would never make fun of the way white people talk." Chen's friend, Anne McSorley, who is white, said minority students are definitely treated differently at the University. "I think I have a different experience with life, being in the majority," said McSorley. "I'll never truly understand it because I never experience it myself." But experiencing racism and discrimination has left some minority students with bitter feelings toward whites. Although she has white friends, Leah Krout also has a problem with how some white people treat minorities. "My problem is with white people in general," said Krout, who is Korean. "That's where all my anger comes from. I won't deny how I feel. She said she has been discriminated against and treated as an object or an alien. "People always come up and ask, 'What are you?' They don't ask what's your nationality or ethnicity."

Although many minority groups face both obvious and not-so-obvious discrimination, some groups face blatant harassment and hatred. Most lesbian, gay and bisexual students said there is little subtlety in the discrimination they face. "It's still socially acceptable to discriminate against LGB groups," said Allan Vives, who is gay. "I can't walk into a bathroom without seeing something like 'Fags should die.' It's an everyday experience. . . ." Unfortunately for gay, lesbian and bisexual students, discrimination is still not socially unacceptable enough that it's reached the point where it's subtle," said Vives. When he first came to the University, Vives went to a club on College Avenue with some other students in the psychology department. As they were coming out of the club, another student walked in. A man Vives was with called the student a "f ***ing faggot" just because the student looked at him. At that time his friend did not know Vives was gay. "That hit me pretty hard," Vives said. "I didn't confront him on it for quite some time." When Vives did talk to him, his friend explained that he was used to being in groups where it was acceptable to express feelings against gay people. "The fact is, I was thinking that is not an adequate answer for a clinical psychology student," Vives said.

Perceiving, Believing, and Knowing

Perceiving
Actively selecting, organizing,
and interpreting sensations

Experiences shape
our perceptions.

We construct beliefs
based on our perceptions.

We view the world through
our own unique lenses,
which shape and influence
our perceptions.

We construct
knowledge based
on our beliefs.

Developing Knowledge
by thinking critically about
our beliefs

Thinking is the way you make sense of the world. By thinking in an active, purposeful, and organized way, you are able to solve problems, work toward your goals, analyze issues, and make decisions. Your experience of the world comes to you by means of your *senses:* sight, hearing, smell, touch, and taste. These senses are your bridges to the world, making you aware of what occurs outside you, and the process of becoming aware of your world through your senses is known as *perceiving.*

In this chapter you will explore the way your perceiving process operates and how it relates to your ability to think effectively. In particular, you will discover the way you shape your personal experience by actively selecting, organizing, and interpreting the sensations provided by the senses. In a way, each of us views the world through a pair of individual eyeglasses or contact lenses that reflect our past experiences and unique personalities. As a critical thinker, you want to become aware of the nature of your own lenses to help eliminate any bias or distortion they may be causing. You also want to become aware of the lenses of others so that you can better understand why they view things the way they do.

At almost every waking moment of your life, your senses are being bombarded by a tremendous number of stimuli: images to see, noises to hear, odors to smell, textures to feel, and flavors to taste. The experience of all these sensations happening at once creates what the nineteenth-century American philosopher William James called "a bloomin' buzzin' confusion." Yet for us, the world usually seems much more orderly and understandable. Why is this so?

In the first place, your sense equipment can receive sensations only within certain limited ranges. For example, there are many sounds and smells that animals can detect but you cannot because their sense organs have broader ranges in these areas than yours do.

A second reason you can handle this sensory bombardment is that from the stimulation available, you *select* only a small amount on which to focus your attention. To demonstrate this, try the following exercise. Concentrate on what you can *see,* ignoring your other senses for the moment. Focus on sensations that you were not previously aware of and then answer the first question. Concentrate on each of your other senses in turn, following the same procedure.

1. What can you *see?* (For example, the shape of the letters on the page, the design of the clothing on your arm)
2. What can you *hear?* (For example, the hum of the air circulator, the rustling of a page)
3. What can you *feel?* (For example, the pressure of the clothes against your skin, the texture of the page on your fingers)

4. What can you *smell?* (For example, the perfume or cologne someone is wearing, the odor of stale cigarette smoke)

5. What can you *taste?* (For example, the aftereffects of your last meal)

Compare your responses with those of the other students in the class. Do your classmates perceive sensations that differ from the ones you perceived? If so, how do you explain these differences?

As you practice this simple exercise, it should become clear that for every sensation that you focus your attention on, there are countless other sensations that you are simply ignoring. If you were aware of *everything* that is happening at every moment, you would be completely overwhelmed. By selecting certain sensations, you are able to make sense of your world in a relatively orderly way. The activity of using your senses to experience and make sense of your world is known as *perceiving.*

perceiving *Actively selecting, organizing, and interpreting what is experienced by your senses*

Actively Selecting, Organizing, and Interpreting Sensations

It is tempting to think that your senses simply record what is happening out in the world as if you were a human camera or tape recorder. You are not, however, a passive receiver of information, a "container" into which sense experience is poured. Instead, you are an *active participant* who is always trying to understand the sensations you are encountering. As you perceive your world, your experience is the result of combining the sensations you are having with the way you understand these sensations. For example, examine the following collection of markings. What do you see?

If all you see is a collection of black spots, try looking at the group sideways. After a while, you will probably perceive a familiar animal.

From this example you can see that when you perceive the world, you are doing more than simply recording what your senses experience. Besides experiencing sensations, you are also *actively making sense* of these sensations. That is why this collection of black spots suddenly became the figure of an animal — because you were able actively to organize these spots into a pattern you recognized. Or think about the times you were able to look up at the white, billowy clouds in the sky and see different figures and designs. The figures you were perceiving were not actually in the clouds but were the result of your giving a meaningful form to the shapes and colors you were experiencing.

The same is true for virtually everything you experience. Your perception of the world results from combining the information provided by your senses with the way you actively make sense of this information. And since making sense of information is what you are doing when you are thinking, you can see that perceiving your world involves using your mind in an active way. Of course, you are usually not aware that you are using your mind to interpret the sensations you are experiencing. You simply see the animal or the figures in the clouds as if they were really there.

When you actively perceive the sensations you are experiencing, you are usually engaged in three distinct activities:

1. *Selecting* certain sensations to pay attention to

2. *Organizing* these sensations into a design or pattern

3. *Interpreting* what this design or pattern means to you

In the case of the figure on page 110, you were able to perceive an animal because you *selected* certain of the markings to concentrate on, *organized* these markings into a pattern, and *interpreted* this pattern as representing a familiar animal.

Of course, when you perceive, these three operations of selecting, organizing, and interpreting are usually performed quickly, automatically, and often simultaneously. Also, you are normally unaware that you are performing these operations because they are so rapid and automatic. This chapter is designed to help you slow down this normally automatic process of perceiving so that you can understand how the process works.

Let's explore more examples that illustrate how you actively select, organize, and interpret your perceptions of the world. Carefully examine the figure at the top of page 112.

Do you see both the young woman and the old woman? If you do, try switching back and forth between the two images. As you switch back and forth, notice how for each image you are:

- *Selecting* certain lines, shapes, and shadings on which to focus your attention

- *Organizing* these lines, shapes, and shadings into different patterns

- *Interpreting* these patterns as representing things that you are able to recognize — a hat, a nose, a chin

Another way for you to become aware of your active participation in perceiving your world is to consider how you see objects. Examine the illustration that follows. Do you perceive different-sized people or the same-sized people at different distances?

When you see someone who is far away, you usually do not perceive a tiny person. Instead, you perceive a normal-sized person who is far away from you. Your experience in the world has enabled you to discover that the farther things are from you, the smaller they look. The moon in the night sky appears about the size of a quarter, yet you perceive it as being considerably larger. As you look down a long stretch of railroad tracks or gaze up at a tall building, the boundary lines seem to come together. Even though these images are what your eyes "see," however, you do not usually perceive the tracks meeting or the building coming to a point. Instead, your mind actively organizes and interprets a world composed of constant shapes and sizes, even though the images you actually see usually vary, depending on how far you are from them and the angle from which you are looking at them.

In short, your mind actively participates in the way you perceive the world. By combining the sensations you are receiving with the way your mind selects, organizes, and interprets these sensations, you perceive a world of things that is stable and familiar, a world that usually makes sense to you.

The process of perceiving takes place at a variety of different levels. At the most basic level, the concept of *perceiving* refers to the selection, organization, and interpretation of sensations: for example, being able to perceive the various objects in your experience, like a basketball. However, you also perceive larger patterns of meaning at more complex levels, as when watching the action of a group of people engaged in a basketball game. Although these are very different contexts, both engage you in the process of actively selecting, organizing, and interpreting what is experienced by your senses — in other words, *perceiving*.

People's Perceptions Differ

Your *active* participation in perceiving your world is something you are not usually aware of. You normally assume that what you are perceiving is what is actually taking place. Only when you find that your perception of the same event differs from the perceptions of others are you forced to examine the manner in which you are selecting, organizing, and interpreting the events in your world.

THINKING ACTIVITY 4.1

Analyzing Perceptions

Carefully examine the picture of a boy sitting at a desk on page 115. What do you think is happening in this picture?

1. Describe as specifically as possible what you perceive is taking place in the picture.
2. Describe what you think will happen next.
3. Identify the details of the picture that led you to your perceptions.
4. Compare your perceptions with the perceptions of other students in the class. List several perceptions that differ from yours.

VISUAL THINKING

The Investigation

- Explain why each witness describes the suspect differently. Have you ever been involved in a situation in which people described an individual or event in contrasting or conflicting ways? What is the artist saying about people's perceptions?

In most cases, people in a group will have a variety of perceptions about what is taking place in the picture in Thinking Activity 4.1. Some will see the boy as frustrated because the work is too difficult. Others will see him concentrating on what has to be done. Still others may see him as annoyed because he is being forced to do something he does not want to do. In each case, the perception depends on how the person is actively using his or her mind to organize and interpret what is taking place. Since the situation pictured is by its nature somewhat puzzling, different people perceive it in different ways.

Thinking Activity 4.2 reveals another example of how people's perceptions can differ.

THINKING ACTIVITY 4.2

Analyzing Perceptions

Closely examine the photograph on page 116.

1. Describe as specifically as possible what you think is taking place in the photograph.
2. Now describe what you think will happen next.
3. Identify the details of the picture that led you to your perceptions.
4. Compare your perceptions with the perceptions of other students in the class. List several perceptions that differ from yours.

VISUAL THINKING

Three for the Road

• Look closely at this photograph: what do you think is taking place? Under what circumstances do you think this photo was taken? Compare notes with another student and see if your interpretations are similar or different. What reasons and evidence led each person to his or her interpretations?

Viewing the World Through Lenses

To understand how various people can be exposed to the same stimuli or events and yet have different perceptions, it helps to imagine that each of us views the world through our own pair of contact lenses. Of course, we are not usually aware of the lenses we are wearing. Instead, our lenses act as *filters* that select and shape what we perceive without our realizing it.

This image of lenses helps explain why people can be exposed to the same stimuli or events and yet perceive different things. This happens because people are wearing *different lenses*, which influence what they are perceiving. For example, in "The Investigation" on page 114, each witness is giving what he or she (or it!) believes is an accurate description of the man in the center, unaware that their descriptions are being influenced by who they are and the way that they see things. When members of your class had different perceptions of the boy at the desk in Thinking Activity 4.1 and of the photograph in Thinking Activity 4.2, their different perceptions were the result of the different lenses through which each views the world.

To understand the way people perceive the world, you have to understand their individual lenses, which influence how they actively select, organize, and interpret the events in their experience. A diagram of the process might look like this:

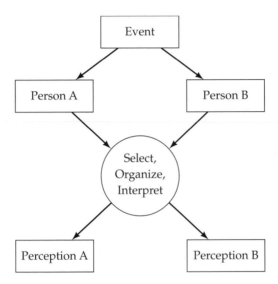

Consider the following pairs of statements. In each of these cases, both people are being exposed to the same basic *stimulus* or event, yet each has a totally different *perception* of the experience. Explain how you think the various perceptions might have developed.

1. a. That chili was much too spicy to eat.
   Explanation:
   b. That chili needed more hot peppers and chili powder to spice it up a little.
   Explanation:
2. a. People who wear lots of makeup and jewelry are very sophisticated.
   Explanation:
   b. People who wear lots of makeup and jewelry are overdressed.
   Explanation:

3. a. The music that young people enjoy listening to is a very creative cultural expression.
   Explanation:

   b. The music that young people enjoy listening to is obnoxious noise.
   Explanation:

To become an effective critical thinker, you have to become aware of the lenses that you — and others — are wearing. These lenses aid you in actively selecting, organizing, and interpreting the sensations in your experience. If you are unaware of the nature of your own lenses, you can often mistake your own perceptions for objective truth without bothering to examine either the facts or others' perceptions on a given issue.

What Factors Shape Perceptions?

Your perceptions of the world are dramatically influenced by your past experiences: the way you were brought up, the relationships you have had, and the training and education you have undergone. Every dimension of "who" you are is reflected in your perceiving lenses: your gender, age, ethnicity, geographical origins, skills, talents, personality characteristics, and so on. Of course, we are generally unaware of the factors that shape our perceptions since they are such a natural part of our lives. It takes a special effort of critical reflection to become aware of these powerful influences on our perceptions of the world and the beliefs we construct based on them.

Your special interests and areas of expertise also affect how you see the world. Consider the case of two people who are watching a football game. One person, who has very little understanding of football, sees merely a bunch of grown men hitting each other for no apparent reason. The other person, who loves football, sees complex play patterns, daring coaching strategies, effective blocking and tackling techniques, and zone defenses with "seams" that the receivers are trying to "split." Both have their eyes focused on the same event, but they are perceiving two entirely different situations. Their perceptions differ because each person is actively selecting, organizing, and interpreting the available stimuli in different ways. The same is true of any situation in which you are perceiving something about which you have special knowledge or expertise. The following are examples:

- A builder examining the construction of a new house

- A music lover attending a concert

- A naturalist experiencing the outdoors

- A cook tasting a dish just prepared

- A lawyer examining a contract

- An art lover visiting a museum

Think about a special area of interest or expertise that you have and how your perceptions of that area differ from those of people who don't share your knowledge. Ask other class members about their areas of expertise. Notice how their perceptions of that area differ from your own because of their greater knowledge and experience.

In all these cases, the perceptions of the knowledgeable person differ substantially from the perceptions of the person who lacks knowledge of that area. Of course, you do not have to be an expert to have more fully developed perceptions. It is a matter of degree. In general, the more understanding you have of a particular area, the more detailed and complete will be your perceptions of all matters related to it.

THINKING ACTIVITY 4.3

Thinking Critically About My Perceiving Lenses

This is an opportunity for you to think about the unique "prescription" of your perceiving lenses. Reflect on the elements in yourself and your personal history that you believe exert the strongest influence on the way that you view the world. These factors will likely include the following categories:

- Demographics (age, gender, race/ethnicity, religion, geographical location)

- Tastes in fashion, music, leisure activities

- Special knowledge, talents, expertise

- Significant experiences in your life, either positive or negative

- Values, goals, aspirations

Create a visual representation of the prescription for your perceiving lenses, highlighting the unique factors that have contributed to your distinctive perspective on the world. Then, compare your "prescription" to those of other students in your class, and discuss the ways in which your lenses result in perceptions and beliefs that are different from those produced by other prescriptions.

THINKING ACTIVITY 4.4

Analyzing Different Accounts of the Assassination of Malcolm X

Let's examine a situation in which a number of different people had somewhat different perceptions about an event they were describing — in this case, the assassination of Malcolm X as he was speaking at a meeting in Harlem. The following are five different accounts of what took place on that day. As you read through the various accounts, pay particular attention to the different perceptions each one presents of this event. After you have finished reading the accounts, analyze some of the differences in these perceptions by answering the questions that follow.

FIVE ACCOUNTS OF THE ASSASSINATION OF MALCOLM X*

The *New York Times* (February 22, 1965)

Malcolm X, the 39-year-old leader of a militant Black Nationalist movement, was shot to death yesterday afternoon at a rally of his followers in a ballroom in Washington Heights. The bearded Negro extremist had said only a few words of greeting when a fusillade rang out. The bullets knocked him over backwards.

A 22-year-old Negro, Thomas Hagan, was charged with the killing. The police rescued him from the ballroom crowd after he had been shot and beaten.

Pandemonium broke out among the 400 Negroes in the Audubon Ballroom at 160th Street and Broadway. As men, women and children ducked under tables and flattened themselves on the floor, more shots were fired. The police said seven bullets struck Malcolm. Three other Negroes were shot. Witnesses reported that as many as 30 shots had been fired. About two hours later the police said the shooting had apparently been a result of a feud between followers of Malcolm and members of the extremist group he broke with last year, the Black Muslims. . . .

Life (March 5, 1965)**

His life oozing out through a half dozen or more gunshot wounds in his chest, Malcolm X, once the shrillest voice of black supremacy, lay dying on the stage of a Manhattan auditorium. Moments before, he had

---

* "On the Assassination of Malcolm X," The *New York Times*, February 22, 1965. Copyright © 1965 by The New York Times *Co.* Reprinted by permission.

** Excerpt from "Assassination of Malcolm X," March 5, 1965. *Life* Magazine. © 1965 Time Inc. Reprinted by permission.

stepped up to the lectern and 400 of the faithful had settled down expectantly to hear the sort of speech for which he was famous — flaying the hated white man. Then a scuffle broke out in the hall and Malcolm's bodyguards bolted from his side to break it up — only to discover that they had been faked out. At least two men with pistols rose from the audience and pumped bullets into the speaker, while a third cut loose at close range with both barrels of a sawed-off shotgun. In the confusion the pistol man got away. The shotgunner lunged through the crowd and out the door, but not before the guards came to their wits and shot him in the leg. Outside he was swiftly overtaken by other supporters of Malcolm and very likely would have been stomped to death if the police hadn't saved him. Most shocking of all to the residents of Harlem was the fact that Malcolm had been killed not by "whitey" but by members of his own race.

The *New York Post* (February 22, 1965)

They came early to the Audubon Ballroom, perhaps drawn by the expectation that Malcolm X would name the men who firebombed his home last Sunday. . . . I sat at the left in the 12th row and, as we waited, the man next to me spoke of Malcolm and his followers: "Malcolm is our only hope. You can depend on him to tell it like it is and to give Whitey hell.". . .

There was a prolonged ovation as Malcolm walked to the rostrum. Malcolm looked up and said, "A salaam aleikum (Peace be unto you)," and the audience replied, "We aleikum salaam (And unto you, peace)."

Bespectacled and dapper in a dark suit, sandy hair glinting in the light, Malcolm said: "Brothers and sisters. . . ." He was interrupted by two men in the center of the ballroom, who rose and, arguing with each other, moved forward. Then there was a scuffle at the back of the room. I heard Malcolm X say his last words: "Now, brothers, break it up," he said softly. "Be cool, be calm."

Then all hell broke loose. There was a muffled sound of shots and Malcolm, blood on his face and chest, fell limply back over the chairs behind him. The two men who had approached him ran to the exit on my side of the room, shooting wildly behind them as they ran. I heard people screaming, "Don't let them kill him." "Kill those bastards."At an exit I saw some of Malcolm's men beating with all their strength on two men. I saw a half dozen of Malcolm's followers bending over his inert body on the stage. Their clothes were stained with their leader's blood.

Four policemen took the stretcher and carried Malcolm through the crowd and some of the women came out of their shock and one said: "I hope he doesn't die, but I don't think he's going to make it."

Associated Press (February 22, 1965)

A week after being bombed out of his Queens home, Black Nationalist leader Malcolm X was shot to death shortly after 3 (P.M.) yesterday at a Washington Heights rally of 400 of his devoted followers. Early today, police brass ordered a homicide charge placed against a 22-year-old man they rescued from a savage beating by Malcolm X supporters after the shooting. The suspect, Thomas Hagan, had been shot in the left leg by one of Malcolm's bodyguards as, police said, Hagan and another assassin fled when pandemonium erupted. Two other men were wounded in the wild burst of firing from at least three weapons. The firearms were a .38, a .45 automatic and a sawed-off shotgun. Hagan allegedly shot Malcolm X with the shotgun, a double-barrelled sawed-off weapon on which the stock also had been shortened, possibly to facilitate concealment. Cops charged Reuben Frances, of 871 E. 179th St., Bronx, with felonious assault in the shooting of Hagan, and with Sullivan Law violation — possession of the .45. Police recovered the shotgun and the .45.

The *Amsterdam News* (February 27, 1965)

"We interrupt this program to bring you a special newscast . . . ," the announcer said as the Sunday afternoon movie on the TV set was halted temporarily. "Malcolm X was shot four times while addressing a crowd at the Audubon Ballroom on 166th Street." "Oh no!" That was my first reaction to the shocking event that followed one week after the slender, articulate leader of the Afro-American Unity was routed from his East Elmhurst home by a bomb explosion. Minutes later we alighted from a cab at the corner of Broadway and 166th St. just a short 15 blocks from where I live on Broadway. About 200 men and women, neatly dressed, were milling around, some with expressions of awe and disbelief. Others were in small clusters talking loudly and with deep emotion in their voices. Mostly they were screaming for vengeance. One woman, small, dressed in a light gray coat and her eyes flaming with indignation, argued with a cop at the St. Nicholas corner of the block. "This is not the end of it. What they were going to do to the Statue of Liberty will be small in comparison. We black people are tired of being shoved around." Standing across the street near the memorial park one of Malcolm's close associates commented: "It's a shame." Later he added that "if it's war they want, they'll get it." He would not say whether Elijah Muhammed's followers had anything to do with the assassination. About 3:30 P.M. Malcolm X's wife, Betty, was escorted by three men and a woman from the Columbia Presbyterian Hospital. Tears streamed down her face. She was screaming, "They killed him!" Malcolm X had no last words. . . . The bombing and burning of the No. 7 Mosque early Tuesday morning was the first blow by those who are seeking revenge for the cold-blooded murder of a man who at 39 might have grown to the stature of respectable leadership.

Questions for Analysis

1. What details of the events has each writer *selected* to focus on?
2. How has each writer *organized* the details that have been selected? Bear in mind that most news organizations present what they consider the most important information first and the least important information last.
3. How does each writer *interpret* Malcolm X, his followers, the gunmen, and the significance of the assassination?
4. How has each writer used *language* to express his or her perspective and to influence the thinking of the reader? Which language styles do you find most effective?

 THINKING ACTIVITY 4.5

Analyzing Different Accounts of the 2001 World Trade Center and Pentagon Attacks

Here's another perspective-taking activity involving critical thinking, this one dealing with the terrorist attacks on the World Trade Center and Pentagon in 2001. The various accounts appeared in news sources in the United States and around the world. After you have finished reading these accounts, analyze some of the differences in perceptions by answering the questions that follow.

Eight Accounts of the World Trade Center and the Pentagon Attacks

The *New York Times* (New York City, September 12, 2001)*

Hijackers rammed jetliners into each of New York's Trade Center towers yesterday, toppling both in a hellish storm of ash, glass, smoke and leaping victims, while a third jetliner crashed into the Pentagon in Virginia.

* "U.S. Attacked: President Vows to Exact Punishment for 'Evil,'" The *New York Times*, September 12, 2001. Copyright © 2001 by The New York Times Co. Reprinted by permission.

VISUAL THINKING

Destruction and Heroism

● What emotions are stirred when you look at this photograph? What does the terrorist destruction of the World Trade Center and the damaging of the Pentagon mean to you? What did New York City mayor Rudolph Giuliani mean when he said the attack displayed "the worst of humanity encountering the best of humanity"?

There was no official count, but President Bush said thousands had perished, and in the immediate aftermath the calamity was already being ranked the worst and most audacious terror attack in American history.

The attacks seemed carefully coordinated. The hijacked planes were all en route to California, and therefore gorged with fuel, and their departures were spaced within an hour and 40 minutes. The first, American Airlines Flight 11, a Boeing 767 out of Boston for Los Angeles, crashed into the north tower at 8:48 A.M. Eighteen minutes later, United Airlines Flight 175, also headed from Boston to Los Angeles, plowed into the south tower. Then an American Airlines Boeing 757, Flight 77, left Washington's Dulles International Airport bound for Los Angeles, but instead hit the western part of the Pentagon, the military headquarters where 24,000 people work, at 9:40 A.M. Finally, United Airlines Flight 93, a Boeing 757 flying from Newark to San Francisco, crashed near Pittsburgh, raising the possibility that its hijackers had failed in whatever their mission was.

In all, 266 people perished in the four planes and several score more were known dead elsewhere. Numerous firefighters, police officers and other rescue workers who responded to the initial disaster in Lower Manhattan were killed or injured when the buildings collapsed. Hundreds were treated for cuts, broken bones, burns and smoke inhalation. But the real carnage was concealed for now by the twisted, smoking, ash-choked carcasses of the twin towers, in which thousands of people used to work on a weekday. The collapse of the towers caused another World Trade Center building to fall 10 hours later, and several other buildings in the area were damaged or aflame. "I have a sense it's a horrendous number of lives lost," said Mayor Rudolph W. Giuliani. "Right now we have to focus on saving as many lives as possible."

Le Monde (Paris, September 12, 2001)

The United States underwent, Tuesday, September 11, the worst attack of their history. The financial, military and policy centers of the country were reached. Terrorists destroyed the two towers of the World Trade Center in New York and tackled the Pentagon. As in Pearl Harbour, the American power was taken by surprise. The dream of invulnerable America definitively ended.

Hamburger Morgenpost (Hamburg, September 12, 2001)

New York, 8:42 A.M.: It is a sunny morning, as the millions-metropolis wakes up, a morning that will change America, and perhaps the entire world, forever. As eyewitnesses later reported, a jetliner flies in a straight line towards the southern of the two 411-meter high towers of the World Trade Center. Flying debris falls in as far as a 5 kilometer radius to the ground, hitting pedestrians in the well-visited streets of Manhattan.

Still the world, which will be informed within only minutes, goes about its business. The news network CNN, whose reach is worldwide, runs live footage with photos of the smoking skyscraper. The damage appears terrible, but overcomable. This impression changes a mere 18 minutes later, as the public, via television, witnesses a second jetliner flying into the second, still stable tower. Incomprehensible: like the special effects in the Hollywood film "Independence Day" the jet penetrates the glass giant, almost slicing all the way through it. TV viewers see how the still-intact glass façade of the opposite side of the tower is destroyed, obviously caused by the jet's explosion in the inside of the tower.

It is only now that the suspicion rises up to awareness: this is the work of terrorists, whose horrific dimensions have until now not been known. Yet for America, the nightmare has not yet ended: Barely an hour after the first attack, there comes a report from the nation's capital, Washington: flames are erupting from the Pentagon. The cause: a passenger aircraft, probably a Boeing 767. Now the terror has struck America's central nervous system. A few minutes later, the Mall outside Congress burns also. A car bomb is the suspected cause. CNN switches from a burning Manhattan to the burning capital — this is war, and the victims are civilians. With the world as a witness, the people behind the shattered glass façade of the WTC gesticulate as the desperate leap out of the burning buildings. A little while later, both towers collapse, transformed in an instant from New York's giants to empty shells.

Pakistani newspaper (Pakistan, September 12, 2001)

A Pakistani newspaper said on Wednesday that Saudi militant Osama bin Laden had issued a denial of responsibility for the devastating terror attacks on the United States. "The terrorist act is the action of some American group. I have nothing to do with it," the newspaper quoted bin Laden as saying through "sources close to the Taliban." The Urdu-language newspaper has a reputation for sensational reporting and there was no independent confirmation of the claim.

Time.com (September 12, 2001)*

Morning came, and everything was changed. The sun rose Wednesday over the absence of a national landmark, a smoldering ruin in lower Manhattan where the World Trade Center towers had stood. In Washington, the Pentagon, still on fire, was deeply scarred, along with America's collective sense of security. After a day in which terrorists had managed to effectively shut down both cities, suspend all air traffic in the U.S. and force evacuations across the country and in U.S. facilities worldwide, a day in which President George W. Bush warned that "the United States will hunt down and punish those responsible for these cowardly acts," there was nothing to do in the bright, crisp fall sunshine but to clean up, search for those responsible, and mourn the dead.

In a tragic and spectacular explosion that engulfed lower Manhattan in thick smoke and gray powder debris, two airplanes crashed into the World Trade Center in New York City at around 9 A.M. EST. . . . The

---

* Time.com (September 12, 2001) "Day of Infamy". © 2001 Time Inc. Reprinted by permission.

planes were loaded with fuel for transcontinental flights, and that jet fuel ignited a hellish blaze that sent temperatures at the point of impact soaring to an estimated 2000 degrees F. Within an hour, the intense heat caused the seemingly invincible steel beams of the towers to melt like cotton candy. At 10 A.M. EST, the southern tower of the World Trade Center was enveloped in smoke after a second gigantic explosion, and part of that tower collapsed and was destroyed. About twenty minutes later, the northern tower imploded.

In Washington, the Pentagon was evacuated after another commercial airliner crashed into the building. A short time later, part of the building collapsed. A fire was also reported on the Mall. The White House, the Capitol and other government buildings were also evacuated, and Washington became a ghost town. If the terrorists sought to undermine the conduct of government, they succeeded at least for the day. They may not, however, have hit all of their targets: Wednesday afternoon, White House officials reported that both the White House and Air Force One were targets of the terrorist attacks; officials speculate the plane that crashed into the Pentagon may have been intended to destroy the White House instead.

The *London Times* (London, September 12, 2001)

It was terrorism by timetable. Morning in America became the darkest of national catastrophes after a carefully co-ordinated attack of grotesque barbarity. The first the world knew of what was to become an unfolding tragedy, which stretched human powers of understanding to breaking point, was just before 9 A.M. U.S. Eastern time (1400 BST). Inside the World Trade Centre, New York's public servants, bankers and industrialists would have been settling into their second working hour when disaster struck. An American Airlines flight crashed directly into the 100-storey building, not just a symbol of American corporate power and capitalism's global sway but the workplace for thousands of New Yorkers. The large passenger jet was careening towards the tower before it embedded itself in the building. Heavy black smoke billowed into the sky above one of New York City's most famous landmarks and debris rained down on the street, one of its busiest work areas.

Before any rational reaction could come, before any judgment about the cause of the disaster could be made, as emergency services were being scrambled and newsrooms alerted, a second jet plunged into the World Trade Centre just after 9 A.M. When the second plane hit, a fireball of flame and smoke erupted, leaving a huge hole in the glass and steel tower. Television stations, alerted to the first crash, caught the second plane ploughing into the second of the twin towers, exploding in a fireball a few minutes after the first impact. The scenario of a Tom Clancy thriller or Spielberg blockbuster was now unfolding live on the world's television screens.

For eyewitnesses, the scale of the devastation was already incomprehensible. John Axisa, who was getting off a commuter train to the World Trade Centre, said he saw "bodies falling out of the building." He ran outside and watched people jump out of the first building. Other witnesses on the street were screaming every time another person leapt. For those below the point of impact, the only thought was flight. People ran down the stairs in panic and fled from the building. And in a grotesque parody of the tickertape parades that characterize New York celebrations, thousands of pieces of office paper were carried on the gusting wind to Brooklyn, about three miles away.

People's Daily (Beijing, September 12, 2001)

At least one Chinese national was injured in the terror attacks against the World Trade Center in New York and the fate of roughly 30 others was unknown on Wednesday morning, China's Foreign Trade Ministry said. China had 14 companies with offices in the building at the heart of the global financial centre which was hit by two aircraft on Tuesday, the ministry said in a statement on its Web site.

Chinese police blocked off the road past the U.S. embassy in Beijing to all but American embassy cars and personnel and doubled the number of guards to about 30.

Ordinary Chinese scrambled for more information, with many trying to access foreign news Web sites. Many condemned the attacks, first reported on the Sina.com, a NASDAQ listed Chinese portal, just several minutes after the event. "I think no matter what, if you play with people's lives, it is too tragic," said Chen Xiao, who works for a Beijing publishing firm, as she bought a morning newspaper. "It doesn't matter who did it or what they were upset about, but taking that many innocent lives is a price that's barbaric." Feng Chang-lin, 63, owner of a downtown hardware store in Shanghai, said the world would never be the same again. "This is just a cowardly act by terrorists," he said. "No matter what problems you might have with another country, you should never resort to such tactics."

China's stock markets dropped sharply at the open on Wednesday, with Shanghai B shares down more than six percent. Chinese investors, who routinely ignore everything from U.S. Fed rate cuts to tumbling Asian bourses, would be unable to shrug off the attacks, brokers and analysts said.

All four flights scheduled from China to the United States on Wednesday had been cancelled. Air China flight CA985 to San Francisco and China Eastern flight MU583 to Los Angeles were both diverted to Vancouver on Tuesday night and China Eastern cargo flight MU5787 was diverted to an American military airport in Anchorage, Alaska.

Chinese President Jiang Zemin sent a message of sympathy to U.S. President George W. Bush at Tuesday's midnight. Jiang also expressed condolences to the family members of the victims of the attacks and "grave concern" for the safety of tens of thousands of Chinese in the United States. Foreign Ministry spokesman Zhu Bangzao said in a statement the Chinese people were "deeply shocked" by the attacks. "The Chinese government has consistently condemned and opposed all manner of terrorist violence," Zhu said.

The *Washington Post* (Washington, D.C., September 12, 2001)*

Terrorists unleashed an astonishing air assault on America's military and financial power centers yesterday morning, hijacking four commercial jets and then crashing them into the World Trade Center in New York, the Pentagon and the Pennsylvania countryside. There were no reliable estimates last night of how many people were killed in the most devastating terrorist operation in American history. The number was certainly in the hundreds and could be in the thousands.

It was the most dramatic attack on American soil since Pearl Harbor, and it created indelible scenes of carnage and chaos. The commandeered jets obliterated the World Trade Center's twin 110-story towers from their familiar perch above Manhattan's skyline and ripped a blazing swath through the Defense Department's imposing five-sided fortress, grounding the domestic air traffic system for the first time and plunging the entire nation into an unparalleled state of anxiety. U.S. military forces at home and abroad were placed on their highest state of alert, and a loose network of Navy warships was deployed along both coasts for air defense.

None of the 266 people aboard the four planes survived. There were even more horrific but still untallied casualties in the World Trade Center

*"Accounts of the 9/11 Terror Attack," by Michael Grunwald. © 2001, The *Washington Post*. Reprinted with permission.

and the Pentagon, which together provided office space for more than 70,000 people. At just one of the firms with offices in the World Trade Center, the Marsh & McLennan insurance brokerage, 1,200 of its 1,700 employees were unaccounted for last night. The spectacular collapse of the Trade Center's historic twin towers and another less recognizable skyscraper during the rescue operations caused even more bloodshed. At least 300 New York firefighters and 85 police officers are presumed dead. The preliminary list of victims included the conservative commentator Barbara K. Olson, "Frasier" executive producer David Angell and two hockey scouts from the Los Angeles Kings.

No one claimed responsibility for the attacks, but federal officials said they suspect the involvement of Islamic extremists with links to fugitive terrorist Osama bin Laden, who has been implicated in the 1998 bombings of two U.S. embassies in Africa and several other attacks. Law enforcement sources said there is already evidence implicating bin Laden's militant network in the attack, and politicians from both parties predicted a major and immediate escalation in America's worldwide war against terrorism. In a grim address to the nation last night, President Bush denounced the attacks as a failed attempt to frighten the United States, and promised to hunt down those responsible. "We will make no distinction," he said, "between the terrorists who committed these acts and those who harbor them."

Questions for Analysis

1. Analyze the perceiving lenses of each account by using the questions on page 123 as a framework.
2. If you were to compose your own account of this catastrophe,
   • Which details would you select to be included?
   • How would you organize the details?
   • What would be your interpretation of the significance of this event? What themes would you want to suggest and elaborate on?
   • Of the language styles displayed in the previous accounts, which style would you choose?
3. Compose your own account of this event, as if you were writing for a major news organization with an international audience.

THINKING PASSAGE

Experiences Shape Your Perceptions

Your ways of viewing the world are developed over a long period of time through the experiences you have and your thinking about these experiences. As you think critically about your perceptions, you learn more from your experiences and about how you make sense of the world. Your perceptions may be strengthened by this understanding, or they may be changed by this understanding. For example, read the following student passage and consider the way the writer's experiences — and her reflection on these experiences — contributed to shaping her perspective on the world.

ACQUIRED KNOWLEDGE
by Anonymous

When news of the Acquired Immune Deficiency Syndrome first began to spread, it was just another one of those issues on the news that I felt did not really concern me. Along with cancer, leukemia, and kidney failure, I knew these diseases ran rampant across the country, but they didn't affect me.

Once the AIDS crisis became a prevalent problem in society, I began to take a little notice of it, but my interest only extended as far as taking precautions to insure that I would not contract the disease. Sure, I felt sorry for all the people who were dying from it, but again, it was not my problem.

My father was an intravenous drug user for as long as I can remember. This was a fact of life when I was growing up. I knew that what he was doing was wrong, and that eventually he would die from it, but I also knew that he would never change.

On July 27th, my father died. An autopsy showed his cause of death as pneumonia and tuberculosis, seemingly natural causes. However, I was later informed that these were two very common symptoms related to carriers of the HIV virus. My father's years of drug abuse had finally caught up with him. He had died from AIDS.

My father's death changed my life. Prior to that, I had always felt that as long as a situation did not directly affect me, it was really no concern of mine. I felt that somewhere, someone would take care of it. Having a crisis strike so close to me made me wake up to reality. Suddenly I became acutely aware of all the things that are wrong in the world. I began to see the problems of AIDS, famine, homelessness, unemployment, and others from a personal point of view, and I began to feel that I had an obligation to join the crusade to do something about these problems.

I organized a youth coalition called UPLIFT INC. In this group, we meet and talk about the problems in society, as well as the everyday problems that any of our members may have in their lives. We organize shows (talent shows, fashion shows) and give a large portion of our proceeds to the American Foundation for AIDS Research, the Coalition for the Homeless, and many other worthy organizations.

Now I feel that I am doing my duty as a human being by trying to help those who are less fortunate than myself. My father's death gave me insight into my own mortality. Now I know that life is too short not to only try to enjoy it, but to really achieve something worthwhile out of it. Material gains matter only if you are willing to take your good fortune and spread it around to those who could use it.

THINKING ACTIVITY 4.6

Describing a Shaping Experience

Think of an experience that has shaped your life. Write an essay describing the experience and the ways it changed your life and how you perceive the world. After writing, analyze your experience by answering the following questions.

1. What were your *initial* perceptions of the situation? As you began the experience, you brought into the situation certain perceptions about the experience and the people involved.

2. What previous experiences had you undergone? Identify some of the influences that helped to shape these perceptions. Describe the actions that you either took or thought about taking.

3. As you became involved in the situation, what experiences in the situation influenced you to question or doubt your initial perceptions?

4. In what new ways did you view the situation that would better explain what was taking place? Identify the revised perceptions that you began to form about the experience.

⊚ Thinking Critically About Perceptions

So far, we have emphasized the great extent to which you actively participate in what you perceive by selecting, organizing, and interpreting. We have suggested that each of us views the world through our own unique lenses. This means that no two of us perceive the world in exactly the same way.

Because we actively participate in selecting, organizing, and interpreting the sensations we experience, however, our perceptions are often incomplete, inaccurate, or subjective. To complicate the situation even more, our own limitations in perceiving are not the only ones that can cause us problems. Other people often purposefully create perceptions and misperceptions. An advertiser who wants to sell a product may try to create the impression that your life will be changed if you use this product. Or a person who wants to discredit someone else may spread untrue rumors about her in order to influence others' perceptions of her.

The only way you can correct the mistakes, distortions, and incompleteness of your perceptions is to *become aware* of this normally unconscious process by which you perceive and make sense of your world. By becoming aware of this process, you can think critically about what is going on and then correct your mistakes and distortions. In other words, you can use your critical thinking abilities to create a clearer and more informed idea of what is taking place. Perception alone cannot be totally relied on, and if you remain unaware of how it operates and of your active role, then you will be unable to exert any control over it. And in that case, you will be convinced that the way *you see* the world is the way the world *is,* even when your perceptions are mistaken, distorted, or incomplete.

The first step in critically examining your perceptions is to be willing to *ask questions* about what you are perceiving. As long as you believe that the way you see things is the only way to see them, you will be unable to recognize when your perceptions are distorted or inaccurate. For instance, if you are certain that your interpretation of the boy at the computer in Thinking Activity 4.1 or of the photograph in Thinking Activity 4.2 is the only correct one, then you will not be likely to try seeing other possible interpretations. But if you are willing to question your perception ("What are some other possible interpretations?"), then you will open the way to more fully developing your perception of what is taking place.

Besides asking questions, you have to try to become aware of the personal factors your lenses bring to your perceptions. As you have seen, each of us brings to every situation a whole collection of expectations, interests, fears, and hopes that can influence what we are perceiving. Consider the following situations:

> You've been fishing all day without a nibble. Suddenly you get a strike! You reel it in, but just as you're about to pull the fish into the boat, it frees itself from the hook and swims away. When you get back home later that night, your friends ask you, "How large was the fish that got away?"

> The teacher asks you to evaluate the performance of a classmate who is giving a report to the class. You don't like this other student because he acts as if he's superior to the rest of the students in the class. How do you evaluate his report?

> You are asked to estimate the size of an audience attending an event that your organization has sponsored. How many people are there?

In each of these cases, you can imagine that your perceptions might be influenced by certain hopes, fears, or prejudices that you brought to the situation, causing your observations to become distorted or inaccurate. Although you usually cannot eliminate the personal feelings that are influencing your perceptions, you can become aware of them and try to control them. For instance, if you are asked to evaluate a group of people, one of whom is a good friend, you should try to keep these personal feelings in mind when making your judgment in order to make your perceptions as accurate as possible.

As you saw in Chapter 2, critical thinkers strive to see things from different perspectives. One of the best ways to do so is by communicating with others and engaging in *dialogue* with them. This means exchanging and critically examining ideas in an open and organized way. Similarly, dialogue is one of the main ways that you check your perceptions — by asking others what their perceptions are and then comparing and contrasting these with your own. This is exactly what you did when you discussed the different possible interpretations of the boy at the computer and the ambiguous photograph. By exchanging your perceptions with the perceptions of other class members, you developed a more complete sense of how these different events could be viewed, as well as the reasons that support these different perspectives.

Looking for reasons that support various perceptions also involves trying to discover any independent proof or evidence regarding the perception. When evidence is available in the form of records, photographs, videotapes, or experimental results, this information will certainly help you evaluate the accuracy of your perceptions. For example, consider the situations just described. What

VISUAL THINKING

Walking on Water?

- What is the artist saying about perceptions with this illustration? If you were writing a caption, what would it be? Describe a situation in which what you perceived to be taking place turned out to be something much different.

are some of the independent forms of evidence you could look for in trying to verify your perceptions?

Thinking critically about your perceptions means trying to avoid developing impulsive or superficial perceptions that you are unwilling to change. As you saw in Chapter 2, critical thinkers are *thoughtful* in approaching the world and *open* to modifying their views in the light of new information or better insight. Consider the following perceptions:

- Women are very emotional.

- Politicians are corrupt.

- Teenagers are wild and irresponsible.

- People who are good athletes are usually poor students.

- Men are thoughtless and insensitive.

These types of general perceptions are known as *stereotypes* because they express a belief about an entire group of people without recognizing the individual differences among members of the group. For instance, it is probably accurate to say that there are *some* politicians who are corrupt, but this is not the same thing as saying that all, or even most, politicians are corrupt. Stereotypes affect your perception of the world because they encourage you to form an inaccurate and superficial idea of a whole group of people ("All teenagers are reckless drivers"). When you meet someone who falls into this group, you automatically perceive that person as having these stereotyped qualities ("This person is a teenager, so he is a reckless driver"). Even if you find that this person does not fit your stereotyped perception ("This teenager is not a reckless driver"), this sort of superficial and unthoughtful labeling does not encourage you to change your perception of the group as a whole. Instead, it encourages you to overlook the conflicting information in favor of your stereotyped perception ("All teenagers are reckless drivers — except for this one"). However, when you are perceiving in a thoughtful fashion, you try to see what a person is like as an individual, instead of trying to fit him or her into a pre-existing category.

THINKING ACTIVITY 4.7

Analyzing Stereotypes

1. Describe an incident in which you were perceived as a stereotype because of your age, ethnic or religious background, employment, accent, or place of residence.

2. Describe how it felt to be stereotyped in this way.

3. Explain what you think are the best ways to overcome stereotypes such as these.

ⓔ Constructing Beliefs

It seems to be a natural human impulse to try to understand the world we live in. This is the overall goal of thinking, which we have defined as the mental process by which we make sense of the world. Perceiving is an important part of this thinking process, but your perceptions, taken by themselves, do not provide a reliable foundation for your understanding of the world. Your perceptions are often incomplete, distorted, and inaccurate. They are shaped and influenced by your perceiving lenses, which reflect your own individual personality, experiences, biases, assumptions, and ways of viewing things. To clarify and validate your perceptions, you must critically examine and evaluate these perceptions.

Thinking critically about your perceptions results in the formation of your beliefs and ultimately in the construction of your knowledge about the world. For example, consider the following statements and answer "Yes," "No," or "Not sure" to each.

1. Humans need to eat to stay alive.
2. Smoking marijuana is a harmless good time.
3. Every human life is valuable.
4. Developing your mind is as important as taking care of your body.
5. People should care about other people, not just about themselves.

Your responses to these statements reflect certain beliefs you have, and these beliefs help you explain why the world is the way it is and how you ought to behave. In this chapter you will see that beliefs are the main tools you use to make sense of the world and guide your actions. The total collection of your beliefs represents your view of the world, your philosophy of life.

What exactly are *beliefs*? Beliefs represent an interpretation, evaluation, conclusion, or prediction about the nature of the world. For example, this statement — "I believe that the whale in the book *Moby Dick* by Herman Melville symbolizes a primal, natural force that men are trying to destroy" — represents an *interpretation* of that novel. To say, "I believe that watching soap operas is unhealthy because they focus almost exclusively on the seamy side of human life" is to express an *evaluation* of soap operas. The statement "I believe that one of the main reasons two out of three people in the world go to bed hungry each night is that industrially advanced nations like the United States have not done a satisfactory job of sharing their knowledge" expresses a *conclusion* about the problem of world hunger. To say, "If drastic environmental measures are not undertaken to slow the global warming trend, then I believe that the polar ice caps will melt and the earth will be flooded" is to make a *prediction* about events that will occur in the future.

Besides expressing an interpretation, evaluation, conclusion, or prediction about the world, beliefs also express an *endorsement* of the accuracy of the beliefs by the speaker or author. In the preceding statements the speakers are not simply expressing interpretations, evaluations, conclusions, and predictions; they are also indicating that they believe these views are *true.* In other words, the speakers are saying that they have adopted these beliefs as their own because they are convinced that they represent accurate viewpoints based on some sort of evidence. This "endorsement" by the speaker is a necessary dimension of beliefs, and we assume it to be the case even if the speaker doesn't directly say, "I believe." For example, the statement "Astrological predictions are meaningless because there is no persuasive reason to believe that the position of the stars and planets has any effect on human affairs" expresses a belief even though it doesn't specifically include the words "I believe. "

beliefs *Interpretations, evaluations, conclusions, or predictions about the world that we endorse as true*

Describe beliefs you have that fall in each of these categories (interpretation, evaluation, conclusion, prediction) and then explain the reason(s) you have for endorsing the beliefs.

1. **Interpretation** (an explanation or analysis of the meaning or significance of something)
   My interpretation is that . . .
   Supporting reason(s):
2. **Evaluation** (a judgment of the value or quality of something, based on certain standards)
   My evaluation is that . . .
   Supporting reason(s):
3. **Conclusion** (a decision made or an opinion formed after consideration of the relevant facts or evidence)
   My conclusion is that . . .
   Supporting reason(s):

4. **Prediction** (a statement about what will happen in the future)
   My prediction is that . . .
   Supporting reason(s):

T H I N K I N G   A C T I V I T Y   4.8

Analyzing a False Perception

Describe an experience of a perception you had that later turned out to be false, based on subsequent experiences or reflection. Address the following questions:

1. What qualities of the perception led you to believe it to be true?
2. How did this perception influence your beliefs about the world?
3. Describe the process that led you to conclude that the perception was false.

Believing and Knowing

The beliefs you develop in living your life help you explain why the world is the way it is, and they guide you in making decisions. But all beliefs are not equal. Some beliefs are certain ("I believe that someday I will die") because they are supported by compelling reasons. Other beliefs are less certain ("I believe that life exists on other planets") because the support is not as solid. As you form and revise your beliefs, based on your experiences and your reflection on these experiences, it is important to make them as accurate as possible. The more accurate your beliefs are, the better you are able to understand what is taking place and to predict what will occur in the future.

The beliefs you form vary tremendously in accuracy. The idea of *knowing* is one of the ways humans have developed to distinguish beliefs supported by strong reasons or evidence from beliefs for which there is less support, as well as from beliefs disproved by evidence to the contrary (such as the belief that the earth is flat). This distinction between "believing" and "knowing" can be illustrated by replacing the word *believe* with the word *know* in statements. For example:

1. I *know* that I will die.
2. I *know* that there is life on other planets.
3. I *know* that working hard will lead me to a happy life.
4. I *know* that the earth is flat.

The only statement with which most people would agree that it clearly makes sense to use the word *know* is the first one, because there is conclusive evidence that this belief is accurate. In the case of statement 2, we might say that, although life on other planets is a possibility, there does not seem to be *conclusive* evidence at present (the *X-Files* notwithstanding) that supports this view. In the case of statement 3, we might say that, although for some people working hard leads to a happy life, this is not always the case. Statement 4 expresses a belief that we "know" is *not* true.

When someone indicates that he or she thinks a belief is completely accurate by saying, "I *know*," your response is often "*How* do you know?" If the person cannot give you a satisfactory answer to this question, you are likely to say something like, "If you can't explain how you know it, then you don't *really* know it — you're just saying it." In other words, when you say that "you know" something, you mean at least two different things.

1. I think this belief is completely accurate.
2. I can explain to you the reasons or evidence that support this belief.

If either of these standards is not met, we would usually say that you do not really "know." Or to state it another way, "You can *believe* what is not so, but you cannot *know* what is not so."

We work at evaluating the accuracy of our beliefs by examining the reasons or evidence that support them (known as the *justification* for the beliefs). Your beliefs can be thought of as forming a continuum based on their accuracy and justification. As you learn more about the world and yourself, you try to form beliefs that are increasingly accurate and justified.

Determining the accuracy and justification of your beliefs is a challenging business. The key point is that as a critical thinker you should continually try to form and revise your beliefs so that you can understand the world in increasingly effective ways. Even when you find that you maintain certain beliefs over a long period of time, you should discover that your explorations result in a deeper and fuller understanding of these beliefs.

THINKING ACTIVITY 4.9

Evaluating the Accuracy of Beliefs

State whether you think that each of the following beliefs is

- *Completely accurate* (so that you would say, "I know this is the case")

- *Generally accurate* but not completely accurate (so that you would say, "This is often, but not always, the case")

- *Generally not accurate* but sometimes accurate (so that you would say, "This is usually not the case but is sometimes true")

- *Definitely not accurate* (so that you would say, "I know that this is not the case")

After determining the *degree of accuracy* in this way, explain why you have selected your answer.

- *Example:* I believe that if you study hard, you will achieve good grades.

- *Degree of accuracy:* Generally, but not completely, accurate.

- *Explanation:* Although many students who study hard achieve good grades, this is not always true. Sometimes students have difficulty understanding the work in a certain subject, no matter how hard they study. And sometimes they just don't know how to study effectively. In other cases, students may lack adequate background or experience in a certain subject area (for example, English may be a second language), or they may have a personality conflict with the instructor.

1. I believe that essay exams are more difficult than multiple-choice exams.
2. I believe that longer prison sentences discourage people from committing crimes.
3. I believe that there are more people on the earth today than there were one hundred years ago.
4. I believe "fate" plays an important role in determining life's events.
5. I believe that people have the freedom to change themselves and their circumstances if they really want to.

Now write some of your most important beliefs on the following subjects and evaluate them in the same way:

- love

- physical health

- happiness

- religion

⊚ Knowledge and Truth

Most people in our culture are socialized to believe that knowledge and truth are absolute and unchanging. One major goal of social institutions, including family, school system, and religion, is to transfer the knowledge that has been developed over the ages. Under this model, the role of learners is to absorb this information passively, like sponges. As you have seen in this text, however, achieving knowledge and truth is a much more complicated process than this. Instead of simply relying on the testimony of authorities like parents, teachers, textbooks, and religious leaders, critical thinkers have a responsibility to engage *actively* in the learning process and participate in developing their own understanding of the world.

The need for this active approach to knowing is underscored by the fact that authorities often disagree about the true nature of a given situation or the best course of action. It is not uncommon, for example, for doctors to disagree about a diagnosis, for economists to differ on the state of the economy, for researchers to present contrasting views on the best approach to curing cancer, for psychiatrists to disagree on whether a convicted felon is a menace to society or a harmless victim of social forces, and for religions to present conflicting approaches to achieving eternal life.

What do we do when experts disagree? As a critical thinker, you must analyze and evaluate all the available information, develop your own well-reasoned beliefs, and recognize when you don't have sufficient information to arrive at well-reasoned beliefs. You must realize that these beliefs may evolve over time as you gain information or improve your insight.

Although there are compelling reasons to view knowledge and truth in this way, many people resist it. Either they take refuge in a belief in the absolute, unchanging nature of knowledge and truth, as presented by the appropriate authorities, or they conclude that there is no such thing as knowledge or truth and that trying to seek either is a futile enterprise. In this latter view of the world, known as *relativism*, all beliefs are considered to be "relative" to the person or context in which they arise. For the relativist, all opinions are equal in validity to all others; we are never in a position to say with confidence that one view is right and another view is wrong. Although a relativistic view is appropriate in some areas of experience — for example, in matters of taste such as fashion — in many other areas it is not. Knowledge, in the form of well-supported beliefs, is often difficult to achieve, but does exist. Some beliefs *are* better than others, not because an authority has proclaimed them so but because they can be analyzed in terms of the following criteria:

- How effectively do your beliefs *explain what is taking place?*

- To what extent are these beliefs *consistent with other beliefs* you have about the world?

- How effectively do your beliefs help you *predict what will happen* in the future?

- To what extent are your beliefs supported by *sound reasons and compelling evidence* derived from *reliable sources?*

Another important criterion for evaluating certain of your beliefs is that the beliefs are *falsifiable.* This means that you can state conditions — tests — under which the beliefs could be disproved and the beliefs nevertheless *pass* those tests. For example, if you believe that you can create ice cubes by placing water-filled trays in a freezer, it is easy to see how you can conduct an experiment to determine if your belief is accurate. If you believe that your destiny is related to the positions of the planets and stars (as astrologers do), it is not clear how you can conduct an experiment to determine if your belief is accurate. Since a belief that is not *falsifiable* can never be *proved,* such a belief is of questionable accuracy.

A critical thinker sees knowledge and truth as goals that we are striving to achieve, processes that we are all actively involved in as we construct our understanding of the world. Developing accurate knowledge about the world is often a challenging process of exploration and analysis in which our understanding grows and evolves over a period of time.

Stages of Knowing

The road to becoming a critical thinker is a challenging journey that involves passing through different Stages of Knowing, in order to achieve an effective understanding of the world. These stages, ranging from simple to complex, characterize people's thinking and the way they understand their world. A critical thinker is a person who has progressed through all of the stages to achieve a sophisticated understanding of the nature of knowledge. This framework is based on the work of Harvard psychologist Dr. William Perry (*Forms of Intellectual and Ethical Development in the College Years: A Scheme*), who used in-depth research to create a developmental model of human thought. I use a condensed three-stage version of Perry's framework.

Stage 1: The Garden of Eden

Stage 2: Anything Goes

Stage 3: Thinking Critically

An individual may be at different stages simultaneously, depending on the subject or area of experience. For example, a person may be at an advanced stage in one area of life (academic work) but at a less sophisticated stage in another area (romantic relationships or conception of morality). In general, however, people tend to operate predominantly within one stage in most areas of their lives.

Stage 1: The Garden of Eden   People in the Garden of Eden stage of thinking tend to see the world in terms of black and white, right and wrong. How do they determine what is right, what to believe? The "authorities" *tell* them. Just like in the biblical Garden of Eden, knowledge is absolute, unchanging, and in the sole possession of authorities. Ordinary people can never determine the truth for themselves; they must rely on the experts. If someone disagrees with what they have been told by their authorities, then that person *must* be wrong. There is no possibility of compromise or negotiation.

Who are the authorities? The first authorities we encounter are usually our parents. When parents are rooted in this stage of thinking, they expect children to do as they're told, not to disagree, not to question. Parents are the authorities, and the role of children is to benefit from their parents' years of experience, their store of knowledge, and their position of authority. Similarly, when children enter a school system built on the foundation of Stage 1 thinking (as most school systems are), they are likely to be told, "We have the questions and the answers; your role is to learn them, not ask questions of your own" — an approach that runs counter to children's natural curiosity.

People who have been raised in a Stage 1 environment often become Stage 1 thinkers themselves when they mature. As parents, supervisors, and even friends they are authoritarian and dogmatic. They believe they know what is right, based on what authorities have told them, and they are convinced that anyone who disagrees with them must be wrong. Organizations ranging from the armed services to "top-down-managed" companies are based on authoritarian principles, and they are often populated by Stage 1 thinkers.

People in this Garden of Eden stage of thinking become dissatisfied with it when they come to realize that they can't simply rely on authorities to tell them what to think and believe because in virtually every arena — medicine, religion, economics, psychology, education, science, law, child-rearing — authorities often disagree with each other. We explored this disturbing phenomenon earlier in the chapter, and it poses a mortal threat to Stage 1 thinking. If the authorities disagree with each other, then how do we figure out what (and whom) to believe? Stage 1 thinkers try to deal with this contradiction by maintaining that *my* authorities know more than *your* authorities. But if we are willing to think clearly and honestly, this explanation simply doesn't hold up: We have to explain *why* we choose to believe one authority over another. And as soon as that happens, we have transcended Stage 1 thinking. Just as Adam and Eve could not go back to blind, uncritical acceptance of authority once they had tasted the fruit of the Tree of the Knowledge of Good and Evil, so it is nearly impossible to return to Stage 1 after recognizing its oversimplifying inadequacies.

Why are some people able to go beyond Stage 1 thinking while others remain more or less stuck there throughout their lives? Part of the answer lies in how diverse their environment is. When people live in predominantly homogeneous environments, surrounded by people who think and believe the same way, it is much easier to maintain the artificially uniform world view of the Garden of Eden thinking.

However, when people are exposed to diverse experiences that challenge them with competing perspectives, it is much more difficult to maintain the unquestioned faith in authoritarian dictates of Stage 1 thinking. For example, in my philosophy of religion classes, the final term project is for students to visit five different places of religious worship selected from a list of thirty I provide; these range from Zen Buddhist to Pentecostal, Catholic to Southern Baptist, Jewish to Hindu. Students are expected to involve themselves in the services to the extent that it is appropriate and then write a report analyzing their experiences and applying the course concepts. Students invariably report that this project transformed their thinking, stimulating them to view religion in a richer, more complex light. It gives them the opportunity to see other people who were just as serious and devout as themselves engage in very different religious practices.

However, simply providing people with diverse experiences does not guarantee that they will be stimulated to question and transcend the limiting confines of Stage 1 thinking. We need to have the *emotional willingness* to open ourselves to new possibilities and the *intellectual ability* to see issues from different perspectives. Very often people are so emotionally entangled in their point of view that they are simply unwilling to question its truth, and so the power of their emotional needs inhibits the potential illumination of their reasoning abilities. Additionally, many people have not developed the flexibility of thinking needed to extricate themselves from their own point of view and look at issues from different perspectives. To become a Stage 2 thinker, both of these conditions must be met: the emotional willingness *and* the cognitive ability to be open-minded.

Stage 2: Anything Goes   Once one has rejected the dogmatic, authoritarian framework of Stage 1, the temptation in Stage 2 is to go to the opposite extreme and believe that anything goes. The reasoning is something like this: If authorities are not infallible and we can't trust their expertise, then no one point of view is ultimately any better than any other. You have your opinion, I have my opinion, and there is no way to determine which is better. In Stage 1 the authorities could resolve such disputes, but if their opinion is on the same level as yours and mine, then there is no rational way to resolve differences.

In the tradition of philosophy, such a view is known as *relativism:* the truth is relative to any individual or situation, and there is no standard we can use to decide which beliefs make most sense. Take the example of fashion. You may believe that an attractive presentation includes loose-fitting clothing in muted colors, a natural hair style, and a minimum of make-up and jewelry. Someone else might prefer tight-fitting black clothing, gelled hair, tattoos, and body piercings. In Stage 2 thinking, there's no way to evaluate these or any other fashion preferences: They are simply "matters of taste." And, in fact, if you examine past photographs of yourself and what you considered to be "attractive" years ago, this relativistic point of view probably makes some sense.

Although we may be drawn to this seemingly open-minded attitude — anything goes — the reality is that we are often not so tolerant. We *do* believe that some appearances are more aesthetically pleasing than others. But there is an even more serious threat to Stage 2 thinking. Imagine the following scenario: As you are strolling down the street, you suddenly feel a gun pushed against your back accompanied by the demand for all your valuables. You protest, arguing with this would-be mugger that he has no right to your possessions. "On the contrary," your philosophically inclined mugger responds, "I believe that 'might makes right,' and since I have a weapon, I am entitled to your valuables. You have your beliefs, I have my beliefs, and as Stage 2 thinkers, there's no way for you to prove me wrong!" Preposterous? Nevertheless, this is the logical conclusion of Anything Goes thinking. If we truly believe this, than we cannot condemn *any* belief or action, no matter how heinous, and we cannot praise *any* belief or action, no matter how laudatory.

When we think things through, it's obvious that the Anything Goes level of thinking simply doesn't work because it leads to absurd conclusions that run counter to our deeply felt conviction that some beliefs *are* better than other beliefs. So while Stage 2 may represent a slight advance over Stage 1 in sophistication and complexity, it's clear to a reflective and discerning eye that a further advance to the next stage is necessary.

Stage 3: Thinking Critically   The two opposite perspectives of Stages 1 and 2 find their synthesis in Stage 3, Thinking Critically. When people achieve this level of understanding, they recognize that some viewpoints *are* better than other viewpoints, not simply because authorities say so but because *there are compelling reasons to support these viewpoints.* At the same time, people in this stage are open-minded toward other viewpoints, especially those that disagree with theirs. They recognize that there are often a number of legitimate perspectives on complex issues, and they accept the validity of these perspectives to the extent that they are supported by persuasive reasons and evidence.

Consider a more complicated issue, like euthanasia ("mercy killing"). A Stage 3 thinker approaches this as she approaches all issues: trying to understand all of the different viewpoints on the issue, evaluating the reasons that support each of these viewpoints, and then coming to her own thoughtful conclusion. When asked, she can explain the rationale for her viewpoint, but she also respects differing viewpoints that are supported by legitimate reasons, even though she feels her viewpoint makes more sense. In addition, a Stage 3 thinker maintains an open mind, always willing to consider new evidence that might convince her to modify or even change her position.

A Stage 3 thinker recognizes that the world is a complex, ambiguous, and evolving place and that our thinking has to be deep, open-minded, and flexible if we are to understand it and make intelligent decisions. But while people in the Thinking Critically stage are actively open to different perspectives, they also *commit* themselves to definite points of view and are *confident* in explaining the reasons and evidence that have led them to their conclusions. Be aware that being open-minded is not the same thing as being intellectually wishy-washy. In addition to having clearly defined views, Stage 3 thinkers are always willing to listen to people who disagree with them. In fact, they actively seek out opposing viewpoints because they know that this is the only way to achieve the clearest, most insightful, most firmly grounded understanding. They also recognize that their views may evolve over time as they learn more.

Stages of Knowing

Stage 1: The Garden of Eden
Knowledge is clear, certain, and absolute and is provided by authorities. Our role is to learn and accept information from authorities without question or criticism. Anyone who disagrees with the authorities must be wrong.

Stage 2: Anything Goes
Since authorities often disagree with each other, no one really "knows" what is true or right. All beliefs are of equal value, and there is no way to determine whether one belief makes more sense than another belief.

Stage 3: Thinking Critically
Some viewpoints *are* better than other viewpoints, not because authorities say so but because there are compelling reasons to support these viewpoints. We have a responsibility to explore every perspective, evaluate the supporting reasons of each, and develop our own informed conclusions that we are prepared to modify or change based on new information or better insight.

Becoming a Stage 3 thinker is certainly a worthy goal, and it is the only way to adequately answer Socrates' challenge to examine our lives thoughtfully and honestly. But to live a life of reflection and action, of open-mindedness and commitment, of purpose and fulfillment, is not a simple endeavor. It requires the full development of our intellectual abilities and positive traits of character, a lifelong journey.

THINKING ACTIVITY 4.10

What Stage of Knowing Am I In?

1. Create a diagram to illustrate the three Stages of Knowing.
2. We all know people who illustrate each of these three Stages of Knowing. Think about the people in your life — professionally and personally — and identify which stage you think they mainly fall into.
3. Consider carefully your beliefs in each of the following areas, and evaluate in which of the three Stages of Knowing you predominantly think.

- education

- professional area of expertise

- science

- moral issues

- religion

- human nature

- social relationships

- child-rearing

- aesthetic areas (beauty)

Example: "My beliefs in the area of my academic classes tend to be Stage 1. I have always trusted the experts, whether they are my teachers or the textbooks we are learning. That's how I see the purpose of education: to learn the facts from those who know them." Or "My beliefs in my area of special interest, health, are Stage 3. When confronted with a set of symptoms, I consider all of the possible diagnoses, carefully evaluate the relevant evidence, get a second opinion if necessary, and then develop a plan that involves holistic and nutritional approaches as well as standard medical treatments."

 THINKING PASSAGE

Perceptions of Patriotism

The terrorist attacks of September 11, 2001, have moved the issue of "patriotism" to the forefront of the American psyche and national dialogue, provoking questions like these:

- What exactly is "patriotism"?

- What thoughts and feelings does patriotism embody?

- When is patriotism a positive force that unites people, creating a sense of community, shared values, and a mutual commitment to one another?

- When is patriotism a negative force that creates divisions between people and fosters distrust and discrimination?

The following selection explores the complex nature of patriotism. After reading and thinking about the issues it raises, complete the questions at the conclusion of the section.

FLAG FEVER: THE PARADOX OF PATRIOTISM*
by Blaine Harden

Until it was uncorked by acts of war on Sept. 11, generations of Americans had never found a compelling reason to take a stiff drink of patriotism or take comfort in its unifying high.

With an ennobling wallop, patriotism has since inspired a deeply felt and classless sense of community. Charitable gifts have skyrocketed, as have sales of flags and stocks of donated blood. Firemen and police officers, who define themselves by sacrifice and service rather than by status and stock options, have become objects of mass adulation. According to some reports, irony has died.

New York City, the erstwhile epicenter of selfishness and sin, has been judged in its time of trial and found good by more than 8 out of 10 Americans. Perhaps boundaries were melting between the Red Zone, the conservative heartland that voted for the Republican president, and the Blue Zone, where coastal liberals had clung to doubts about President Bush's work ethic, his judgment and his intelligence.

Yet, from the moment suicide terrorists steered airplanes into the World Trade Center and the Pentagon, the invidious paradox of American patriotism came back into play. Constitutional rights, which supposedly form the core of patriotism's appeal, suddenly lost ground to fear. As it has during every major military conflict since World War I, a nationalist undertow that is culturally conformist, ethnically exclusive and belligerently militaristic began to silence dissent, spread fear among immigrants and lock up people without explanation.

The White House press secretary, Ari Fleischer, warned reporters that in times like these "people have to watch what they say and watch what they do." In lock step with times like these, loose lips have been slapped shut. As an Oregon columnist, a University of New Mexico professor and a late-night talk show host all discovered last week, the country is suddenly thick with self-appointed censors. They are firing, disciplining and pulling advertising from those whose commentary or jokes sound insufficiently loyal.

VISUAL THINKING

The Red, White, and Blue

● Focus on just the large American flag: what are your thoughts and feelings? Now consider the photograph as a whole: what is your reaction? What do you think is the source of patriotic feelings? Do you consider these feelings to be positive or destructive? Why?

Patriotism's extraordinary power to expand and constrain the American spirit is hardly new. But it seems novel now because so many people —including many among that huge bulge of the population that came of age during and after the Vietnam War — have never lived it themselves.

A heartfelt and reinvigorating love of country has not been universally experienced in the United States since the Kennedy assassination, said Gary Gerstle, a professor of history at the University of Maryland and author of "American Crucible: Race and Nation in the Twentieth Century" (Princeton University Press, 2001). "After the civil rights movement and the war in Vietnam, there was a sustained cultural crisis," he said. "Many Americans did not waver, but a lot did. They asked, 'Who are we?' 'Are we good?' What is emerging now is something completely different. It's a broadly based consensus on the value of America."

Patriotism seems particularly potent and purely felt among the tens of millions of Americans who came of age after the 1960s and early 70s. Unlike many of their parents, they can wave the flag without the mixed feelings of a generation that did its darndest to dodge military service in an unpopular war and, in more than a few cases, burned flags rather than waved them. Unburdened by such memories — the wars of the 90s were all too short and decisive to stir such passions — Americans under 40 suddenly have a chance to reimagine themselves, to participate selflessly in a world-rousing conflict that might define them as something other than Generation X, Y or Z.

For all its ennobling kick, historians agree that patriotism has almost always been at odds with itself. It reinforces a sense of community by erecting strong walls to comfort those on the inside. But outside those exclusive walls, it has a history of denying equal protection under the law and making life seem scary.

The flag, as much as any symbol, embodies the paradox. As surprisingly reassuring as it has been to many baby boomers who had never before viewed themselves as flag-wavers, it has been unnerving for Arab-Americans and other immigrant groups, like Sikhs. "I see flags everywhere, yet my first instinct is apprehension," said Nabeel Abraham, an American-born anthropologist of Palestinian descent who is a co-author of "Arab Detroit" (Wayne State University Press, 2000), an examination of the country's oldest and largest Arab-American community. He said most Arab-Americans and many Asians who could be mistaken for Arabs are staying home as much as possible and keeping quiet. "We don't know what to expect," he said. "We expect the worst."

For other Americans, not just those whose ethnicity makes them feel coerced by patriotism, the proliferation of flags and "God Bless America" signage can seem a bit too simplistic, a feel-good distraction from trying to understand a monstrously precise act of simultaneous suicide.

A contentious and still unresolved struggle over what the flag should symbolize has been going on since at least 1863, when President Lincoln issued the Emancipation Proclamation. Since then, according to Cecilia Elizabeth O'Leary, a history professor at California State University in Monterey Bay, there have been Americans who define the flag as primarily a symbol of equal rights and social justice under the law. It was not until World War I, she said, when federal and state governments joined forces with right-wing organizations and vigilantes, that the flag's egalitarian resonance was drowned out by jingoism.

In 1918, a Montana court sentenced E. V. Starr to 20 years in prison for refusing to kiss a flag. As Professor O'Leary noted in "To Die For: The Paradox of American Patriotism" (Princeton University Press, 1999), an appeals judge reluctantly decided he could not reverse the sentence. But he did condemn the way that patriotism, with the approval of government authorities, had devolved into a kind of "fanaticism."

Since then, the strength of exclusionary patriotism has waxed and waned, usually as a corollary of fear, with abuses most widespread when the federal government plays a supporting role. In the frenzy that followed World War I, the Palmer raids, led by an attorney general whose house had been bombed, included the detention, beatings and deportations of thousands of people, most of them immigrants. Each successive war featured its own shameful excess. World War II had the internment of 110,000 Japanese, the Korean War coincided with McCarthyism, and during the Vietnam conflict the F.B.I. infiltrated antiwar groups.

Less than three weeks into America's latest flush of flag waving fervor, it's too early to know if patriotism's undertow will cause systemic abuses of civil liberties. The signals, so far, are mixed.

The Bush administration's request for authority to detain suspected terrorists indefinitely has run into opposition from senior Democrats and Republicans in Congress. Even harsh critics of the administration, like Michael Maggio, an immigration expert, say the White House seems to be able to sense when it has gone too far.

"I have been impressed by the administration's willingness to back away from some of its most outlandish proposals," he said, referring to an earlier plan, now discarded, to deport foreign-born legal residents suspected of terrorist involvement.

Perhaps most reassuring, for Americans who thirst for a brand of patriotism that elevates their spirits and protects minorities, are President Bush's repeated calls for ethnic and religious tolerance, along with his highly publicized meetings with Arab, Muslim and Sikh leaders.

"As long as this continues, it bodes well for inclusion and tolerance," said Professor Gerstle, at the University of Maryland. "But this is a very fluid moment. What happens if another airliner hits a building? Many people are going to be out for revenge if American boys get killed."

The worst abuses against immigrant Americans occurred not at the beginning of World War I, but at the end, when the federal government lost touch with Constitutional protections and briefly joined forces with the mob.

President Bush and his senior advisers have warned Americans to expect a war that is long, murky and unsatisfying. As months stretch into years, it is also likely to be a conflict that periodically screams for the clarifying blood of a scapegoat. If the president is going to continue to insist on an inclusive kind of patriotism, home-front defense of tolerance could prove as formidable as the war itself.

Reporting, Inferring, and Judging

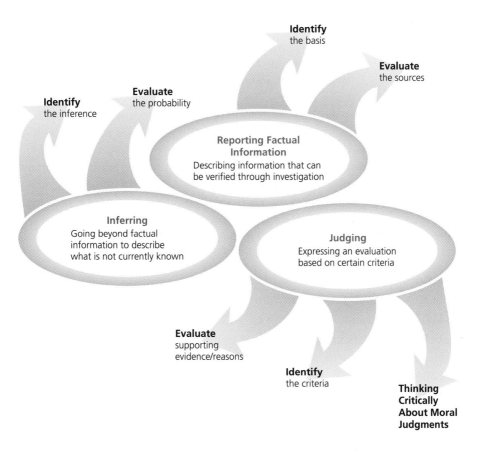

Identify
the basis

Evaluate
the sources

Evaluate
the probability

Identify
the inference

Reporting Factual Information
Describing information that can be verified through investigation

Inferring
Going beyond factual information to describe what is not currently known

Judging
Expressing an evaluation based on certain criteria

Evaluate
supporting evidence/reasons

Identify
the criteria

Thinking Critically About Moral Judgments

The main goal of your thinking process is to organize the world into intelligible relationships that help you understand what is going on. The relationships that you compose and discover express the basic thinking patterns you use to make sense of the world, including the following thinking patterns:

- Chronological and process

- Comparative and analogical

- Causal

In this chapter we will be exploring the way that we use these thinking patterns, and others, to organize our beliefs and knowledge about the world. Beliefs are the main tools you use to make sense of the world and guide your actions, as explained in Chapter 4. The total collection of your beliefs represents your view of the world, your philosophy of life. More specifically, beliefs are interpretations, evaluations, conclusions, and predictions about the world that you endorse as true.

All beliefs are not equal. In fact, beliefs differ from one another in many kinds of ways, including their accuracy. The belief "The earth is surrounded by stars and planets" is considerably more certain than the belief "The positions of the stars and planets determine our personalities and destinies."

Beliefs differ in other respects besides accuracy. Review the following beliefs, and then describe some of their differences:

1. I believe that I have hair on my head.
2. I believe that the sun will rise tomorrow.
3. I believe that there is some form of life after death.
4. I believe that dancing is more fun than jogging and that jogging is preferable to going to the dentist.
5. I believe that you should always act toward others in ways that you would like to have them act toward you.

In this chapter you will be thinking critically about three basic types of beliefs you use to make sense of the world:

- Reports

- Inferences

- Judgments

These beliefs are expressed in both your thinking and your use of language, as illustrated in the following sentences:

1. My bus was late today.
   Type of belief: reporting
2. My bus will probably be late tomorrow.
   Type of belief: inferring
3. The bus system is unreliable.
   Type of belief: judging

Now try the activity with a different set of statements.

1. Each modern atomic warhead has over one hundred times the explosive power of the bomb dropped on Hiroshima.
   Type of belief:
2. With all of the billions of planets in the universe, the odds are that there are other forms of life in the cosmos.
   Type of belief:
3. In the long run, the energy needs of the world will best be met by solar energy technology rather than nuclear energy or fossil fuels.
   Type of belief:

As you examine these various statements, you can see that they provide you with different types of information about the world. For example, the first statement in each list reports aspects of the world that you can verify — that is, check for accuracy. By doing the appropriate sort of investigating, you can determine whether the bus was actually late today and whether modern atomic warheads really have the power attributed to them. When you describe the world in ways that can be verified through investigation, you are said to be *reporting* factual information about the world.

reporting factual information *Describing the world in ways that can be verified through investigation*

Looking at the second statement in each list, you can see immediately that each provides a different sort of information from the first one. These statements cannot be verified. There is no way to investigate and determine with certainty whether the bus will indeed be late tomorrow or whether there is in fact life on other planets. Although these conclusions may be based on factual information, they go beyond factual information to make statements about what is not currently known. When you describe the world in ways that are based on factual information yet go beyond this information to make statements regarding what is not currently known, you are said to be *inferring* conclusions about the world.

> **inferring** *Describing the world in ways that are based on factual information yet going beyond this information to make statements about what is not currently known*

Finally, as you examine the third statement in both lists, it is apparent that these statements are different from both factual reports and inferences. They describe the world in ways that express the speaker's evaluation — of the bus service and of energy sources. These evaluations are based on certain standards (criteria) that the speaker is using to judge the bus service as unreliable and solar energy as more promising than nuclear energy or fossil fuels. When you describe the world in ways that express your evaluation based on certain criteria, you are said to be *judging.*

> **judging** *Describing the world in ways that express an evaluation based on certain criteria*

You continually use these various ways of describing and organizing your world — reporting, inferring, judging — to make sense of your experience. In most cases, you are not aware that you are actually performing these activities, nor are you usually aware of the differences among them. Yet these three activities work together to help you see the world as a complete picture.

 THINKING   ACTIVITY   5.1

Identifying Reports, Inferences, and Judgments

1. Compose six sentences that embody these three types of beliefs: two reports, two inferences, and two evaluations.
2. Locate a short article from a newspaper or magazine and identify the reports, inferences, and judgments it contains.

VISUAL THINKING

Observing a Street Scene

● Carefully examine this photograph of a street scene. Then write five statements based on your observations of the scene. Identify each statement as reporting, inferring, or judging, and explain why you classify each one as such.

◎ Reporting Factual Information

The statements that result from the activity of reporting express the most accurate beliefs you have about the world. Factual beliefs have earned this distinction because they are verifiable, usually with one or more of your senses. For example, consider the following factual statement:

> That young woman is wearing a brown hat in the rain.

This statement about an event in the world is considered to be factual because it can be verified by your immediate sense experience — what you can (in principle or in theory) see, hear, touch, feel, or smell. It is important to say *in principle* or *in theory* because you often do not use all of your relevant senses to check out what you are experiencing. Look again at your example of a factual statement: You would normally be satisfied to *see* this event, without insisting on touching the hat or giving the person a physical examination. If necessary, however, you could perform these additional actions — in principle or in theory.

You use the same reasoning when you believe factual statements from other people that you are not in a position to check out immediately. For instance:

- The Great Wall of China is more than fifteen hundred miles long.

- There are large mountains and craters on the moon.

- Your skin is covered with germs.

You consider these to be factual statements because, even though you cannot verify them with your senses at the moment, you could in principle or in theory verify them with your senses *if* you were flown to China, *if* you were rocketed to the moon, or *if* you were to examine your skin with a powerful microscope. The process of verifying factual statements involves *identifying* the sources of information on which they are based and *evaluating* the reliability of these sources, topics examined in some detail in Chapter 4.

You communicate factual information to others by means of reports. A *report* is a description of something experienced that is communicated in as accurate and complete a way as possible. Through reports you can share your sense experiences with other people, and this mutual sharing enables you to learn much more about the world than if you were confined to knowing only what you experience. The *recording* (making records) of factual reports also makes possible the accumulation of knowledge learned by previous generations.

Because factual reports play such an important role in our exchange and accumulation of information about the world, it is important that they be as accurate and complete as possible. This brings us to a problem. We have already seen in previous chapters that our perceptions and observations are often *not* accurate or complete. What this means is that often when we think we are making true, factual reports, our reports are actually inaccurate or incomplete. For instance, consider our earlier "factual statement":

That young woman is wearing a brown hat in the rain.

Here are some questions you could ask concerning the accuracy of the statement:

- Is the woman really young, or does she merely look young?

- Is the woman really a woman, or a man disguised as a woman?

- Is that really a hat the woman/man is wearing or something else (e.g., a paper bag)?

Of course, there are methods you could use to clear up these questions with more detailed observations. Can you describe some of these methods?

Besides difficulties with observations, the "facts" that you see in the world actually depend on more general *beliefs* that you have about how the world operates. Consider the question

Why did the man's body fall from the top of the building to the sidewalk?

Having had some general science courses, you might say something like, "The body was simply obeying the law of gravity," and you would consider this to be a "factual statement." But how did people account for this sort of event before Newton formulated the law of gravity? Some popular responses might have included the following:

- Things always fall down, not up.

- The spirit in the body wanted to join with the spirit of the earth.

When people made statements like these and others, such as "Humans can't fly," they thought that they were making "factual statements." Increased knowledge and understanding have since shown these "factual beliefs" to be inaccurate, and so they have been replaced by "better" beliefs. These "better beliefs" are able to explain the world in a way that is more accurate and predictable. Will many of the beliefs you now consider to be factually accurate also be replaced in the future by beliefs that are *more* accurate and predictable? If history is any indication, this will most certainly happen. (Already Newton's formulations have been replaced by Einstein's, based on the latter's theory of relativity. And Einstein's have been refined and modified as well and may be replaced someday.)

VISUAL THINKING

Telescoping Visions

● What concept is the artist depicting in this illustration? What do you think he means to suggest by the woman standing on one telescope and holding another in her hands?

THINKING ACTIVITY 5.2

Evaluating Factual Information

1. Locate and carefully read an article that deals with an important social issue.
2. Summarize the main theme and key points of the article.
3. Describe the factual statements that are used to support the major theme.
4. Evaluate the accuracy of the factual information.
5. Evaluate the reliability of the sources of the factual information.

⊚ Inferring

Imagine yourself in the following situations:

1. Your roommate has just learned that she passed a math exam for which she had done absolutely no studying. Humming the song "I Did It My Way," she comes bouncing over to you with a huge grin on her face and says, "Let me buy you dinner to celebrate!" What do you conclude about how she is feeling?
2. It is midnight and the library is about to close. As you head for the door, you spy your roommate shuffling along in an awkward waddle. His coat bulges out in front like he's pregnant. When you ask, "What's going on?" he gives you a glare and hisses, "Shhh!" Just before he reaches the door, a pile of books slides from under his coat and crashes to the floor. What do you conclude?

In these examples, it would be reasonable to make the following conclusions:

1. Your roommate is happy.
2. Your roommate is stealing library books.

Although these conclusions are reasonable, they are not factual reports; they are *inferences.* You have not directly experienced your roommate's "happiness" or "stealing." Instead, you have inferred it based on your roommate's behavior and the circumstances. What are the clues in these situations that might lead to these conclusions?

One way of understanding the inferential nature of these views is to ask yourself the following questions:

1. Have you ever pretended to be happy when you weren't? Could other people tell?
2. Have you ever been accused of stealing something when you were perfectly innocent? How did this happen?

From these examples you can see that whereas factual beliefs can in principle be verified by direct observation, *inferential beliefs* go beyond what can be directly observed. For instance, in the examples given, your observation of certain of your roommate's actions led you to infer things that you were *not* observing directly — "She's happy"; "he's stealing books." Making such simple inferences is something you do all the time. It is so automatic that usually you are not even aware that you are going beyond your immediate observations, and you may have difficulty drawing a sharp line between what you *observe* and what you *infer*. Making such inferences enables you to see the world as a complete picture, to fill in the blanks and round out the fragmentary sensations being presented to your senses. In a way, you become an artist, painting a picture of the world that is consistent, coherent, and predictable.

Your picture also includes *predictions* of what will be taking place in the near future. These predictions and expectations are also inferences because you attempt to determine what is currently unknown from what is already known.

Of course, your inferences may be mistaken, and in fact they frequently are. You may infer that the woman sitting next to you is wearing two earrings and then discover that she has only one. Or you may expect the class to end at noon and find that the teacher lets you go early — or late. In the last section we concluded that not even factual beliefs are ever absolutely certain. Comparatively speaking, inferential beliefs are a great deal more uncertain than factual beliefs, and it is important to distinguish between the two.

For example, do you ever cross streets with cars heading toward you, expecting them to stop because the light is red or because you have the right of way? Is this a factual belief or an inference? Considered objectively, are you running a serious risk when you do this? In evaluating the risk, think of all the motorists who may be in a hurry, not paying attention, drunk, ill, and so on.

Consider the following situations, analyzing each one by asking these questions: Is the action based on a factual belief or an inference? In what ways might the inference be mistaken? What is the degree of risk involved?

- Placing your hand in a closing elevator door to reopen it
- Taking an unknown drug at a party
- Jumping out of an airplane with a parachute on
- Riding on the back of a motorcycle
- Taking a drug prescribed by your doctor

Having an accurate picture of the world depends on your being able to evaluate how *certain* your beliefs are. Therefore, it is crucial that you *distinguish* inferences from factual beliefs and then *evaluate* how certain or uncertain your inferences are. This is known as "calculating the risks," and it is very important to solving problems successfully and deciding what steps to take.

The distinction between what is observed and what is inferred is paid particular attention in courtroom settings, where defense lawyers usually want witnesses to describe *only what they observed* — not what they *inferred* — as part of the observation. When a witness includes an inference such as "I saw him steal it," the lawyer may object that the statement represents a "conclusion of

VISUAL THINKING

"Only Two More Steps . . . ?"

● What aspect of working with inferences does this illustration fancifully depict?

the witness" and move to have the observation stricken from the record. For example, imagine that you are a defense attorney listening to the following testimony. At what points would you make the objection "This is a conclusion of the witness"?

> I saw Harvey running down the street, right after he knocked the old lady down. He had her purse in his hand and was trying to escape as fast as he could. He was really scared. I wasn't surprised because Harvey has always taken advantage of others. It's not the first time that he's stolen either, I can tell you that. Just last summer he robbed the poor box at St. Anthony's. He was bragging about it for weeks.

Finally, you should be aware that even though in *theory* facts and inferences can be distinguished, in *practice* it is almost impossible to communicate with others by sticking only to factual observations. A reasonable approach is to state your inference along with the observable evidence on which the inference is based (e.g., John *seemed* happy because . . .). Our language has an entire collection of terms *(seems, appears, is likely,* etc.) that signal when we are making an inference and not expressing an observable fact.

Many of the predictions that you make are inferences based on your past experiences and on the information that you presently have. Even when there appear to be sound reasons to support these inferences, they are often wrong due to incomplete information or unanticipated events. The fact that even people considered by society to be "experts" regularly make inaccurate predictions with absolute certainty should encourage you to exercise caution when making your own inferences. Here are some examples:

- *"So many centuries after the Creation, it is unlikely that anyone could find hitherto unknown lands of any value."* — the advisory committee to King Ferdinand and Queen Isabella of Spain, before Columbus's voyage in 1492

- *"What will the soldiers and sailors, what will the common people say to 'George Washington, President of the United States'? They will despise him to all eternity."* — John Adams, 1789

- *"What use could the company make of an electrical toy?"* — Western Union's rejection of the telephone in 1878

- *"The actual building of roads devoted to motor cars is not for the near future in spite of many rumors to that effect."* — a 1902 article in *Harper's Weekly*

- *"This game will never be successful because it contains 38 major errors in design."* — Parker Brothers' initial rejection of the proposed game Monopoly in 1931, which went on to become the most successful board game of the twentieth century

- *"The energy produced by the breaking down of the atom is a very poor kind of thing. Anyone who expects a source of power from the transformation of the atom is talking moonshine."* — Lord Rutherford, Nobel laureate, after the first experimental splitting of the atom, 1933

- *"The [atom] bomb will never go off, and I speak as an expert in explosives."* — Vannevar Bush, presidential adviser, 1945

- *"Among the really difficult problems of the world, [the Arab-Israeli conflict is] one of the simplest and most manageable."* — Walter Lippmann, newspaper columnist, 1948

- *"Space travel is utter bilge."* — British astronomer Dr. R. Woolsey, 1958

- *"The Wankel will . . . dwarf such major post-war technological developments as xerography, the Polaroid camera and color television."* — a statement by General Motors announcing its commitment to the rotary engine, 1969

- *"You ain't goin' nowhere, son. You ought to go back to driving a truck."* — Jim Denny, Grand Ole Opry manager, firing Elvis Presley after one performance, 1954

Examine the following list of statements, noting which statements are *factual beliefs* (based on observations) and which are *inferential beliefs* (conclusions that go beyond observations). For each factual statement, describe how you might go about verifying the information. For each inferential statement, describe a factual observation on which the inference could be based. (Note: Some statements may contain both factual beliefs and inferential beliefs.)

- When my leg starts to ache, that means snow is on the way.

- The grass is wet — it must have rained last night.

- I think that it's pretty clear from the length of the skid marks that the accident was caused by that person's driving too fast.

- Fifty men lost their lives in the construction of the Queensboro Bridge.

- Nancy said she wasn't feeling well yesterday — I'll bet that she's out sick today.

Now consider the following situations. What inferences might you be inclined to make based on what you are observing? How could you investigate the accuracy of your inference?

- A student in your class is consistently late for class.

- You see a friend of yours driving a new car.

- A teacher asks the same student to stay after class several times.

- You don't receive any birthday cards.

So far we have been exploring relatively simple inferences. Many of the inferences people make, however, are much more complicated. In fact, much of our knowledge about the world rests on our ability to make complicated inferences in a systematic and logical way. However, just because an inference is more complicated does not mean that it is more accurate; in fact, the opposite is often the case. One of the masters of inference is the legendary Sherlock Holmes. In the following passage, Holmes makes an astonishing number of inferences upon meeting Dr. Watson. Study carefully the conclusions he comes to. Are they reasonable? Can you explain how he reaches these conclusions?

"You appeared to be surprised when I told you, on our first meeting, that you had come from Afghanistan."

"You were told, no doubt."

"Nothing of the sort. I *knew* you came from Afghanistan. From long habit the train of thoughts ran so swiftly through my mind that I arrived at the conclusion without being conscious of intermediate steps. There were such steps, however. The train of reasoning ran, 'Here is a gentleman of a medical type, but with the air of a military man. Clearly an army doctor, then. He is just come from the tropics, for his face is dark, and that is not the natural tint of his skin, for his wrists are fair. He has undergone hardship and sickness, as his haggard face says clearly. His left arm has been injured. He holds it in a stiff and unnatural manner. Where in the tropics could an English army doctor have seen much hardship and got his arm wounded? Clearly in Afghanistan.' The whole train of thought did not occupy a second. I then remarked that you came from Afghanistan, and you were astonished."

— Sir Arthur Conan Doyle, *A Study in Scarlet*

 THINKING ACTIVITY 5.3

Analyzing an Incorrect Inference

Describe an experience in which you made an *in*correct inference that resulted in serious consequences. For example, it might have been a situation in which you mistakenly accused someone, you were in an accident because of a miscalculation, or you made a poor decision based on an inaccurate prediction. Analyze that experience by answering the following questions:

1. What was (were) your mistaken inference(s)?
2. What was the factual evidence on which you based your inference(s)?
3. Looking back, what could you have done to avoid the erroneous inference(s)?

◎ Judging

Identify and describe a friend you have, a course you have taken, and the college you attend. Be sure your descriptions are specific and include *what you think* about the friend, the course, and the college.

1. _____ is a friend whom I have.
 He or she is . . .

2. _____ is a course I have taken.
 It was . . .

3. _____ is the college I attend.
 It is . . .

Now review your responses. Do they include factual descriptions? For each response, note any factual information that can be verified.

 In addition to factual reports, your descriptions may contain inferences based on factual information. Can you identify any inferences? In addition to inferences, your descriptions may include judgments about the person, course, and school — descriptions that express your evaluation based on certain criteria. Facts and inferences are designed to help you figure out what is actually happening (or will happen); the purpose of judgments is to express your evaluation about what is happening (or will happen). For example:

- My new car has broken down three times in the first six months. *(Factual report)*

- My new car will probably continue to have difficulties. *(Inference)*

- My new car is a lemon. *(Judgment)*

When you pronounce your new car a "lemon," you are making a judgment based on certain criteria you have in mind. For instance, a "lemon" is usually a newly purchased item — generally an automobile — with which you have repeated problems.

 To take another example of judging, consider the following statements:

- Carla always does her work thoroughly and completes it on time. *(Factual report)*

- Carla will probably continue to do her work in this fashion. *(Inference)*

- Carla is a very responsible person. *(Judgment)*

By judging Carla to be responsible, you are evaluating her on the basis of the criteria or standards that you believe indicate a responsible person. One such criterion is completing assigned work on time. Can you identify additional criteria for judging someone to be responsible?

Review your previous descriptions of a friend, a course, and your college. Can you identify any judgments in your descriptions?

1. Judgments about your friend:

2. Judgments about your course:

3. Judgments about your college:

For each judgment you have listed, identify the criteria on which the judgment is based.

1. Criteria for judgments about your friend:

2. Criteria for judgments about your course:

3. Criteria for judgments about your college:

When we judge, we are often expressing our feelings of approval or disapproval. Sometimes, however, we make judgments that conflict with what we personally approve of. For example:

- I think a woman should be able to have an abortion if she chooses to, although I don't believe abortion is right.

- I can see why you think that person is very beautiful, even though she is not the type that appeals to me.

In fact, at times it is essential to disregard your personal feelings of approval or disapproval when you judge. For instance, a judge in a courtroom should render evaluations based on the law, not on his or her personal preferences.

Differences in Judgments

Many of our disagreements with other people focus on differences in judgments. As a critical thinker, you need to approach such differences in judgments intelligently. You can do so by following these guidelines:

- Make explicit the criteria or standards used as a basis for the judgment.

- Try to establish the reasons that justify these criteria.

For instance, if I make the judgment "Professor Andrews is an excellent teacher," I am basing my judgment on certain criteria of teaching excellence.

Once these standards are made explicit, we can discuss whether they make sense and what the justification is for them. Identify some of your standards for teaching excellence.

Of course, your idea of what makes an excellent teacher may be different from someone else's, a conclusion you can test by comparing your criteria with those of other class members. When these disagreements occur, your only hope for resolution is to use the two steps previously identified:

- Make explicit the standards you are using.

- Give reasons that justify these standards.

For example, "Professor Andrews really gets my mind working, forcing me to think through issues on my own and then defend my conclusions. I earn what I learn, and that makes it really 'mine.'"

In short, not all judgments are equally good or equally poor. The credibility of a judgment depends on the criteria used to make the judgment and the evidence or reasons that support these criteria. For example, there may be legitimate disagreements about judgments on the following points:

- Who was the greatest U.S. president?

- Which movie deserves the Oscar this year?

- Who should win the Miss America Pageant or the Mr. America Contest?

- Which is the best baseball team this year?

- Which music is best for dancing?

However, in these and countless other cases, the quality of your judgments depends on your identifying the criteria used for the competing judgments and then demonstrating that your candidate best meets those criteria by providing supporting evidence and reasons. With this approach, you can often engage in intelligent discussion and establish which judgments are best supported by the evidence.

Understanding how judgments function is also important for encouraging you to continue thinking critically about a situation. For instance, the judgment "This course is worthless!" does not encourage further exploration and critical analysis. In fact, it may prevent such an analysis by discouraging further exploration. Judgments seem to summarize the situation in a final sort of way. And because judgments are sometimes made before you have a clear and complete understanding of the situation, they can serve to prevent you from seeing the situation as clearly and completely as you might. Of course, if you understand

that all judgments are based on criteria that may or may not be adequately justified, you can explore these judgments further by making the criteria explicit
and examining the reasons that justify them.

THINKING   ACTIVITY   5.4

Analyzing Judgments

Review the following passages, which illustrate various judgments. For each
passage

1. Identify the evaluative criteria on which the judgments are based.

2. Describe the reasons or evidence the author uses to support the criteria.

3. Explain whether you agree or disagree with the judgments and give your
rationale.

> One widely held misconception concerning pizza should be laid to rest.
> Although it may be characterized as fast food, pizza is *not* junk food.
> Especially when it is made with fresh ingredients, pizza fulfills our basic
> nutritional requirements. The crust provides carbohydrates; from the
> cheese and meat or fish comes protein; and the tomatoes, herbs, onions,
> and garlic supply vitamins and minerals.
>   — Louis Philip Salamone, "Pizza: Fast Food, Not Junk Food"

> Let us return to the question of food. Responsible agronomists report that
> before the end of the year millions of people if unaided might starve to
> death. Half a billion deaths by starvation is not an uncommon estimate.
> Even though the United States has done more than any other nation to
> feed the hungry, our relative affluence makes us morally vulnerable in
> the eyes of other nations and in our own eyes. Garrett Hardin, who has
> argued for a "lifeboat" ethic of survival (if you take all the passengers
> aboard, everybody drowns), admits that the decision *not* to feed all the
> hungry requires of us "a very hard psychological adjustment." Indeed it
> would. It has been estimated that the 3.5 million tons of fertilizer spread
> on American golf courses and lawns could provide up to 30 million tons
> of food in overseas agricultural production. The nightmarish thought
> intrudes itself. If we as a nation allow people to starve while we could,
> through some sacrifice, make more food available to them, what hope

can any person have for the future of international relations? If we cannot agree on this most basic of values — feed the hungry — what hopes for the future can we entertain?

— James R. Kelly, "The Limits of Reason"

Thinking Critically About Moral Judgments

Many of the judgments with which you are involved are moral judgments, decisions regarding "right" and "wrong" behavior in your relationships with others. These judgments are often based on criteria that you have absorbed from your parents and the surrounding culture. If you have critically examined the ethical beliefs with which you were raised, however, you may have found that some of your views diverge from the views of those around you. Of course, critical evaluation may also strengthen your endorsement of the beliefs with which you were raised by deepening your understanding of the reasons on which they are based. These influences create a "moral compass" that each of us possesses to guide our decisions in moral situations.

THINKING ACTIVITY 5.5

Analyzing Moral Dilemmas

The following are several dilemmas that ask you to respond with decisions based on moral reasoning. After thinking carefully about each situation, do the following:

- Describe the decision that you would make in this situation and explain why.

- Identify the moral value(s) or principle(s) on which you based your decision.

- At the conclusion of the activity, compare the moral values that you used. Did you find that you consistently used the same values to make decisions, or did you use different values? If you used different ones, how did the various values relate to one another?

- Based on this analysis, describe your general conclusions about your own "moral compass."

1. *The Lifeboat:* You are the captain, and your ship struck an iceberg and sank. There are thirty survivors, but they are crowded into a lifeboat designed to hold just seven. With the weather stormy and getting worse, it is obvious that many of the passengers will have to be thrown out of the lifeboat, or it will sink and everyone will drown. Will you have people thrown over the side? If so, on what basis will you decide who will go? Age? Health? Strength? Gender? Size?

2. *The Whistle-Blower:* You are employed by a large corporation that manufactures baby formula. You suspect that a flaw in the manufacturing process has resulted in contamination of the formula in a small number of cases. This contamination can result in serious illness, even death. You have been told by your supervisor that "everything is under control" and warned that if you "blow the whistle" by going public, you will be puting the entire company in jeopardy from multimillion-dollar lawsuits. You will naturally be fired and blackballed in the industry. As the sole provider in your household, your family depends on you.

3. *The Mad Bomber:* You are a police lieutenant heading up an investigation of a series of bombings that have resulted in extensive damage, injuries, and deaths. Your big break comes when you capture the person whom you are certain is the "mad bomber." However, he tauntingly tells you that he has placed a number of devices in public locations that will explode at the cost of many innocent lives and injuries. You believe that your only chance of extracting the location of these bombs is to torture this person until he tells. If you decide to do this, both your career and the legal case against the bomber will be placed in jeopardy. What do you do?

4. *The Patient:* As a clinical psychologist, you are committed to protecting the privacy of your patients. One afternoon a patient tells you that her husband, who has been abusing her physically and mentally for years, has threatened to kill her, and she believes he would. You try to convince her to leave him, but she tells you that she has decided to kill *him*. She is certain that he would find her wherever she went and feels that she will be safe only when he is dead. What do you do?

5. *The Friend:* As the director of your department, you are in charge of filling an important vacancy. Many people have applied, including your best friend, who has been out of work for over a year and needs a job desperately. Although your friend would likely perform satisfactorily, there are several more experienced and talented candidates who would

undoubtedly perform better. You have always prided yourself on hiring the best people, and you have earned a reputation as someone with high standards who will not compromise your striving for excellence. Whom do you hire?

As you think your way through these moral dilemmas, you will probably find yourself appealing to the basic moral principles that you typically use to guide your actions. Of course, what makes these examples moral *dilemmas* is the fact that they involve a *conflict* of traditional moral principles.

1. The Lifeboat involves a conflict between these moral beliefs:

- It is wrong to take any innocent life.
- It is right to save *some* lives rather than threaten *all* the lives on board.

2. The Whistle-Blower involves a conflict between these moral beliefs:

- It is wrong to knowingly jeopardize the health of children.
- It is right to protect the welfare of your family and your career.

3. The Mad Bomber involves a conflict between these moral beliefs:

- It is wrong to harm a human being.
- It is right to save the lives of many innocent people.

4. The Patient involves a conflict between these moral beliefs:

- It is wrong to violate the confidentiality of a professional relationship.
- It is right to prevent someone from committing murder.

5. The Friend involves a conflict between these moral beliefs:

- It is wrong to hire someone who is not the best-qualified candidate for the job.
- It is right to try to help and support your friends.

What makes each of these examples dilemmas is that both of the moral principles to which you are appealing seem ethically sound and appropriate; the problem is that they contradict each other. What should you do when this happens? How do you decide which principle is *more* right? There is no simple answer to this question, just as there is no easy answer to the question "What do you do when experts disagree?" In both cases, you need to *think critically* in order to arrive at intelligent and informed conclusions.

Naturally, the moral dilemmas just described are specifically designed to provoke intense angst and vigorous debate, but the situations nevertheless contain elements also found in everyday moral deliberations. For example, though you are unlikely to find yourself in a similar Lifeboat situation, you might be faced with the decision of which employees to fire in order to keep your company afloat. And though the Whistle-Blower example may seem extreme, employees working for companies that manufacture baby formula, contraceptives like the Dalkon Shield, and tobacco products have often found themselves in precisely this moral dilemma. You yourself may have been in a job situation where telling the truth or objecting to an unethical practice would have jeopardized your position or opportunity for advancement. Many therapists, clergy, lawyers, and doctors wrestle daily with issues of confidentiality analogous to the one described in the Patient. And we all have to deal with the question of under what circumstances it is morally appropriate to break our promises to avoid a greater evil or achieve a greater good. It requires little imagination to identify the issues of the Friend. There are countless instances in which we are forced to balance our feelings of personal obligation with our objective or professional analysis.

In addition to these kinds of ethical situations, you will undoubtedly confront other types of moral dilemmas that are at least as problematic. It is likely that at some point in your life you will have to make a "right to die" decision regarding a loved one nearing the end of life. You might also find yourself in a situation in which you are torn between ending a difficult marriage or remaining as a full-time parent of young children. Or you might be tempted to take advantage of an investment opportunity that, while not completely illegal, is clearly unethical. Dealing with complicated, ambiguous moral challenges is an inescapable part of the human condition. Since these situations can't be avoided, you need to develop the insight and conceptual tools to deal with them effectively.

The Thinker's Guide to Moral Decision-Making

After wrestling with the moral dilemmas presented in the previous section, you might be wondering exactly how we *do* develop a clear sense of right and wrong to guide us through complex moral situations. The answer is found by applying to moral issues the same critical thinking abilities we have been developing in the activities presented throughout this book to create **The Thinker's Guide to Moral Decision-Making.** Consider this guide a moral blueprint for constructing your own personal moral code. Using the concepts and principles provided by this guide, you can create a moral philosophy to analyze successfully virtually any moral situation and to make informed decisions that you can justify with confidence.

Make Morality a Priority   To live a life that achieves your moral potential, you must work to *become aware* of the moral issues that you face and strive to make choices that are grounded in thoughtful reflection and supported by persuasive reasoning. By living a morally enlightened life, you are defining yourself as a person of substance, a person with a vision that informs the quality of your relationships with others.

> *Strategy: During the next week, identify the moral issues that you encounter in your daily life that involve other people — choices related to right and wrong, good and evil, matters just and unjust. Select several of these moral choices, and think about the approach that you used in making each decision: What was the issue? What choices could you have made? Why did you make the choice that you did? If you had it to do over again, would you make the same choice? Why or why not?*

Adopt the "Ethic of Justice"   A critical thinking approach to ethics is founded on the principle of *justice* or *impartiality:* It is our moral obligation to treat everyone equally, with the same degree of consideration and respect, unless there is some persuasive reason not to do so. This is the basic principle of the ethic of justice. For example, differences among people that are based on race, religion, gender, or sexual orientation pose no threat to society as a whole. Therefore, people whose traits, beliefs, or practices differ from those of the majority deserve to be treated with the same respect to which everyone is entitled. It is both illogical and immoral to discriminate against other people.

> *Strategy: Think about your own biases toward others and begin working to treat these people with the respect they are due.*

Adopt the "Ethic of Care"   The ethic of care expresses a moral responsibility to others that is based on your ability to empathize — to put yourself in other people's situations and view the world from their perspectives. This ability to empathize enables you to feel compassion and sympathy toward others and serves as the foundation of all your healthy relationships. According to an empathic point of view, achieving happiness and fulfillment in life does not mean pursuing your own narrow desires; instead, it involves pursuing your aspirations in a context of genuine understanding of other people. When you actively work to transcend your own perspective and think within other

VISUAL THINKING

"What Homeless Person?"

- How is the couple in this photo behaving in relation to the homeless woman on the sidewalk? Why? What kinds of moral judgments do people make about homeless people? Do you think these judgments are justified? Why or why not?

points of view, particularly those with which you disagree, you are gaining a deeper and richer understanding of others.

> *Strategy: Increase your ability to empathize by making a special effort to transcend your own perspective and to place yourself in other people's "shoes." In your dealings with others, use your imagination to experience what you believe they are thinking and feeling, and observe whether this viewpoint influences your attitudes and actions toward them.*

Universalize Your Moral Choices   A very effective strategy to employ during your moral deliberations is to ask yourself if you would be willing for everyone in situations similar to your own to make the same choice that you are making — in other words, to "universalize" your choice. This moral principle was best articulated by the German philosopher Immanuel Kant in the "categorical imperative" that he believed every virtuous person should obey: "Act only according to that maxim by which you can at the same time will that it should become a universal law." Should you spread unflattering gossip about an unpopular acquaintance or coworker because you think the person "deserves" it? By applying this principle, you would determine that you should do so only if you believe that all people in all situations should spread unflattering gossip. Most people would be reluctant to sign on to this sort of universal rule.

Reason dictates that everyone's interests must be treated in the same way, without special consideration. We should all be willing to make every personal choice a universal law.

> *Strategy: As you deliberate the various moral choices in your life, both small ("Should I cut ahead in line?") and large ("Should I pursue my own self-interest at the risk of hurting someone else?"), make a conscious effort to universalize your anticipated actions. Would you be willing to have everyone take this same action in similar circumstances? If not, evaluate whether the action is truly morally justified and consistent with the other moral values you hold.*

Treat People as Ends, Not Means   Kant also formulated a second version of the categorical imperative: "Act so that you treat humanity, whether in your own person or in that of another, always as an end and never as a means only." Since all people possess the same *intrinsic value,* a value that is defined by the ability to understand their options and to make free choices, we should always act in a way that respects their inherent dignity as rational agents. Imagine, for example, that you want to sell something. Is it all right to manipulate people's feelings so that they will buy your product? Or suppose that your child or friend is planning to do something that you don't think is in her best interests.

Is it permissible to manipulate her thinking indirectly so that she will make a different choice? According to Kant, both of these actions are morally wrong because you are not treating the people involved as "ends" — that is, as rational agents who are entitled to make their own choices. Instead, you are treating them as *means to an end,* even though you may believe that your manipulation is in their best interests.

> *Strategy: Think about some recent instances in which you attempted to influence someone's thoughts, feelings, or behavior. Did you make a clear case for your recommendation, respecting the person's right to make a free choice? Or did you try to manipulate him or her by using techniques designed to influence the person without his or her knowledge or to coerce the person against his or her wishes? If you discover examples of such manipulation, try to imagine how things would have turned out if you had taken a more forthright approach.*

Accept Responsibility for Your Moral Choices   From a critical thinking perspective, morality makes sense only if we assume that people are able to make free choices for which they are responsible. When people choose courses of action that we consider to be right, we judge them as morally good. When they choose courses of action that we consider to be wrong, we condemn them as morally evil. It is impossible to achieve genuine moral stature without admitting responsibility for the choices that you make. If you are to create yourself as a person of moral integrity, you must have the courage to acknowledge your own moral failures as well as the humility to accept your moral successes.

> *Strategy: Strengthen your moral integrity by actively seeking to acknowledge your moral failings and then by committing yourself to improve. Self-honesty will build your inner strength and moral fiber, and you will find that moral integrity of this sort is both rewarding and habit forming.*

Seek to Promote Human Happiness   Promoting human happiness and its corollary, diminishing human suffering, have been mainstays of many ethical systems through the ages. Most people are perfectly willing to pursue their own happiness. However, you don't receive moral accolades solely for pursuing your own interests. Moral recognition is typically earned by devoting your time and resources to enhancing the happiness of others, sometimes at the expense of your own interests.

All things being equal, it makes sense to promote the happiness of others through your words and actions. Being friendly, generous, supportive, understanding, sympathetic, or helpful — exhibiting these and other similar traits can enhance the quality of others' lives, usually at a minimal cost to yourself. Happiness breeds happiness in the same way that aggression escalates aggression and negativity inspires more negativity. When you actively employ your words and actions to help other people become happy, their happiness will reflect back onto you, instilling a sense of satisfaction and fulfillment. Happiness and goodwill are not limited commodities. There are, in fact, inexhaustible supplies.

> **Strategy:** *Think about specific ways in which you can increase the happiness of the people in your life. These may involve bestowing a small kindness on someone you know casually or making a more significant commitment to someone to whom you are very close. Create and implement a plan for doing this during the next few days, and then evaluate the results of your efforts. How did applying the extra effort to make others happy make you feel? How did they respond? Doesn't it make sense to continue this effort and even to increase it?*

Develop an Informed Moral Intuition   An informed moral intuition is the product of thoughtful exploration and reflection on moral issues throughout your life. Developing an informed, reliable moral intuition involves achieving insight into the essential nature of humans: What are the basic qualities that define what kind of individuals we ought to be and how we should treat others?

Once you have developed an intuition in which you have confidence, you need to *use* it to help you think your way through moral dilemmas. If your moral intuition is *informed*, the product of a great deal of thought and reflection, then it will have a high degree of credibility. But if your moral intuition is *uninformed*, the product of inaccurate information or inadequate experience, then your intuition will not be credible.

> **Strategy:** *Imagine an ideal, perfect human being. What personal qualities would such a person possess? How would such a person treat other people? What moral vision and specific moral values would such a person display? Using these explorations, construct a composite portrait of an ideal person that you can use to guide your own moral intuitions.*

Choose to Be a Moral Person   Just as a person can possess an array of critical thinking abilities and yet choose not to use them, so also can a person be a walking compendium of moral theory and yet choose not to apply it to her or his own life. To achieve an enlightened moral existence in your own life, you need to decide to be a moral person struggling to live a moral life. You need to *value* morality, to aspire to an enhanced moral awareness, to exert the motivation and commitment required to reach this lofty but attainable goal.

Each day confronts you with new choices and unexpected challenges, many of which you cannot possibly anticipate. With your moral code in hand to guide you, you will need to commit yourself to making the choices that best express your moral philosophy of life. Achieving moral enlightenment is an ongoing process, and it is a struggle that cannot be avoided if you are to live a life of purpose and meaning, one created by a self that is authentic and, as Aristotle would say, "great souled."

> **Strategy:** *Develop the habit of conducting a regular appraisal of your self and your life. Ask — and answer — questions such as these: Am I achieving my goals as a moral person? As a critical thinker? As a creative individual? Then use this evaluation regularly to maintain a much-needed perspective on your life, reminding yourself of the "big picture" and applying it to guide your evolution into the most worthy person you can become.*

Why Be Moral?

The considerations that we have been discussing provide a convincing answer to a pertinent question: Why be moral? As it turns out, becoming a moral person can help you become a psychologically healthy person; promoting the happiness of others frequently enhances your own happiness. Often adages are clichéd and empty of meaning, but in this case "Virtue is its own reward" contains a substantial measure of truth, a point noted by Socrates in his observation that doing wrong "will harm and corrupt that part of ourselves that is improved by just actions and destroyed by unjust actions."

As a free individual, you create yourself through the choices that you make, much as a sculptor gradually forms a figure through countless cuts of the chisel. If you create yourself as a moral person, you create a person of character and worth, someone with an acute sense of right and wrong and the power to make appropriate choices. But if you *don't* choose to create yourself as a moral person, you will gradually become corrupted. You will lose your moral sensitivity, developing a moral blindness that will handicap your ability to see yourself or the world clearly. It is no wonder that Socrates believed that "it is better to suffer wickedness than to commit it." You gain true power when you possess the unfettered and unrestrained ability to choose freely. Conversely, choosing immorality binds your hands, one loop of thread at a time, until your freedom of movement disappears. In the same way that substance abusers gradually surrender their freedom of choice to their destructive cravings, so also do immoral people have only the illusion of genuine freedom in their lives. While moral people enjoy healthy personalities and spiritual wholeness, immoral people are corrupted at their core, progressively ravaged by a disease of the spirit.

THINKING ACTIVITY 5.6

Nurturing Your Moral Growth

No matter how highly evolved you are as a moral person, you can achieve a more enlightened state by choosing to nurture your moral growth. Your critical thinking abilities will give you the means to explore the moral dimensions of your experience with insight, and your personal dedication to moral improvement will provide you with the ongoing motivation. Remember that becoming a moral person is both a daily and a lifetime project. Nurture your continued moral growth by cultivating the qualities that we have been exploring in this section.

- Make morality a priority.
- Adopt the "ethic of justice."
- Adopt the "ethic of care."
- Universalize your moral choices.
- Treat people as ends, not means.
- Accept responsibility for your moral choices.
- Seek to promote human happiness.
- Develop an informed moral intuition.
- Choose to be a moral person.

Final Thoughts

This chapter has explored the thinking processes that create three of the fundamental types of beliefs that you use to make sense of your world. These processes are

Reporting   Describing information that can be verified through investigation

Inferring   Going beyond factual information to describe what is not known

Judging   Expressing an evaluation based on certain criteria

Each of these types of beliefs has an important and distinctive role to play in your ongoing efforts to organize and make sense of your world. As a critical thinker, you must learn to recognize each of these different types of beliefs and use them properly. Of course, it is often difficult and confusing to distinguish among these types of beliefs because you rarely make an effort to try to separate them. Instead, the thinking activities of reporting, inferring, and judging tend to be woven together, organizing your world into a seamless fabric. Only when you make a special effort to reflect and think critically are you able to recognize these activities as being distinct.

In addition to recognizing and using these types of beliefs appropriately, thinking critically about these beliefs involves evaluating their basis and reliability: What is the reliability of the sources providing information for the *factual reports?* What is the probability that the *inference* is correct? What are the evidence and reasons that support the criteria used in the *judgment?* By distinguishing and critically evaluating these fundamental types of beliefs, you will be able to improve their accuracy and effectiveness as you seek to make sense of your world.

THINKING PASSAGE

Character and Intellect

Robert Coles is a professor of psychiatry and medical humanities at Harvard University who specializes in issues of moral development. In 1973, Coles won a Pulitzer Prize for his book Children of Crisis. More recently he published "In the Deep Heart's Core."

THE DISPARITY BETWEEN INTELLECT AND CHARACTER
by Robert Coles

Over 150 years ago, Ralph Waldo Emerson gave a lecture at Harvard University, which he ended with the terse assertion: "Character is higher than intellect." Even then, this prominent man of letters was worried (as many other writers and thinkers of succeeding generations would be)

about the limits of knowledge and the nature of a college's mission. The intellect can grow and grow, he knew, in a person who is smug, ungenerous, even cruel. Institutions originally founded to teach their students how to become good and decent, as well as broadly and deeply literate, may abandon the first mission to concentrate on a driven, narrow book learning — a course of study in no way intent on making a connection between ideas and theories on one hand and, on the other, our lives as we actually live them.

Students have their own way of realizing and trying to come to terms with the split that Emerson addressed. A few years ago, a sophomore student of mine came to see me in great anguish. She had arrived at Harvard from a Midwestern, working-class background. She was trying hard to work her way through college, and, in doing so, cleaned the rooms of some of her fellow students. Again and again, she encountered classmates who apparently had forgotten the meaning of *please,* or *thank you* — no matter how high their Scholastic Assessment Test scores — students who did not hesitate to be rude, even crude toward her.

One day she was not so subtly propositioned by a young man she knew to be a very bright, successful pre-med student and already an accomplished journalist. This was not the first time he had made such an overture, but now she had reached a breaking point. She had quit her job and was preparing to quit college in what she called "fancy, phony Cambridge."

The student had been part of a seminar I teach, which links Raymond Carver's fiction and poetry with Edward Hopper's paintings and drawings — the thematic convergence of literary and artistic sensibility in exploring American loneliness, both its social and its personal aspects. As she expressed her anxiety and anger to me, she soon was sobbing hard. After her sobs quieted, we began to remember the old days of that class. But she had some weightier matters on her mind and began to give me a detailed, sardonic account of college life, as viewed by someone vulnerable and hardpressed by it. At one point, she observed of the student who had propositioned her: "That guy gets all A's. He tells people he's in Group I [the top academic category]. I've taken two moral-reasoning courses with him, and I'm sure he's gotten A's in both of them — and look at how he behaves with me, and I'm sure with others."

She stopped for a moment to let me take that in. I happened to know the young man and could only acknowledge the irony of his behavior, even as I wasn't totally surprised by what she'd experienced. But I was at a loss to know what to say to her. A philosophy major, with a strong interest in literature, she had taken a course on the Holocaust and described for me the ironies she also saw in that tragedy — mass murder of unparalleled historical proportion in a nation hitherto known as one of the most civilized in the world, with a citizenry as well educated as that of any country at the time.

Drawing on her education, the student put before me names such as Martin Heidegger, Carl Jung, Paul De Man, Ezra Pound — brilliant and accomplished men (a philosopher, a psychoanalyst, a literary critic, a poet) who nonetheless had linked themselves with the hate that was Nazism and Fascism during the 1930s. She reminded me of the willingness of the leaders of German and Italian universities to embrace Nazi and Fascist ideas, of the countless doctors and lawyers and judges and journalists and schoolteachers, and, yes, even members of the clergy — who were able to accommodate themselves to murderous thugs because the thugs had political power. She pointedly mentioned, too, the Soviet Gulag, that expanse of prisons to which millions of honorable people were sent by Stalin and his brutish accomplices — prisons commonly staffed by psychiatrists quite eager to label those victims of a vicious totalitarian state with an assortment of psychiatric names, then shoot them up with drugs meant to reduce them to zombies.

I tried hard, toward the end of a conversation that lasted almost two hours, to salvage something for her, for myself, and, not least, for a university that I much respect, even as I know its failings. I suggested that if she had learned what she had just shared with me at Harvard — why, *that* was itself a valuable education acquired. She smiled, gave me credit for a "nice try," but remained unconvinced. Then she put this tough, pointed, unnerving question to me: "I've been taking all these philosophy courses, and we talk about what's true, what's important, what's *good.* Well, how do you teach people to *be* good?" And she added: "What's the point of *knowing* good, if you don't keep trying to *become* a good person?"

I suddenly found myself on the defensive, although all along I had been sympathetic to her, to the indignation she had been directing toward some of her fellow students, and to her critical examination of the limits of abstract knowledge. Schools are schools, colleges are colleges, I averred, a complaisant and smug accommodation in my voice. Thereby I meant to say that our schools and colleges these days don't take major responsibility for the moral values of their students, but, rather, assume that their student acquire those values at home. I topped off my surrender to the *status quo* with a shrug of my shoulders, to which she responded with an unspoken but barely concealed anger. This she expressed through a knowing look that announced that she'd taken the full moral measure of me.

Suddenly, she was on her feet preparing to leave. I realized that I'd stumbled badly. I wanted to pursue the discussion, applaud her for taking on a large subject in a forthright, incisive manner, and tell her she was right in understanding that moral reasoning is not to be equated with moral conduct. I wanted, really, to explain my shrug — point out that there is only so much that any of us can do to affect others' behavior, that institutional life has its own momentum. But she had no interest in that kind of self-justification — as she let me know in an unforgetable aside as she was departing my office: "I wonder whether Emerson was just being 'smart' in that lecture he gave here. I wonder if he ever had any ideas about what to *do* about what was worrying him — or did he think he'd done enough because he'd spelled the problem out to those Harvard professors?"

She was demonstrating that she understood two levels of irony: One was that the study of philosophy — even moral philosophy or moral reasoning — doesn't necessarily prompt in either the teacher or the student a determination to act in accordance with moral principles. And, further, a discussion of that very irony can prove equally sterile — again carrying no apparent consequences as far as one's everyday actions go.

When that student left my office (she would soon leave Harvard for good), I was exhausted and saddened — and brought up short. All too often those of us who read books or teach don't think to pose for ourselves the kind of ironic dilemma she had posed to me. How might we teachers encourage our students (encourage *ourselves*) to take that big step from thought to action, from moral analysis to fulfilled moral commitments? Rather obviously, community service offers us all a chance to put our money where our mouths are; and, of course, such service can enrich our understanding of the disciplines we study. A reading of *Invisible Man* (literature), *Tally's Corners* (sociology and anthropology), or *Childhood and Society* (psychology and psychoanalysis) takes on new meaning after some time spent in a ghetto school or a clinic. By the same token, such books can prompt us to think pragmatically about, say, how the wisdom that Ralph Ellison worked into his fiction might shape the way we get along with the children we're tutoring — affect our attitudes toward them, the things we say and do with them.

Yet I wonder whether classroom discussion, *per se*, can't also be of help, the skepticism of my student notwithstanding. She had pushed me hard, and I started referring again and again in my classes on moral introspection to what she had observed and learned, and my students more than got the message. Her moral righteousness, her shrewd eye and ear for hypocrisy hovered over us, made us uneasy, goaded us.

She challenged us to prove that what we think intellectually can be connected to our daily deeds. For some of us, the connection was established through community service. But that is not the only possible way. I asked students to write papers that told of particular efforts to honor through action the high thoughts we were discussing. Thus goaded to a certain self-consciousness, I suppose, students made various efforts. I felt that the best of them were small victories, brief epiphanies that might otherwise have been overlooked, but had great significance for the students in question.

"I thanked someone serving me food in the college cafeteria, and then we got to talking, the first time," one student wrote. For her, this was a decisive break with her former indifference to others she abstractly regarded as "the people who work on the serving line." She felt that she had learned something about another's life and had tried to show respect for that life.

The student who challenged me with her angry, melancholy story had pushed me to teach differently. Now, I make an explicit issue of the more than occasional disparity between thinking and doing, and I ask my students to consider how we all might bridge that disparity. To be sure, the task of connecting intellect to character is daunting, as Emerson and others well knew. And any of us can lapse into cynicism, turn the moral challenge of a seminar into yet another moment of opportunism: I'll get an A this time, by writing a paper cannily extolling myself as a doer of this or that "good deed"!

Still, I know that college administrators and faculty members everywhere are struggling with the same issues that I was faced with, and I can testify that many students will respond seriously, in at least small ways, if we make clear that we really believe that the link between moral reasoning and action is important to us. My experience has given me at least a measure of hope that moral reasoning and reflection can somehow be integrated into students' — and teachers' — lives as they actually live them.

Questions for Analysis

1. What does Robert Coles mean by the term *character* when he quotes Ralph Waldo Emerson, "Character is higher than intellect"?

2. "The intellect can grow and grow . . . in a person who is smug, ungenerous, even cruel. Institutions originally founded to teach their students how to become good and decent, as well as broadly and deeply literate, may abandon the first mission to concentrate on a driven, narrow book learning — a course of study in no way intent on making a connection between ideas and theories on one hand and, on the other, our lives as we actually live them." To what extent do you believe this indictment of the lack of moral instruction applies to your college? Do you believe that colleges should do more to encourage the development of moral character on the part of students? Why or why not?

3. The student who comes to visit Coles is profoundly disturbed by what she perceived to be the disparity between academic learning and moral values on the part of students and faculty at Harvard. Do you think her criticisms are legitimate? If you had been in Coles's position, how would you have responded?

4. According to Aristotle, "The ultimate purpose in studying ethics is not as it is in other inquiries, the attainment of theoretical knowledge; we are not conducting this inquiry in order to know what virtue is, but in order to become good, else there would be no advantage in studying it" (Nichomachean Ethics, Bk. 2, Ch. 2). Do you agree with Aristotle? Why or why not?

5. The student who comes to Coles poses this question: "I've been taking all these philosophy courses, and we talk about what's true, what's important, what's *good*." Well, how do you teach people to *be* good? What's the point of *knowing* good, if you don't keep trying to *become* a good person?" How do you think colleges should respond to the challenge of teaching people to be good?

Recognizing Arguments

Cue words

Constructing Arguments

Decide
Explain
Predict
Persuade

Argument
A form of thinking in which certain reasons are offered to support a conclusion

Constructing Extended Arguments

Identifying a thesis
Conducting research
Evaluating sources
Organizing ideas

Evaluating Arguments

Truth
Validity
Soundness

Understanding Deductive Arguments

Application of a general rule
Modus ponens
Modus tollens
Disjunctive syllogism

Consider carefully the following dialogue about whether marijuana should be legalized:

Dennis: Did you hear about the person who was sentenced to fifteen years in prison for possessing marijuana? I think this is one of the most outrageously unjust punishments I've ever heard of! In most states, people who are convicted of armed robbery, rape, or even murder don't receive fifteen-year sentences. And unlike the possession of marijuana, these crimes violate the rights of other people.

Caroline: I agree that this is one case in which the punishment doesn't seem to fit the crime. But you have to realize that drugs pose a serious threat to the young people of our country. Look at all the people who are addicted to drugs, who have their lives ruined, and who often die at an early age of overdoses. And think of all the crimes committed by people to support their drug habits. As a result, sometimes society has to make an example of someone — like the person you mentioned — to convince people of the seriousness of the situation.

Dennis: That's ridiculous. In the first place, it's not right to punish someone unfairly just to provide an example. At least not in a society that believes in justice. And in the second place, smoking marijuana is nothing like using drugs such as heroin or even cocaine. It follows that smoking marijuana should not be against the law.

Caroline: I don't agree. Although marijuana might not be as dangerous as some other drugs, smoking it surely isn't good for you. And I don't think that anything that is a threat to your health should be legal.

Dennis: What about cigarettes and alcohol? We *know* that they are dangerous. Medical research has linked smoking cigarettes to lung cancer, emphysema, and heart disease, and alcohol damages the liver. No one has proved that marijuana is a threat to our health. And even if it does turn out to be somewhat unhealthy, it's certainly not as dangerous as cigarettes and alcohol.

Caroline: That's a good point. But to tell you the truth, I'm not so sure that cigarettes and alcohol should be legal. And in any case, they are already legal. Just because cigarettes and alcohol are bad for your health is no reason to legalize another drug that can cause health problems.

Dennis: Look — life is full of risks. We take chances every time we cross the street or climb into our car. In fact, with all of these loonies on the road, driving is a lot more hazardous to our health than any of the drugs around. And many of the foods we eat can kill. For example, red meat contributes to heart disease, and artificial sweeteners can cause cancer. The point is, if people want to take chances with their health, that's up to them. And many

VISUAL THINKING

"Let Herbs Grow Free!"

- Would you be inclined to join a "Legalize Marijuana" protest like this one? Why do some people believe that marijuana should be legalized? Why do others believe it shouldn't?

people in our society like to mellow out with marijuana. I read somewhere that over 70 percent of the people in the United States think that marijuana should be legalized.

Caroline: There's a big difference between letting people drive cars and letting them use dangerous drugs. Society has a responsibility to protect people from themselves. People often do things that are foolish if they are encouraged or given the opportunity to. Legalizing something like marijuana encourages people to use it, especially young people. It follows that many more people would use marijuana if it were legalized. It's like society saying, "This is all right — go ahead and use it."

Dennis: I still maintain that marijuana isn't dangerous. It's not addictive — like heroin is — and there is no evidence that it harms you. Consequently, anything that is harmless should be legal.

Caroline: Marijuana may not be physically addictive like heroin, but I think that it can be psychologically addictive, because people tend to use more and more of it over time. I know a number of people who spend a lot of their time getting high. What about Carl? All he does is lie around and get high. This shows that smoking it over a period of time definitely affects your mind. Think about the people you know who smoke a lot — don't they seem to be floating in a dream world? How are they ever going to make anything of their lives? As far as I'm concerned, a pothead is like a zombie — living but dead.

Dennis: Since you have had so little experience with marijuana, I don't think that you can offer an informed opinion on the subject. And anyway, if you do too much of anything it can hurt you. Even something as healthy as exercise can cause problems if you do too much of it. But I sure don't see anything wrong with toking up with some friends at a party or even getting into a relaxed state by yourself. In fact, I find that I can even concentrate better on my schoolwork after taking a little smoke.

Caroline: If you believe that, then marijuana really *has* damaged your brain. You're just trying to rationalize your drug habit. Smoking marijuana doesn't help you concentrate — it takes you away from reality. And I don't think that people can control it. Either you smoke and surrender control of your life, or you don't smoke because you want to retain control. There's nothing in between.

Dennis: Let me point out something to you: Because marijuana is illegal, organized crime controls its distribution and makes all the money from it. If marijuana were legalized, the government could tax the sale of it — like cigarettes and alcohol — and then use the money for some worthwhile purpose. For example, many states have legalized gambling and use the money to support education. In fact, the major tobacco companies have already copyrighted names for different marijuana brands — like "Acapulco Gold." Obviously, they believe that marijuana will soon become legal.

Caroline: Just because the government can make money out of something doesn't mean that they should legalize it. We could also legalize prostitution or muggings and then tax the proceeds. Also, simply because the cigarette companies are prepared to sell marijuana doesn't mean that it makes sense to. After all, they're the ones who are selling us cigarettes.

Continue this dialogue, incorporating other views on the subject of legalizing marijuana.

⊚ Recognizing Arguments

The preceding discussion is an illustration of two people engaging in *dialogue*, which we have defined (in Chapter 2) as the systematic exchange of ideas. Participating in this sort of dialogue with others is one of the keys to thinking critically because it stimulates you to develop your mind by carefully examining the way you make sense of the world. Discussing issues with others encourages you to be mentally active, to ask questions, to view issues from different perspectives, and to develop reasons to support conclusions. It is this last quality of thinking critically — supporting conclusions with reasons — that we will focus on in this chapter and the next.

When we offer reasons to support a conclusion, we are considered to be presenting an *argument*.

argument *A form of thinking in which certain statements (reasons) are offered in support of another statement (a conclusion)*

At the beginning of the dialogue, Dennis presents the following argument against imposing a fifteen-year sentence for possession of marijuana (argument 1):

Reason: Possessing marijuana is not a serious offense because it hurts no one.

Reason: There are many other more serious offenses in which victims' basic rights are violated — such as armed robbery, rape, and murder — for which the offenders don't receive such stiff sentences.

Conclusion: Therefore, a fifteen-year sentence is an unjust punishment for possessing marijuana.

Can you identify an additional reason that supports this conclusion?

Reason:

The definition of *argument* given here is somewhat different from the meaning of the concept in our ordinary language. In common speech, "argument" usually refers to a dispute or quarrel between people, often involving intense feelings (for example: "I got into a terrible argument with the idiot who hit the back of my car"). Very often these quarrels involve people presenting arguments in the sense in which we have defined the concept, although the arguments are usually not carefully reasoned or clearly stated because the people are so angry. Instead of this common usage, in this chapter we will use the word's more technical meaning.

Using our definition, we can define the main ideas that make up an argument.

reasons *Statements that support another statement (known as a conclusion), justify it, or make it more probable*

conclusion *A statement that explains, asserts, or predicts on the basis of statements (known as reasons) that are offered as evidence for it*

The type of thinking that uses argument — reasons in support of conclusions — is known as *reasoning,* and it is a type of thinking you have been doing throughout this book, as well as in much of your life. We are continually trying to explain, justify, and predict things through the process of reasoning.

Of course, our reasoning — and the reasoning of others — is not always correct. For example, the reasons someone offers may not really support the conclusion they are supposed to. Or the conclusion may not really follow from the reasons stated. These difficulties are illustrated in a number of the arguments contained in the discussion on marijuana. Nevertheless, whenever we accept a conclusion as likely or true based on certain reasons or whenever we offer reasons to support a conclusion, we are using arguments to engage in reasoning — even if our reasoning is weak or faulty and needs to be improved. In this chapter and the next, we will be exploring both the way we construct effective arguments and the way we evaluate arguments to develop and sharpen our reasoning ability.

Let us return to the discussion about marijuana. After Dennis presents the argument with the conclusion that the fifteen-year prison sentence is an unjust punishment, Caroline considers that argument. Although she acknowledges that in this case "the punishment doesn't seem to fit the crime," she goes on to offer another argument (argument 2), giving reasons that lead to a conclusion that conflicts with the one Dennis drew:

Reason: Drugs pose a very serious threat to the young people of our country.

Reason: Many crimes are committed to support drug habits.

Conclusion: As a result, sometimes society has to make an example of someone to convince people of the seriousness of the situation.

Can you identify an additional reason that supports this conclusion?

Reason:

Cue Words for Arguments

Our language provides guidance in our efforts to identify reasons and conclusions. Certain key words, known as *cue words*, signal that a reason is being offered in support of a conclusion or that a conclusion is being announced on the basis of certain reasons. For example, in response to Caroline's conclusion that society sometimes has to make an example of someone to convince people of the seriousness of the situation, Dennis gives the following argument (argument 3):

Reason: In the first place, it's not right to punish someone unfairly just to provide an example.

Reason: In the second place, smoking marijuana is nothing like using drugs such as heroin or even cocaine.

Conclusion: It follows that smoking marijuana should not be against the law.

In this argument, the phrases *in the first place* and *in the second place* signal that reasons are being offered in support of a conclusion. Similarly, the phrase *it follows that* signals that a conclusion is being announced on the basis of certain reasons. Here is a list of the most commonly used cue words for reasons and conclusions:

Cue Words Signaling Reasons

since	in view of
for	first, second
because	in the first (second) place
as shown by	may be inferred from
as indicated by	may be deduced from
given that	may be derived from
assuming that	for the reason that

Cue Words Signaling Conclusions

therefore	then
thus	it follows that
hence	thereby showing
so	demonstrates that
(which) shows that	allows us to infer that
(which) proves that	suggests very strongly that
implies that	you see that

points to	leads me to believe that
as a result	allows us to deduce that
consequently	

Of course, identifying reasons, conclusions, and arguments involves more than looking for cue words. The words and phrases listed here do not always signal reasons and conclusions, and in many cases arguments are made without the use of cue words. However, cue words do help alert us that an argument is being made.

THINKING ACTIVITY 6.1

Identifying Arguments with Cue Words

1. Review the discussion on marijuana, and underline any cue words signaling that reasons are being offered or that conclusions are being announced.
2. With the aid of cue words, identify the various arguments contained in the discussion on marijuana. For each argument, describe
   a. The *reasons* offered in support of a conclusion
   b. The *conclusion* announced on the basis of the reasons

   Before you start, review the three arguments we have examined thus far in this chapter.
3. Go back to the additional arguments you wrote on page 193. Reorganize and add cue words if necessary to clearly identify your reasons as well as the conclusion you drew from those reasons.

THINKING PASSAGES

Legalizing Drugs

The following two essays discuss the issue of whether drugs should be legalized. The first passage, "Drugs," is written by Gore Vidal, a well-known essayist and novelist. The second, "The Case for Slavery," is authored by New York Times editor and columnist A. M. Rosenthal. After carefully reading the essays, answer the questions that follow.

Drugs*
by Gore Vidal

It is possible to stop most drug addiction in the United States within a very short time. Simply make all drugs available and sell them at cost. Label each drug with a precise description of what effect — good and bad — the drug will have on the taker. This will require heroic honesty. Don't say that marijuana is addictive or dangerous when it is neither, as millions of people know — unlike "speed," which kills most unpleasantly, or heroin, which is addictive and difficult to kick.

For the record, I have tried — once — almost every drug and liked none, disproving the popular Fu Manchu theory that a single whiff of opium will enslave the mind. Nevertheless many drugs are bad for certain people to take and they should be told why in a sensible way.

Along with exhortation and warning, it might be good for our citizens to recall (or learn for the first time) that the United States was the creation of men who believed that each man has the right to do what he wants with his own life as long as he does not interfere with his neighbor's pursuit of happiness. (That his neighbor's idea of happiness is persecuting others does confuse matters a bit.)

This is a startling notion to the current generation of Americans. They reflect a system of public education which has made the Bill of Rights, literally, unacceptable to a majority of high school graduates who now form the "silent majority" — a phrase which that underestimated wit Richard Nixon took from Homer who used it to describe the dead.

Now one can hear the warning rumble begin: If everyone is allowed to take drugs everyone will and the GNP will decrease, the Commies will stop us from making everyone free, and we shall end up a race of zombies, passively murmuring "groovy" to one another. Alarming thought. Yet it seems most unlikely that any reasonably sane person will become a drug addict if he knows in advance what addiction is going to be like.

Is everyone reasonably sane? No. Some people will always become drug addicts just as some people will always become alcoholics, and it is just too bad. Every man, however, has the power (and should have the legal right) to kill himself if he chooses. But since most men don't, they won't be mainliners either. Nevertheless, forbidding people things they like or think they might enjoy only makes them want those things all the more. This psychological insight is, for some mysterious reason, perennially denied our governors.

It is a lucky thing for the American moralist that our country has always existed in a kind of time-vacuum: We have no public memory of anything that happened before last Tuesday. No one in Washington today recalls what happened during the years alcohol was forbidden to the people by a Congress that thought it had a divine mission to stamp out Demon Rum — launching, in the process, the greatest crime wave in the country's history, causing thousands of deaths from bad alcohol, and creating a general (and persisting) contempt among the citizenry for the laws of the United States.

The same thing is happening today. But the government has learned nothing from past attempts at prohibition, not to mention repression.

Last year when the supply of Mexican marijuana was slightly curtailed by the Feds, the pushers got the kids hooked on heroin and deaths increased dramatically, particularly in New York. Whose fault? Evil men like the Mafiosi? Permissive Dr. Spock? Wild-eyed Dr. Leary? No.

The Government of the United States was responsible for those deaths. The bureaucratic machine has a vested interest in playing cops and robbers. Both the Bureau of Narcotics and the Mafia want strong laws against the sale and use of drugs because if drugs are sold at cost there would be no money in it for anyone.

If there was no money in it for the Mafia, there would be no friendly playground pushers, and addicts would not commit crimes to pay for the next fix. Finally, if there was no money in it, the Bureau of Narcotics would wither away, something they are not about to do without a struggle.

Will anything sensible be done? Of course not. The American people are as devoted to the idea of sin and its punishment as they are to making money —and fighting drugs is nearly as big a business as pushing them. Since the combination of sin and money is irresistible (particularly to the professional politician), the situation will only grow worse.

THE CASE FOR SLAVERY*
by A. M. Rosenthal

Across the country, a scattered but influential collection of intellectuals is intensely engaged in making the case for slavery.

With considerable passion, these Americans are repeatedly expounding the benefits of not only tolerating slavery but legalizing it:

* "The Case for Slavery," by A. M. Rosenthal, The *New York Times*, September 26, 1989. Copyright © 1989 by the New York Times Co. Reprinted by permission.

It would make life less dangerous for the free. It would save a great deal of money. And since the economies could be used to improve the lot of the slaves, in the end they would be better off.

The new antiabolitionists, like their predecessors in the nineteenth century, concede that those now in bondage do not themselves see the benefits of legalizing their status.

But in time they will, we are assured, because the beautiful part of legalization is that slavery would be designed so as to keep slaves pacified with the very thing that enslaves them!

The form of slavery under discussion is drug addiction. It does not have every characteristic of more traditional forms of bondage. But they have enough in common to make the comparison morally valid — and the campaign for drug legalization morally disgusting.

Like the plantation slavery that was a foundation of American society for so long, drug addiction largely involves specifiable groups of people. Most of the enchained are children and adolescents of all colors and black and Hispanic adults.

Like plantation slavery, drug addiction is passed on from generation to generation. And this may be the most important similarity: Like plantation slavery, addiction can destroy among its victims the social resources most valuable to free people for their own betterment — family life, family traditions, family values.

In plantation-time America, mothers were taken from their children. In drug-time America, mothers abandon their children. Do the children suffer less, or the mothers?

Antiabolitionists argue that legalization would make drugs so cheap and available that the profit for crime would be removed. Well-supplied addicts would be peaceful addicts. We would not waste billions for jails and could spend some of the savings helping the addicted become drug-free.

That would happen at the very time that new millions of Americans were being enticed into addiction by legalization — somehow.

Are we really foolish enough to believe that tens of thousands of drug gang members would meekly steal away, foiled by the marvels of the free market?

Not likely. The pushers would cut prices, making more money than ever from the ever-growing mass market. They would immediately increase the potency and variety beyond anything available at any government-approved narcotics counters.

Crime would increase. Crack produces paranoid violence. More permissiveness equals more use equals more violence.

And what will legalization do to the brains of Americans drawn into drug slavery by easy availability?

Earlier this year, an expert drug pediatrician told me that after only a few months babies born with crack addiction seemed to recover. Now we learn that stultifying behavioral effects last at least through early childhood. Will they last forever?

How long will crack affect neurological patterns in the brains of adult crack users? Dr. Gabriel G. Nahas of Columbia University argues in his new book, *Cocaine: The Great White Plague,* that the damage may be irreversible. Would it not be an act of simple intelligence to drop the legalization campaign until we find out?

Then why do a number of writers and academicians, left to right, support it? I have discussed this with antidrug leaders like Jesse Jackson, Dr. Mitchell Rosenthal of Phoenix House, and William J. Bennett, who search for answers themselves.

Perhaps the answer is that the legalizers are not dealing with reality in America. I think the reason has to do with class.

Crack is beginning to move into the white middle and upper classes. That is a tragedy for those addicted.

However, it has not yet destroyed the communities around which their lives revolve, not taken over every street and doorway. It has not passed generation to generation among them, killing the continuity of family.

But in ghetto communities poverty and drugs come together in a catalytic reaction that is reducing them to social rubble.

The antiabolitionists, virtually all white and well-to-do, do not see or do not care. Either way they show symptoms of the callousness of class. That can be a particularly dangerous social disorder.

Questions for Analysis

1. Identify and rewrite the arguments that each of the authors uses to support his position regarding the legalization of drugs, using the following format:

   Reason:

   Reason:

   Conclusion:

   Use cue words to help you identify arguments.
2. Construct one new argument to support each side of this issue, using the form shown in question 1.
3. State whether or not you believe drugs should be legalized and provide reasons to support your conclusion.

Arguments Are Inferences

When you construct arguments, you are composing and relating to the world by means of your ability to infer. As you saw in Chapter 5, *inferring* is a thinking process that you use to reason from what you already know (or believe to be the case) to form new knowledge or beliefs. This is usually what you do when you construct arguments. You work from reasons you know or believe in to form conclusions based on these reasons.

Just as you can use inferences to make sense of different types of situations, so you can also construct arguments for different purposes. In a variety of situations, you construct arguments to do the following:

* decide

* explain

* predict

* persuade

An example of each of these different types of arguments follows. After examining each example, construct an argument of the same type related to issues in your own life.

We Construct Arguments to Decide

Reason: Throughout my life, I've always been interested in all different kinds of electricity.

Reason: There are many attractive job opportunities in the field of electrical engineering.

Conclusion: I will work toward becoming an electrical engineer.

Reason:

Reason:

Conclusion:

We Construct Arguments to Explain

Reason: I was delayed in leaving my house because my dog needed an emergency walking.

Reason: There was an unexpected traffic jam caused by motorists slowing down to view an overturned chicken truck.

Conclusion: Therefore, I was late for our appointment.

Reason:

Reason:

Conclusion:

We Construct Arguments to Predict

Reason: Some people will always drive faster than the speed limit allows, no matter whether the limit is 55 or 65 mph.

Reason: Car accidents are more likely to occur at higher speeds.

Conclusion: It follows that the newly reinstated 65 mph limit will result in more accidents.

Reason:

Reason:

Conclusion:

We Construct Arguments to Persuade

Reason: Chewing tobacco can lead to cancer of the mouth and throat.

Reason: Boys sometimes are led to begin chewing tobacco by ads for the product that feature sports heroes they admire.

Conclusion: Therefore, ads for chewing tobacco should be banned.

Reason:

Reason:

Conclusion:

Evaluating Arguments

To construct an effective argument, you must be skilled in evaluating the effectiveness, or soundness, of arguments that have already been constructed. You must investigate two aspects of each argument independently to determine the soundness of the argument as a whole:

1. How true are the reasons being offered to support the conclusion?

2. To what extent do the reasons support the conclusion, or to what extent does the conclusion follow from the reasons offered?

We will first examine each of these ways of evaluating arguments separately and then see how they work together.

Truth: How True Are the Supporting Reasons?

The first aspect of the argument you must evaluate is the truth of the reasons that are being used to support a conclusion. Does each reason make sense? What evidence is being offered as part of each reason? Do you know each rea-

VISUAL THINKING

Sound Construction

● The scene in this illustration evokes two popular instructional tales — one from children's stories and one from the Bible (New Testament) — to depict the soundness of arguments. What other metaphors or symbols could be pictured to show the same concept?

son to be true based on your experience? Is each reason based on a source that can be trusted? You use these questions and others like them to analyze the reasons offered and to determine how true they are. As you saw in Chapter 4, "Believing, Perceiving, and Knowing," evaluating the sort of beliefs usually found as reasons in arguments is a complex and ongoing challenge. Let us evaluate the truth of the reasons presented in the discussion at the beginning of this chapter about whether marijuana should be legalized.

Argument 1

Reason: Possessing marijuana is not a serious offense.

Evaluation: As it stands, this reason needs further evidence to support it. The major issue of the discussion is whether possessing (and using) marijuana

is in fact a serious offense or no offense at all. This reason would be strengthened by stating: "Possessing marijuana is not as serious an offense as armed
robbery, rape, and murder, according to the overwhelming majority of legal
statutes and judicial decisions."

Reason: There are many other more serious offenses — such as armed robbery,
rape, and murder — for which criminals don't receive such stiff sentences.

Evaluation: The accuracy of this reason is highly doubtful. It is true that there
is wide variation in the sentences handed down for the same offense. The
sentences vary from state to state and also vary within states and even
within the same court. Nevertheless, on the whole, serious offenses like
armed robbery, rape, and murder do receive long prison sentences.

The real point here is that a fifteen-year sentence for possessing marijuana is
extremely unusual when compared with other sentences for marijuana possession.

Argument 2

Reason: Drugs pose a very serious threat to the young people of our country.

Evaluation: As the later discussion points out, this statement is much too
vague. "Drugs" cannot be treated as being all the same. Some drugs (such
as aspirin) are beneficial, while other drugs (such as heroin) are highly dangerous. To strengthen this reason, we would have to be more specific, stating, "Drugs like heroin, amphetamines, and cocaine pose a very serious
threat to the young people of our country." We could increase the accuracy
of the reason even more by adding the qualification "*some* of the young people of our country" because many young people are not involved with dangerous drugs.

Reason: Many crimes are committed to support drug habits.

Evaluation:

Argument 3

Reason: It's not right to punish someone unfairly just to provide an example.

Evaluation: This reason raises an interesting and complex ethical question that
has been debated for centuries. The political theorist Machiavelli stated that
"the ends justify the means," which implies that if we bring about desirable
results, it does not matter how we go about doing so. He would therefore
probably disagree with this reason since using someone as an example
might bring about desirable results, even though it might be personally
unfair to the person being used as an example. In our society, however,
which is based on the idea of fairness under the law, most people would
probably agree with this reason.

Reason: Smoking marijuana is nothing like using drugs such as heroin or even cocaine.

Evaluation:

T H I N K I N G   A C T I V I T Y   6.2

Evaluating the Truth of Reasons

Review the other arguments from the discussion on marijuana that you identified in Thinking Activity 6.1 (p. 197). Evaluate the truth of each of the reasons contained in the arguments.

Validity: Do the Reasons Support the Conclusion?

In addition to determining whether the reasons are true, evaluating arguments involves investigating the *relationship* between the reasons and the conclusion. When the reasons support the conclusion so that the conclusion follows from the reasons being offered, the argument is *valid.** If, however, the reasons do *not* support the conclusion so that the conclusion does *not* follow from the reasons being offered, the argument is *invalid.*

> **valid argument** *An argument in which the reasons support the conclusion so that the conclusion follows from the reasons offered*

> **invalid argument** *An argument in which the reasons do not support the conclusion so that the conclusion does not follow from the reasons offered*

One way to focus on the concept of validity is to *assume* that all the reasons in the argument are true and then try to determine how probable they make the conclusion. The following is an example of one type of valid argument:

---

* In formal logic, the term *validity* is reserved for deductively valid arguments in which the conclusions follow necessarily from the premises. (See the discussion of deductive arguments later in this chapter.)

Reason: Anything that is a threat to our health should not be legal.

Reason: Marijuana is a threat to our health.

Conclusion: Therefore, marijuana should not be legal.

This is a valid argument because if we assume that the reasons are true, then the conclusion necessarily follows. Of course, we may not agree that either or both of the reasons are true and thus not agree with the conclusion. Nevertheless, the *structure* of the argument is valid. This particular form of thinking is known as *deduction,* and we will examine deductive reasoning more closely in the pages ahead.

The following is a different type of argument:

Reason: As part of a project in my social science class, we selected 100 students in the school to be interviewed. We took special steps to ensure that these students were representative of the student body as a whole (total students: 4,386). We asked the selected students whether they thought the United States should actively try to overthrow foreign governments that the United States disapproves of. Of the 100 students interviewed, 88 students said the United States should definitely *not* be involved in such activities.

Conclusion: We can conclude that most students in the school believe the United States should not be engaged in attempts to actively overthrow foreign governments that the United States disapproves of.

This is a persuasive argument because if we assume that the reason is true, then it provides strong support for the conclusion. In this case, the key part of the reason is the statement that the 100 students selected were representative of the entire 4,386 students at the school. To evaluate the truth of the reason, we might want to investigate the procedure used to select the 100 students to determine whether this sample was in fact representative of all the students. This particular form of thinking is an example of *induction,* and we will explore inductive reasoning more fully in Chapter 7, "Reasoning Critically."

The following argument is an example of an invalid argument:

Reason: George W. Bush believes that the "Star Wars" missile defense shield should be built to ensure America's national defense, because it provides the capability to intercept incoming nuclear missiles.

Reason: George W. Bush is the president of the United States.

Conclusion: Therefore, the "Star Wars" missile defense shield should be built.

This argument is *not* valid because even if we assume that the reasons are true, the conclusion does not follow. Although George W. Bush is the president of the United States, that fact does not give him any special expertise on the subject of sophisticated radar designs for weapons systems. Indeed, this is a subject of such complexity and global significance that it should not be based on any one person's opinion, no matter who that person is. This form of invalid thinking is a type of *fallacy*, and we will investigate fallacious reasoning in Chapter 7.

The Soundness of Arguments

When an argument includes both true reasons and a valid structure, the argument is considered to be *sound*. When an argument has either false reasons or an invalid structure, however, the argument is considered to be *unsound*.

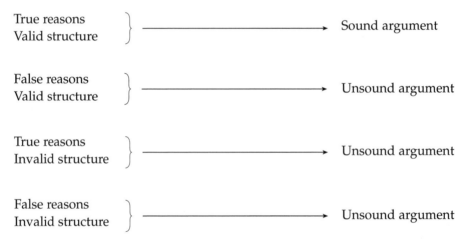

From this chart, we can see that in terms of arguments "truth" and "validity" are not the same concepts. An argument can have true reasons and an invalid structure or false reasons and a valid structure. In both cases the argument is *unsound*. To be sound, an argument must have both true reasons and a valid structure. For example, consider the following argument:

Reason: For a democracy to function most effectively, its citizens should be able to think critically about the important social and political issues.

Reason: Education plays a key role in developing critical thinking abilities.

Conclusion: Therefore, education plays a key role in ensuring that a democracy is functioning most effectively.

A good case could be made for the soundness of this argument because the reasons are persuasive and the argument structure is valid. Of course, someone might contend that one or both of the reasons are not completely true, which illustrates an important point about the arguments we construct and evaluate.

Many of the arguments we encounter in life fall somewhere between complete soundness and complete unsoundness because we are often not sure if our reasons are completely true. Throughout this book we have found that developing accurate beliefs is an ongoing process and that our beliefs are subject to clarification and revision. As a result, the conclusion of any argument can be only as certain as the reasons supporting the conclusion.

To sum up, evaluating arguments effectively involves both the truth of the reasons and the validity of the argument's structure. The degree of soundness an argument has depends on how accurate our reasons turn out to be and how valid the argument's structure is.

@ Understanding Deductive Arguments

We use a number of basic argument forms to organize, relate to, and make sense of the world. As already noted, two of the major types of argument forms are *deductive arguments* and *inductive arguments.* In the remainder of this chapter, we will explore various types of deductive arguments, reserving our analysis of inductive arguments for Chapter 7.

The deductive argument is the one most commonly associated with the study of logic. Though it has a variety of valid forms, they all share one characteristic: If you accept the supporting reasons (also called *premises*) as true, then you must necessarily accept the conclusion as true.

> **deductive argument** *An argument form in which one reasons from premises that are known or assumed to be true to a conclusion that follows necessarily from these premises*

For example, consider the following famous deductive argument:

Reason/Premise: All men are mortal.

Reason/Premise: Socrates is a man.

Conclusion: Therefore, Socrates is mortal.

In this example of deductive thinking, accepting the premises of the argument as true means that the conclusion necessarily follows; it cannot be false. Many deductive arguments, like the one just given, are structured as *syllogisms,* an argument form that consists of two supporting premises and a conclusion. There are also, however, a large number of *invalid* deductive forms, one of which is illustrated in the following syllogism:

Reason/Premise: All men are mortal.

Reason/Premise: Socrates is a man.

Conclusion: Therefore, all men are Socrates.

In the next several pages, we will briefly examine some common valid deductive forms.

Application of a General Rule

Whenever we reason with the form illustrated by the valid Socrates syllogism, we are using the following argument structure:

Premise: All *A* (men) are *B* (mortal).

Premise: *S* is an *A* (Socrates is a man).

Conclusion: Therefore, *S* is *B* (Socrates is mortal).

This basic argument form is valid no matter what terms are included. For example:

Premise: All politicians are untrustworthy.

Premise: Bill White is a politician.

Conclusion: Therefore, Bill White is untrustworthy.

Notice again that with any valid deductive form, *if* we assume that the premises are true, then we must accept the conclusion. Of course, in this case there is considerable doubt that the first premise is actually true.

When we diagram this argument form, it becomes clear why it is a valid way of thinking:

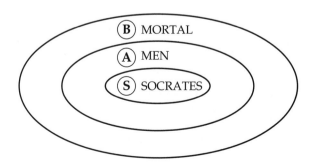

The *first premise* states that classification *A* (men) falls within classification *B* (mortal).

The *second premise* states that *S* (Socrates) is a member of classification *A* (men).

The *conclusion* simply states what has now become obvious — namely, that *S* (Socrates) must fall within classification *B* (mortal).

Although we are usually not aware of it, we use this basic type of reasoning whenever we apply a general rule in the form *All A is B*. For instance:

Premise: All children eight years old should be in bed by 9:30 P.M.

Premise: You are an eight-year-old child.

Conclusion: Therefore, you should be in bed by 9:30 P.M.

Review the dialogue at the beginning of this chapter and see if you can identify a deductive argument that uses this form.

Premise:

Premise:

Conclusion:

Describe an example from your own experience in which you use this deductive form.

Modus Ponens

A second valid deductive form that we commonly use in our thinking goes by the name *modus ponens* — that is, "affirming the antecedent" — and is illustrated in the following example:

Premise: If I have prepared thoroughly for the final exam, then I will do well.

Premise: I prepared thoroughly for the exam.

Conclusion: Therefore, I will do well on the exam.

When we reason like this, we are using the following argument structure:

Premise: If *A* (I have prepared thoroughly), then *B* (I will do well).

Premise: *A* (I have prepared thoroughly).

Conclusion: Therefore, *B* (I will do well).

Like all valid deductive forms, this form is valid no matter what specific terms are included. For example:

Premise: If the Democrats are able to register 20 million new voters, then they will win the presidential election.

Premise: The Democrats were able to register more than 20 million new voters.

Conclusion: Therefore, the Democrats will win the presidential election.

As with other valid argument forms, the conclusion will be true *if* the reasons are true. Although the second premise in this argument expresses information that can be verified, the first premise would be more difficult to establish.

Review the dialogue at the beginning of this chapter, and see if you can identify any deductive arguments that use this form.

Modus Tollens

A third commonly used valid deductive form has the name *modus tollens* — that is, "denying the consequence" — and is illustrated in the following example:

Premise: If Michael were a really good friend, he would lend me his car for the weekend.

Premise: Michael refuses to lend me his car for the weekend.

Conclusion: Therefore, Michael is not a really good friend.

When we reason in this fashion, we are using the following argument structure:

Premise: If A (Michael is a really good friend), then B (He will lend me his car).

Premise: Not B (He won't lend me his car).

Conclusion: Therefore, not A (He's not a really good friend).

Again, like other valid reasoning forms, this form is valid no matter what subject is being considered. For instance:

Premise: If Iraq were genuinely interested in world peace, it would not have invaded Kuwait.

Premise: Iraq did invade Kuwait (that is, Iraq did not "not invade" Kuwait).

Conclusion: Therefore, Iraq is not genuinely interested in world peace.

This conclusion — and any other conclusion produced by this form of reasoning — can be considered accurate if the reasons are true. In this case, the second premise would be easier to verify than the first.

Review the dialogue at the beginning of this chapter, and see if you can identify any deductive arguments that use this reasoning form.

Disjunctive Syllogism

A fourth common form of a valid deductive argument is known as a *disjunctive syllogism.* The term *disjunctive* means presenting several alternatives. This form is illustrated in the following example:

Premise: Either I left my wallet on my dresser, or I have lost it.

Premise: The wallet is not on my dresser.

Conclusion: Therefore, I must have lost it.

When we reason in this way, we are using the following argument structure:

Premise: Either A (I left my wallet on my dresser) or B (I have lost it).

Premise: Not A (I didn't leave it on my dresser).

Conclusion: Therefore, B (I have lost it).

This valid reasoning form can be applied to any number of situations and still yield valid results. For example:

Premise: Either your stomach trouble is caused by what you are eating, or it is caused by nervous tension.

Premise: You tell me that you have been taking special care with your diet.

Conclusion: Therefore, your stomach trouble is caused by nervous tension.

To determine the accuracy of the conclusion, we must determine the accuracy of the premises. If they are true, then the conclusion must be true.

Review the dialogue at the beginning of this chapter, and see if you can identify any deductive arguments that use this reasoning form.

All these basic argument forms — application of a general rule, *modus ponens, modus tollens,* and disjunctive syllogism — are found not only in informal, everyday conversations but also at more formal levels of thinking. They appear in academic disciplines, in scientific inquiry, in debates on social issues, and elsewhere. Many other argument forms — both deductive and inductive — also constitute human reasoning. By sharpening your understanding of these ways of thinking, you will be better able to make sense of the world by constructing and evaluating effective arguments.

THINKING ACTIVITY 6.3

Evaluating Arguments

Analyze the following arguments by completing these steps:

1. Summarize the reasons and conclusions given.

2. Identify which, if any, of the following deductive argument forms are used.

- Application of a general rule
- *Modus ponens* (affirming the antecedent)
- *Modus tollens* (denying the consequence)
- Disjunctive syllogism

3. Evaluate the truth of the reasons that support the conclusion.

For if the brain is a machine of ten billion nerve cells and the mind can somehow be explained as the summed activity of a finite number of chemical and electrical reactions, [then] boundaries limit the human prospect — we are biological and our souls cannot fly free.

— *Edward O. Wilson,* On Human Nature

The state is by nature clearly prior to the family and to the individual, since the whole is of necessity prior to the part.

— *Aristotle,* Politics

There now is sophisticated research that strongly suggests a deterrent effect [of capital punishment]. Furthermore, the principal argument against the deterrent effect is weak. The argument is that in most juris-dictions where capital punishment has been abolished there has been no immediate, sharp increase in what had been capital crimes. But in those jurisdictions, the actual act of abolition was an insignificant event because for years the death penalty had been imposed rarely, if at all. Common sense — which deserves deference until it is refuted—suggests that the fear of death can deter some premeditated crimes, including some murders.

— *George F. Will,* Cleveland Plain-Dealer, *March 13, 1981*

If the increased power which science has conferred upon human voli-tions is to be a boon and not a curse, the ends to which these volitions are directed must grow commensurately with the growth of power to carry them out. Hitherto, although we have been told on Sundays to love our neighbor, we have been told on weekdays to hate him, and there are six times as many weekdays as Sundays. Hitherto, the harm that we could do to our neighbor by hating him was limited by our incompetence, but in the new world upon which we are entering there will be no such limit, and the indulgence of hatred can lead only to ultimate and complete disaster.

— *Bertrand Russell, "The Expanding Mental Universe"*

The extreme vulnerability of a complex industrial society to intelligent, targeted terrorism by a very small number of people may prove the fatal challenge to which Western states have no adequate response. Counterforce alone will never suffice. The real challenge of the true terrorist is to the basic values of a society. If there is no commitment to shared values in Western society — and if none are imparted in our amoral institutions of higher learning — no increase in police and burglar alarms will suffice to preserve our society from the specter that haunts us — not a bomb from above but a gun from within.

— *James Billington, "The Gun Within"*

To fully believe in something, to truly understand something, one must be intimately acquainted with its opposite. One should not adopt a creed by default, because no alternative is known. Education should prepare students for the "real world" not by segregating them from evil but by urging full confrontation to test and modify the validity of the good.

— *Robert Baron, "In Defense of 'Teaching' Racism, Sexism, and Fascism"*

The inescapable conclusion is that society secretly *wants* crime, *needs* crime, and gains definite satisfactions from the present mishandling of it! We condemn crime; we punish offenders for it; but we need it. The crime and punishment ritual is a part of our lives. We need crimes to wonder at, to enjoy vicariously, to discuss and speculate about, and to publicly deplore. We need criminals to identify ourselves with, to envy secretly, and to punish stoutly. They do for us the forbidden, illegal things we *wish* to do and, like scapegoats of old, they bear the burdens of our displaced guilt and punishment — "the iniquities of us all."

— *Karl Menninger, "The Crime of Punishment"*

Final Thoughts

In this chapter we have focused mainly on deductive arguments, an argument form in which it is claimed that the premises constitute conclusive evidence for the truth of the conclusion. In a correct deductive argument, which is organized into a valid deductive form, if the premises are true, the conclusion must be true; it cannot be false.

Although *deductive* forms of reasoning are crucial to our understanding of the world and making informed decisions, much of our reasoning is nondeductive. The various nondeductive argument forms are typically included under the general category of *inductive* reasoning. In contrast to deductive arguments, inductive arguments rarely provide conclusions that are totally certain. The premises offer evidence in support of the conclusion, but the conclusion does not follow necessarily from the premises. We will explore the area of inductive reasoning more fully in the next chapter, "Reasoning Critically."

     THINKING   PASSAGE

Human Cloning

Evaluate the following article which carefully examines the repercussions of cloning a human embryo. The National Bioethics Advisory Commission (NBAC) was established by President Clinton in 1995 to provide guidance and suggestions regarding bioethical issues; this report details their conclusions.

CLONING HUMAN BEINGS*
by National Bioethics Advisory Commission

There is one basis of opposition to somatic cell nuclear transfer cloning on which almost everyone can agree. [A somatic cell is any cell of the embryo, fetus, child, or adult which contains a full complement of two sets of chromosomes; in contrast with a germ cell, i.e., an egg or a sperm, which contains only one set of chromosomes. During somatic cell nuclear transfer cloning, the nucleus — which contains a full set of chromosomes — is removed from the somatic cell and transferred to an egg cell which has had its nucleus removed.] There is virtually universal concern

---

* Reprinted from *Cloning Human Beings: Report and Recommendations of the National Bioethics Advisory Commission*, Rockville, Maryland, June 1997.

regarding the current safety of attempting to use this technique in human beings. Even if there were a compelling case in favor of creating a child in this manner, it would have to yield to one fundamental principle of both medical ethics and political philosophy — the injunction, as it is stated in the Hippocratic canon, to "first, do no harm." In addition, the avoidance of physical and psychological harm was established as a standard for research in the Nuremberg Code, 1946–49. At this time, the significant risks to the fetus and physical well-being of a child created by somatic cell nuclear transplantation cloning outweigh arguably beneficial uses of the technique.

It is important to recognize that the technique that produced Dolly the sheep was successful in only 1 of 277 attempts. If attempted in humans, it would pose the risk of hormonal manipulation in the egg donor; multiple miscarriages in the birth mother; and possibly severe developmental abnormalities in any resulting child. Clearly the burden of proof to justify such an experimental and potentially dangerous technique falls on those who would carry out the experiment. Standard practice in biomedical science and clinical care would never allow the use of a medical drug or device on a human being on the basis of such a preliminary study and without much additional animal research. Moreover, when risks are taken with an innovative therapy, the justification lies in the prospect of treating an illness in a patient; whereas, here no patient is at risk until the innovation is employed. Thus, no conscientious physician or Institutional Review Board should approve attempts to use somatic cell nuclear transfer to create a child at this time. For these reasons, prohibitions are warranted on all attempts to produce children through nuclear transfer from a somatic cell at this time.

A Difference of Opinion

Even on this point, however, NBAC [National Bioethics Advisory Committee] has noted some difference of opinion. Some argue, for example, that prospective parents are already allowed to conceive, or to carry a conception to term, when there is a significant risk — or even certainty — that the child will suffer from a serious genetic disease. Even when others think such conduct is morally wrong, the parents' right to reproductive freedom takes precedence. Since many of the risks believed to be associated with somatic cell nuclear transfer may be no greater than those associated with genetic disorders, some contend that such cloning should be subject to no more restriction than other forms of reproduction.

And, as in any new and experimental clinical procedure, harms cannot be accurately determined until trials are conducted in humans. Law professor John Robertson noted before NBAC on March 13, 1997 that:

> [The] first transfer [into a uterus] of a human [embryo] clone [will occur] before we know whether it will succeed. . . . [Some have argued therefore] that the first transfers are somehow unethical . . . experimentation on the resulting child, because one does not know what is going to happen, and one is . . . possibly leading to a child who could be disabled and have developmental difficulties. . . . [But the] child who would result would not have existed but for the procedure at issue, and [if] the intent there is actually to benefit that child by bringing it into being . . . [this] should be classified as experimentation for [the child's] benefit and thus it would fall within recognized exceptions. . . . We have a very different set of rules for experimentation intended to benefit [the experimental subject].

But the argument that somatic cell nuclear transfer cloning experiments are "beneficial" to the resulting child rest on the notion that it is a "benefit" to be brought into the world as compared to being left unconceived and unborn. This metaphysical argument, in which one is forced to compare existence with non-existence, is problematic. Not only does it require us to compare something unknowable — non-existence — with something else, it also can lead to absurd conclusions if taken to its logical extreme. For example, it would support the argument that there is no degree of pain and suffering that cannot be inflicted on a child, provided that the alternative is never to have been conceived. Even the originator of this line of analysis rejects this conclusion.

In addition, it is true that the actual risks of physical harm to the child born through somatic cell nuclear transfer cannot be known with certainty unless and until research is conducted on human beings. It is likewise true that if we insisted on absolute guarantees of no risk before we permitted any new medical intervention to be attempted in humans, this would severely hamper if not halt completely the introduction of new therapeutic interventions, including new methods of responding to infertility. The assertion that we should regard attempts at human cloning as "experimentation for [the child's] benefit" is not persuasive. . . .

Cloning and Individuality

The concept of creating a genetic twin, although separated in time, is one aspect of somatic cell nuclear transfer cloning that most find both troubling and fascinating. The phenomenon of identical twins has intrigued human cultures across the globe, and throughout history. It is easy to understand why identical twins hold such fascination. Common experience demonstrates how distinctly different twins are, both in personality and in personhood. At the same time, observers cannot help but imbue identical bodies with some expectation that identical persons occupy those bodies, since body and personality remain intertwined in human intuition. With the prospect of somatic cell nuclear transfer cloning comes a scientifically inaccurate but nonetheless instinctive fear of multitudes of identical bodies, each housing personalities that are somehow less than distinct, less unique, and less autonomous than usual.

Is there a moral or human right to a unique identity, and if so would it be violated by this manner of human cloning? For such somatic cell nuclear transfer cloning to violate a right to a unique identity, the relevant sense of identity would have to be genetic identity, that is, a right to a unique unrepeated genome. Even with the same genes, two individuals — for example, homozygous twins — are distinct and not identical, so what is intended must be the various properties and characteristics that make each individual qualitatively unique and different than others. Does having the same genome as another person undermine that unique qualitative identity?

Ignorance and Knowledge

Along these lines of inquiry some question whether reproduction using somatic cell nuclear transfer would violate what philosopher Hans Jonas called a right to ignorance, or what philosopher Joel Feinberg called a right to an open future, or what Martha Nussbaum called the quality of "separateness." Jonas argued that human cloning, in which there is a substantial time gap between the beginning of the lives of the earlier and later twin, is fundamentally different from the simultaneous beginning of the lives of homozygous twins that occur in nature.

Although contemporaneous twins begin their lives with the same genetic inheritance, they also begin their lives or biographies at the same time, in ignorance of what the twin who shares the same genome will by his or her choices make of his or her life. To whatever extent one's genome determines one's future, each life begins ignorant of what that determination will be, and so remains as free to choose a future as are individuals who do not have a twin. In this line of reasoning, ignorance of the effect of one's genome on one's future is necessary for the spontaneous, free, and authentic construction of a life and self.

A later twin created by cloning, Jonas argues, knows, or at least believes he or she knows, too much about him- or herself. For there is already in the world another person, one's earlier twin, who from the same genetic starting point has made the life choices that are still in the later twin's future. It will seem that one's life has already been lived and layed out by another, that one's fate is already determined, and so the later twin will lose the spontaneity of authentically creating and becoming his or her own self. One will lose the sense of human possibility in freely creating one's own future. It is tyrannical, Jonas claims, for the earlier twin to try to determine another's fate in this way.

And even if it is a mistake to believe such crude genetic determinism according to which one's genes determine one's fate, what is important for one's experience of freedom and ability to create a life for oneself is whether one thinks one's future is open and undetermined, and so still to be largely determined by one's own choices. One might try to interpret Jonas' objection so as not to assume either genetic determinism, or a belief in it. A later twin might grant that he or she is not destined to follow in his or her earlier twin's footsteps, but that nevertheless the earlier twin's life would always haunt the later twin, standing as an undue influence on the latter's life, and shaping it in ways to which others' lives are not vulnerable. . . .

Potential Harms to Important Social Values

Those with grave reservations about somatic cell nuclear transfer cloning ask us to imagine a world in which cloning human beings via somatic cell nuclear transfer were permitted and widely practiced. What kind of people, parents, and children would we become in such a world? Opponents fear that such cloning to create children may disrupt the interconnected web of social values, practices, and institutions that support the healthy growth of children. The use of such cloning techniques might encourage the undesirable attitude that children are to be valued according to how closely they meet parental expectations, rather than loved for their own sake. In this way of looking at families and parenting, certain values are at the heart of those relationships, values such as love, nurturing, loyalty, and steadfastness. In contrast, a world in which such cloning were widely practiced would give, the critics claim, implicit approval to vanity, narcissism, and avarice. To these critics, changes that undermine those deeply prized values should be avoided if possible. At a minimum, such undesirable changes should not be fostered by public policies. . . .

Treating People as Objects

Some opponents of somatic cell nuclear cloning fear that the resulting children will be treated as objects rather than as persons. This concern often underlies discussions of whether such cloning amounts to "making" rather than "begetting" children, or whether the child who is created in this manner will be viewed as less than a fully independent moral agent. In sum, will being cloned from the somatic cell of an existing person result in the child being regarded as less of a person whose humanity and dignity would not be fully respected?

One reason this discussion can be hard to capture and to articulate is that certain terms, such as "person," are used differently by different people. What is common to these various views, however, is a shared understanding that being a "person" is different from being the manipulated "object" of other people's desires and expectations. Writes legal scholar Margaret Radin,

> The person is a subject, a moral agent, autonomous and self-governing.
> An object is a non-person, not treated as a self-governing moral agent.
> . . . [By] "objectification of persons," we mean, roughly, "what Kant would not want us to do."

That is, to objectify a person is to act towards the person without regard for his or her own desires or well-being, as a thing to be valued according to externally imposed standards, and to control the person rather than to engage her or him in a mutually respectful relationship. Objectification, quite simply, is treating the child as an object — a creature less deserving of respect for his or her moral agency. Commodification is sometimes distinguished from objectification and concerns treating persons as commodities, including treating them as a thing that can be exchanged, bought or sold in the marketplace. To those who view the intentional choice by another of one's genetic makeup as a form of manipulation by others, somatic cell nuclear transfer cloning represents a form of objectification or commodification of the child.

Some may deny that objectification is any more a danger in somatic cell nuclear transfer cloning than in current practices such as genetic screening or, in the future perhaps, gene therapy. These procedures aim either to avoid having a child with a particular condition, or to compensate for a genetic abnormality. But to the extent that the technology is used to benefit the child by, for example, allowing early preventive measures with phenylketonuria, no objectification of the child takes place.

When such cloning is undertaken not for any purported benefit of the child himself or herself, but rather to satisfy the vanity of the nucleus donor, or even to serve the need of someone else, such as a dying child in need of a bone marrow donor, then some would argue that it goes yet another step toward diminishing the personhood of the child created in this fashion. The final insult, opponents argue, would come if the child created through somatic cell nuclear transfer is regarded as somehow less than fully equal to the other human beings, due to his or her diminished physical uniqueness and the diminished mystery surrounding some aspects of his or her future physical development.

Eugenic Concerns

The desire to improve on nature is as old as humankind. It has been played out in agriculture through the breeding of special strains of domesticated animals and plants. With the development of the field of genetics over the past 100 years came the hope that the selection of advantageous inherited characteristics — called eugenics, from the Greek *eugenes* meaning wellborn or noble in heredity — could be as beneficial to humankind as selective breeding in agriculture.

The transfer of directed breeding practices from plants and animals to human beings is inherently problematic, however. To begin, eugenic proposals require that several dubious and offensive assumptions be made. First, that most, if not all people would mold their reproductive behavior to the eugenic plan; in a country that values reproductive freedom, this outcome would be unlikely absent compulsion. Second, that means exist for deciding which human traits and characteristics would be favored, an enterprise that rests on notions of selective human superiority that have long been linked with racist ideology.

Equally important, the whole enterprise of "improving" humankind by eugenic programs oversimplifies the role of genes in determining human traits and characteristics. Little is known about the correlation between genes and the sorts of complex behavioral characteristics that are associated with successful and rewarding human lives; moreover, what little is known indicates that most such characteristics result from complicated interactions among a number of genes and the environment. While cows can be bred to produce more milk and sheep to have softer fleece, the idea of breeding humans to be superior would belong in the realm of science fiction even if one could conceive how to establish the metric of superiority, something that turns not only on the values and prejudices of those who construct the metric but also on the sort of a world they predict these specially bred persons would face.

Nonetheless, at the beginning of this century eugenic ideas were championed by scientific and political leaders and were very popular with the American public. It was not until they were practiced in such a grotesque fashion in Nazi Germany that their danger became apparent. Despite this sordid history and the very real limitations in what genetic selection could be expected to yield, the lure of "improvement" remains very real in the minds of some people. In some ways, creating people through somatic cell nuclear transfer offers eugenicists a much more powerful tool than any before. In selective breeding programs, such as the "germinal choice" method urged by the geneticist H. J. Muller a generation ago, the outcome depended on the usual "genetic lottery" that occurs each time a sperm fertilizes an egg, fusing their individual genetic heritages into a new individual. Cloning, by contrast, would allow the selection of a desired genetic prototype which would be replicated in each of the "offspring," at least on the level of the genetic material in the cell nucleus.

Objections to a Eugenics Program

It might be enough to object to the institution of a program of human eugenic cloning — even a voluntary program — that it would rest on false scientific premises and hence be wasteful and misguided. But that argument might not be sufficient to deter those people who want to push the genetic traits of a population in a particular direction. While acknowledging that a particular set of genes can be expressed in a variety of ways and therefore that cloning (or any other form of eugenic selection) does not guarantee a particular phenotypic manifestation of the genes, they might still argue that certain genes provide a better starting point for the next generation than other genes.

The answer to any who would propose to exploit the science of cloning in this way is that the moral problems with a program of human eugenics go far beyond practical objections of infeasibility. Some objections are those that have already been discussed in connection with the possible desire of individuals to use somatic cell nuclear transfer that the creation of a child under such circumstances could result in the child being objectified, could seriously undermine the value that ought to attach to each individual as an end in themselves, and could foster inappropriate efforts to control the course of the child's life according to expectations based on the life of the person who was cloned.

In addition to such objections are those that arise specifically because what is at issue in eugenics is more than just an individual act; it is a collective program. Individual acts may be undertaken for singular and often unknown or even unknowable reasons, whereas a eugenics program would propagate dogma about the sorts of people who are desirable and those who are dispensable. That is a path that humanity has tread before, to its everlasting shame. And it is a path to whose return the science of cloning should never be allowed to give even the slightest support. . . .

Cloning Is Unethical

In summary, the Commission reached several conclusions in considering the appropriateness of public policies regarding the creation of children through somatic cell nuclear transfer. First and foremost, creating children in this manner is unethical at this time because available scientific evidence indicates that such techniques are not safe at this time. Even if concerns about safety are resolved, however, significant concerns remain about the negative impact of the use of such a technology on both individuals and society. Public opinion on this issue may remain divided. Some people believe that cloning through somatic cell nuclear transfer will always be unethical because it . . . will always risk causing psychological or other harms to the resulting child. In addition, although the Commission acknowledged that there are cases for which the use of such cloning might be considered desirable by some people, overall these cases were insufficiently compelling to justify proceeding with the use of such techniques. . . .

Finally, many scenarios of creating children through somatic cell nuclear transfer are based on the serious misconception that selecting a child's genetic makeup is equivalent to selecting the child's traits or accomplishments. A benefit of more widespread discussion of such cloning would be a clearer recognition that a person's traits and achievements depend heavily on education, training, and the social environment, as well as on genes. Should this type of cloning proceed, however, any children born as a result of this technique should be treated as having the same rights and moral status as any other human being.

Questions for Analysis

After reading this article on human cloning, do the following:

1. Identify the arguments that were used, and summarize the reasons and conclusion for each.
2. Describe the types of argument forms that you identified.
3. Evaluate the *truth* of the reasons that support the conclusion for each of the arguments that you identified and the *validity* of the logical form.
4. Imagine that you have been asked by the president to prepare a position paper on human cloning that he can use to shape the government's policy. Construct an extended argument regarding human cloning. Be sure to include arguments on both sides of the issue, and conclude with your own reasoned analysis and conclusion. Be sure to include specific policy recommendations that you believe the government should take with respect to cloning.

7 Reasoning Critically

Inductive Reasoning
Reasoning from premises assumed
to be true to a conclusion supported
(but not logically) by the premises

Empirical Generalization
Drawing conclusions about a target
population based on observing
a sample population

Is the sample known?
Is the sample sufficient?
Is the sample representative?

Causal Reasoning
Concluding that an event is
the result of another event

Scientific Method
1. Identify an event for
   investigation
2. Gather information
3. Develop a theory/hypothesis
4. Test/experiment
5. Evaluate results

Fallacies
Unsound arguments
that can appear logical

**Fallacies of False
Generalization**

Hasty generalization
Sweeping generalization
False dilemma

Fallacies of Relevance
Appeal to authority
Appeal to tradition
Bandwagon
Appeal to pity
Appeal to fear
Appeal to flattery
Special pleading
Appeal to ignorance
Begging the question
Straw man
Red herring
Appeal to personal attack
Two wrongs make a right

Causal Fallacies
Questionable cause
Misidentification of
   the cause
*Post hoc ergo
   propter hoc*
Slippery slope

The Critical Thinker's Guide to Reasoning

Reasoning is the type of thinking that uses arguments — reasons in support of conclusions — to decide, explain, predict, and persuade. Effective reasoning involves using all of the intellectual skills and critical attitudes we have been developing in this book, and in this chapter we will further explore various dimensions of the reasoning process.

@ Inductive Reasoning

Chapter 6 focused primarily on *deductive reasoning*, an argument form in which one reasons from premises that are known or assumed to be true to a conclusion that follows necessarily from the premises. In this chapter we will examine *inductive reasoning*, an argument form in which one reasons from premises that are known or assumed to be true to a conclusion that is supported by the premises but does not follow logically from them.

> **inductive reasoning** *An argument form in which one reasons from premises that are known or assumed to be true to a conclusion that is supported by the premises but does not necessarily follow from them*

When you reason inductively, your premises provide evidence that makes it more or less probable (but not certain) that the conclusion is true. The following statements are examples of conclusions reached through inductive reasoning.

1. A recent Gallup poll reported that 74 percent of the American public believes that abortion should remain legalized.
2. On the average, a person with a college degree will earn over $1,140,000 more in his or her lifetime than a person with just a high school diploma.
3. In a recent survey twice as many doctors interviewed stated that if they were stranded on a desert island, they would prefer Bayer Aspirin to Extra Strength Tylenol.
4. The outbreak of food poisoning at the end-of-year school party was probably caused by the squid salad.
5. The devastating disease AIDS is caused by a particularly complex virus that may not be curable.

6. The solar system is probably the result of an enormous explosion — a "big bang" — that occurred billions of years ago.

The first three statements are forms of inductive reasoning known as *empirical generalization,* a general statement about an entire group made on the basis of observing some members of the group. The final three statements are examples of *causal reasoning,* a form of inductive reasoning in which it is claimed that an event (or events) is the result of the occurrence of another event (or events). We will be exploring the ways each of these forms of inductive reasoning functions in our lives and in various fields of study.

In addition to examining various ways of reasoning logically and effectively, we will also explore certain forms of reasoning that are not logical and, as a result, are usually not effective. These ways of pseudo-reasoning (false reasoning) are often termed *fallacies:* arguments that are not sound because of various errors in reasoning. Fallacious reasoning is typically used to influence others. It seeks to persuade not on the basis of sound arguments and critical thinking but rather on the basis of emotional and illogical factors.

> **fallacies** *Unsound arguments that are often persuasive and appearing to be logical because they usually appeal to our emotions and prejudices, and because they often support conclusions that we want to believe are accurate*

Empirical Generalization

One of the most important tools used by both natural and social scientists is empirical generalization. Have you ever wondered how the major television and radio networks can accurately predict election results hours before the polls close? These predictions are made possible by the power of *empirical generalization,* a first major type of inductive reasoning that is defined as reasoning from a limited sample to a general conclusion based on this sample.

> **empirical generalization** *A form of inductive reasoning in which a general statement is made about an entire group (the "target population") based on observing some members of the group (the "sample population")*

Network election predictions, as well as public opinion polls that occur throughout a political campaign, are based on interviews with a select number of people. Ideally, pollsters would interview everyone in the *target population* (in this case, voters), but this, of course, is hardly practical. Instead, they select a relatively small group of individuals from the target population, known as a *sample*, who they have determined will adequately represent the group as a whole. Pollsters believe that they can then generalize the opinions of this smaller group to the target population. And with a few notable exceptions (such as in the 1948 presidential election, when New York governor Thomas Dewey went to bed believing he had been elected president and woke up a loser to Harry Truman, and the 2000 election, when Al Gore was briefly declared the presidential winner over George W. Bush), these results are highly accurate.

There are three key criteria for evaluating inductive arguments:

- Is the sample known?
- Is the sample sufficient?
- Is the sample representative?

Is the Sample Known?

An inductive argument is only as strong as the sample on which it is based. For example, sample populations described in vague and unclear terms — "highly placed sources" or "many young people interviewed," for example — provide a treacherously weak foundation for generalizing to larger populations. In order for an inductive argument to be persuasive, the sample population should be explicitly *known* and clearly identified. Natural and social scientists take great care in selecting the members in the sample groups, and this is an important part of the data that is available to outside investigators who may wish to evaluate and verify the results.

Is the Sample Sufficient?

The second criterion for evaluating inductive reasoning is to consider the *size* of the sample. It should be sufficiently large enough to give an accurate sense of the group as a whole. In the polling example discussed earlier, we would be concerned if only a few registered voters had been interviewed, and the results of these interviews were then generalized to a much larger population. Overall, the larger the sample, the more reliable the inductive conclusions. Natural and social scientists have developed precise guidelines for determining the size of the sample needed to achieve reliable results. For example, poll results are often accompanied by a qualification such as "These results are subject to an error factor of ± 3 percentage points." This means that if the sample reveals that 47 percent of those interviewed prefer candidate X, then we can reliably state that 44 to 50 percent of the target population prefer candidate X. Because a sample is usually a small portion of the target population, we can rarely state that the two match each other exactly — there must always be some room for variation. The exceptions to this are situations in which the target population is completely homogeneous. For example, tasting one cookie from a bag of cookies is usually enough to tell us whether or not the entire bag is stale.

Is the Sample Representative?

The third crucial element in effective inductive reasoning is the *representativeness* of the sample. If we are to generalize with confidence from the sample to the target population, then we have to be sure the sample is similar to the larger group from which it is drawn in all relevant aspects. For instance, in the polling example the sample population should reflect the same percentage of men and women, of Democrats and Republicans, of young and old, and so on, as the target population. It is obvious that many characteristics, such as hair color, favorite food, and shoe size, are not relevant to the comparison. The better the sample reflects the target population in terms of *relevant* qualities, the better the accuracy of the generalizations. However, when the sample is *not* representative of the target population — for example, if the election pollsters interviewed only females between the ages of thirty and thirty-five — then the sample is termed *biased*, and any generalizations about the target population will be highly suspect.

How do we ensure that the sample is representative of the target population? One important device is *random selection*, a selection strategy in which every member of the target population has an equal chance of being included in the sample. For example, the various techniques used to select winning lottery tickets are supposed to be random — each ticket is supposed to have an equal chance of winning. In complex cases of inductive reasoning — such as polling — random selection is often combined with the confirmation that all of the important categories in the population are adequately represented. For example, an election pollster would want to be certain that all significant geographical areas are included and then would randomly select individuals from within those areas to compose the sample.

Understanding the principles of empirical generalization is of crucial importance to effective thinking because we are continually challenged to construct and evaluate this form of inductive argument in our lives.

THINKING ACTIVITY 7.1

Evaluating Inductive Arguments

Review the following examples of inductive arguments. For each argument, evaluate the quality of the thinking by answering the following questions:

1. Is the sample known?
2. Is the sample sufficient?
3. Is the sample representative?
4. Do you believe the conclusions are likely to be accurate? Why or why not?

Link Between Pornography and Antisocial Behavior?   In a study of a possible relationship between pornography and antisocial behavior, questionnaires went out to 7,500 psychiatrists and psychoanalysts whose listing in the directory of the American Psychological Association indicated clinical experience. Over 3,400 of these professionals responded. The result: 7.4 percent of the psychiatrists and psychologists had cases in which they were convinced that pornography was a causal factor in antisocial behavior; an additional 9.4 percent were suspicious; 3.2 percent did not commit themselves; and 80 percent said they had no cases in which a causal connection was suspected.

To Sleep, Perchance to Die?   A survey by the Sleep Disorder Clinic of the VA hospital in La Jolla, California (involving more than one million people), revealed that people who sleep more than ten hours a night have a death rate 80 percent higher than those who sleep only seven or eight hours. Men who sleep less than four hours a night have a death rate 180 percent higher, and women with less [than four hours] sleep have a rate 40 percent higher. This might be taken as indicating that too much or too little sleep causes death.

"U.S. Wastes Food Worth Millions"   Americans in the economic middle waste more food than their rich and poor counterparts, according to a study published Saturday. Carried out in Tucson, Arizona, by University of Arizona students under the direction of Dr. William L. Rathje, the study analyzed 600 bags of garbage each week for three years from lower-, middle-, and upper-income neighborhoods. They found that city residents throw out around 10 percent of the food they took home — about 9,500 tons of food each year. The figure amounts to $9 to $11 million worth of food. Most of the waste occurred in middle-class neighborhoods. Both the poor and the wealthy were significantly more frugal.

One in Four British Couples Regret Marriage   One in four British married couples regret the day they tied the knot, a national poll conducted for *Reader's Digest* magazine showed. Middle-aged couples were five times more likely to dream of having a dog rather than fantasize about having an affair. Forty-four percent of women surveyed admitted having a secret they would never tell their husband, against 39 percent of men. Some 22 percent of men under 45 wanted their wives to be more affectionate, and 40 percent wanted to spend more time with their wives. "Men want to talk more — we'd always thought it was women," the editor-in-chief of *Reader's Digest* said. "The state of marriage in Britain in 2002 is puzzling and contradictory," he added.

Young People's Moral Compass   A recent survey of 5,012 students from fourth grade through high school yields important insights about how young people make moral decisions. Asked how they would decide what to do if "unsure of what was right or wrong in a particular situation," these were the responses and how they were described by the researchers:

- 23 percent said they would "do what was best for everyone involved," an orientation the researchers labeled "civic humanist."

- 20 percent would "follow the advice of an authority, such as a parent, teacher, or youth leader" — "conventionalist."

- 18 percent of respondents said they would do what would make them "happy" — "expressivist."

- 16 percent would "do what God or Scriptures" say "is right" — "theistic."

- 10 percent would "do what would improve their own situations" — "utilitarian."

- 9 percent did not know, and 3 percent wrote that they would follow their "conscience."

When young people were asked their beliefs about anything from lying, stealing, and using drugs to abortion or reasons for choosing a job, these rudimentary ethical systems or "moral compasses" turned out to be more important than the background factors that social scientists habitually favor in their search for explanations, like economic status, sex, race, and even religious practice.

THINKING ACTIVITY 7.2

Designing a Poll

Select an issue that you would like to poll a group of people about — for example, the population of your school or your neighborhood. Describe in specific terms how you would go about constructing a sample both large and representative enough for you to generalize the results to the target population accurately.

Fallacies of False Generalization

Although generalizing and interpreting are useful in forming concepts, they also can give rise to fallacious ways of thinking, including the following:

- Hasty generalization
- Sweeping generalization
- False dilemma

Hasty Generalization

Consider the following examples of reasoning. Do you think that the arguments are sound? Why or why not?

> My boyfriends have never shown any real concern for my feelings. My conclusion is that men are insensitive, selfish, and emotionally superficial.

> My mother always gets upset over insignificant things. This leads me to believe that women are very emotional.

In both of these cases, a general conclusion has been reached that is based on a very small sample. As a result, the reasons provide very weak support for the conclusions that are being developed. It just does not make good sense to generalize from a few individuals to all men or all women. The conclusions are *hasty* because the samples are not large enough and/or not representative enough to provide adequate justification for the generalization.

Of course, many generalizations are more warranted than the two given here because the conclusion is based on a sample that is larger and more representative of the group as a whole. For example:

> I have done a lot of research in a variety of automotive publications on the relationship between the size of cars and the gas mileage they get. In general, I think it makes sense to conclude that large cars tend to get fewer miles per gallon than smaller cars.

In this case, the conclusion is generalized from a larger and more representative sample than those in the preceding two arguments. As a result, the reason for the last argument provides much stronger support for the conclusion.

Sweeping Generalization

Whereas the fallacy of hasty generalization deals with errors in the process of generalizing, the fallacy of *sweeping generalization* focuses on difficulties in the process of interpreting. Consider the following examples of reasoning. Do you think that the arguments are sound? Why or why not?

> Vigorous exercise contributes to overall good health. Therefore, vigorous exercise should be practiced by recent heart attack victims, people who are out of shape, and women who are about to give birth.

> People should be allowed to make their own decisions, providing that their actions do not harm other people. Therefore, people who are trying to commit suicide should be left alone to do what they want.

In both of these cases, generalizations that are true in most cases have been deliberately applied to instances that are clearly intended to be exceptions to the generalizations because of special features that the exceptions possess. Of course, the use of sweeping generalizations stimulates us to clarify the generalization, rephrasing it to exclude instances, like those given here, that have special features. For example, the first generalization could be reformulated as

"Vigorous exercise contributes to overall good health, *except for* recent heart attack victims, people out of shape, and women who are about to give birth." Sweeping generalizations become dangerous only when they are accepted without critical analysis and reformulation.

Review the following examples of sweeping generalizations, and in each case (a) explain *why* it is a sweeping generalization and (b) reformulate the statement so that it becomes a legitimate generalization.

1. A college education stimulates you to develop as a person and prepares you for many professions. Therefore, all persons should attend college, no matter what career they are interested in.

2. Drugs such as heroin and morphine are addictive and therefore qualify as dangerous drugs. This means that they should never be used, even as painkillers in medical situations.

3. Once criminals have served time for the crimes they have committed, they have paid their debt to society and should be permitted to work at any job they choose.

False Dilemma

The fallacy of the *false dilemma* — also known as the "either/or" fallacy or the "black-or-white" fallacy — occurs when we are asked to choose between two extreme alternatives without being able to consider additional options. For example, we may say, "Either you're for me or against me," meaning that a choice has to be made between these alternatives. Sometimes giving people only two choices on an issue makes sense ("If you decide to swim the English Channel, you'll either make it or you won't"). At other times, however, viewing situations in such extreme terms may be a serious oversimplification — for it would mean viewing a complicated situation in terms that are too simple.

The following statements are examples of false dilemmas. After analyzing the fallacy in each case, suggest different alternatives than those being presented.

Example: "Everyone in Germany is a National Socialist — the few outside the party are either lunatics or idiots." (Adolf Hitler, quoted by the New York Times, *April 5, 1938)*

Analysis: This is an oversimplification. Hitler is saying that if you are not a Nazi, then you are a lunatic or an idiot. By limiting the population to these groups, Hitler was simply ignoring all the people who did not qualify as Nazis, lunatics, or idiots.

1. America — love it or leave it!
2. She loves me; she loves me not.
3. Live free or die.
4. If you're not part of the solution, then you're part of the problem. (Eldridge Cleaver)
5. If you know about BMW, you either own one or you want to.

◎ Causal Reasoning

A second major type of inductive reasoning is *causal reasoning,* a form in which an event (or events) is claimed to be the result of the occurrence of another event (or events).

causal reasoning *A form of inductive reasoning in which an event (or events) is claimed to be the result of another event (or events)*

As you use your thinking abilities to try to understand the world you live in, you often ask the question "Why did that happen?" For example, if the engine of your car is running roughly, your natural question is "What's wrong?" If you wake up one morning with an upset stomach, you usually ask yourself, "What's the cause?" Or maybe the softball team you belong to has been losing recently. You typically wonder, "What's going on?" In each of these cases you assume that there is some factor (or factors) responsible for what is occurring, some *cause* (or causes) that results in the *effect* (or effects) you are observing (the rough engine, the upset stomach, the losing team).

Causality is one of the basic patterns of thinking we use to organize and make sense of our experience. For instance, imagine how bewildered you would feel if a mechanic looked at your car and told you there was no explanation for the poorly running engine. Or suppose you go to the doctor with an upset stomach, he examines you and then concludes that there is no possible causal explanation for the malady. In each case you would be understandably skeptical of the diagnosis and would probably seek another opinion.

The Scientific Method

Causal reasoning is also the backbone of the natural and social sciences; it is responsible for the remarkable understanding of our world that has been achieved. The *scientific method* works on the assumption that the world is constructed in a complex web of causal relationships that can be discovered through systematic investigation. Scientists have devised an organized approach for discovering causal relationships and testing the accuracy of conclusions. The sequence of steps is as follows:

1. Identify an event or a relationship between events to be investigated.
2. Gather information about the event (or events).
3. Develop a hypothesis or theory to explain what is happening.
4. Test the hypothesis or theory through experimentation.
5. Evaluate the hypothesis or theory based on experimental results.

How does this sequence work when applied to the situation of the rough-running engine mentioned earlier?

1. *Identify an event or a relationship between events to be investigated.* In this case, the event is obvious — your car's engine is running poorly, and you want to discover the cause of the problem so that you can fix it.
2. *Gather information about the event (or events).* This step involves locating any relevant information about the situation that will help solve the problem. You initiate this step by asking and trying to answer a variety of questions: When did the engine begin running poorly? Was this change abrupt or gradual? When did the car last have a tune-up? Are there other mechanical difficulties that might be related? Has anything unusual occurred with the car recently?
3. *Develop a hypothesis or theory to explain what is happening.* After reviewing the relevant information, you will want to identify the most likely explanation of what has happened. This possible explanation is known as a *hypothesis*. (A *theory* is normally a more complex model that involves a number of interconnected hypotheses, such as the theory of quantum mechanics in physics.)

hypothesis *A possible explanation that is introduced to account for a set of facts and that can be used as a basis for further investigation*

VISUAL THINKING

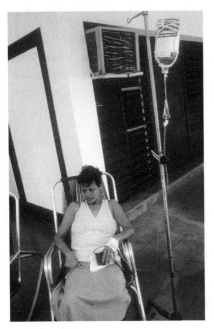 

Curing Disease

- The woman in the photo on the left is an AIDS patient living under quarantine. As depicted in the photo on the right, many thousands of scientists around the world are actively seeking cures for a wide range of human illnesses, including AIDS, the plague of our times. Do you know anyone who is engaged in disease-related research?

Although your hypothesis may be suggested by the information you have, it goes beyond the information as well and so must be tested before you commit yourself to it. In this case the hypothesis you might settle on is "water in the gas." This hypothesis was suggested by your recollection that the engine troubles began right after you bought gas in the pouring rain. This hypothesis may be correct or it may be incorrect — you have to test it to find out.

When you devise a plausible hypothesis to be tested, you should keep three general guidelines in mind:

- *Explanatory power:* The hypothesis should effectively explain the event you are investigating. The hypothesis that damaged windshield wipers are causing the engine problem doesn't seem to provide an adequate explanation of the difficulties.

- *Economy:* The hypothesis should not be unnecessarily complex. The explanation that your engine difficulty is the result of sabotage by an unfriendly neighbor is possible but unlikely. There are simpler and more direct explanations you should test first.

- *Predictive power:* The hypothesis should allow you to make various predictions to test its accuracy. If the "water in the gas" hypothesis is accurate, you can predict that removing the water from the gas tank and gas line should clear up the difficulty.

4. *Test the hypothesis or theory through experimentation.* Once you identify a hypothesis that meets these three guidelines, the next task is to devise an experiment to test its accuracy. In the case of your troubled car you would test your hypothesis by pouring several containers of "dry gas" into the tank, blowing out the gas line, and cleaning the carburetor. By removing the moisture in the gas system, you should be able to determine whether your hypothesis is correct.

5. *Evaluate the hypothesis or theory based on experimental results.* After reviewing the results of your experiment, you usually can assess the accuracy of your hypothesis. If the engine runs smoothly after you remove moisture from the gas line, then this strong evidence supports your hypothesis. If the engine does *not* run smoothly after your efforts, then this persuasive evidence suggests that your hypothesis is not correct. There is, however, a third possibility. Removing the moisture from the gas system might improve the engine's performance somewhat but not entirely. In that case you might want to construct a *revised* hypothesis along the lines of "Water in the gas system is partially responsible for my rough-running engine, but another cause (or causes) might be involved as well."

If the evidence does not support your hypothesis or supports a revised version of it, you then begin the entire process again by identifying and testing a new hypothesis. The natural and social sciences engage in an ongoing process of developing theories and hypotheses and testing them through experimental design. Many theories and hypotheses are much more complex than our "moisture in the gas" example and take years of generating, revising, and testing. Determining the subatomic structure of the universe and finding cures for various kinds of cancers, for example, have been the subjects of countless theories and hypotheses, as well as experiments to test their accuracy. We might diagram this operation of the scientific process as follows:

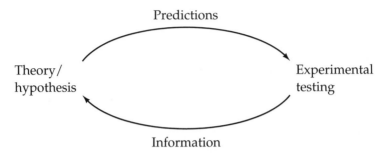

Acceptance, rejection, or revision
of the theory/hypothesis

THINKING ACTIVITY 7.3

Applying the Scientific Method

Select one of the following situations, or describe a situation of your own choosing. Then analyze the situation by working through the various steps of the scientific method listed directly after.

- Situation 1: You wake up in the morning with an upset stomach.

- Situation 2: Your grades have been declining all semester.

- Situation 3: (Your own choosing)

1. *Identify an event or a relationship between events to be investigated.* Describe the situation you have selected.

2. *Gather information about the event (or events).* Elaborate the situation by providing additional details. Be sure to include a variety of possible causes for the event. (For example, an upset stomach might be the result of food poisoning, the flu, anxiety, etc.).

3. *Develop a theory or hypothesis to explain what is happening.* Based on the information you have described, identify a plausible hypothesis that (a) explains what occurred, (b) is clear and direct, and (c) leads to predictions that can be tested.

4. *Test the theory or hypothesis through experimentation.* Design a way of testing your hypothesis that results in evidence proving or disproving it.

5. *Evaluate the theory or hypothesis.* Describe the results of your experiment and explain whether the results lead you to accept, reject, or revise your hypothesis.

THINKING ACTIVITY 7.4

Evaluating Experimental Results

Read the following experimental situations. For each situation

1. Describe the proposed causal relationship (the theory or hypothesis).

2. Evaluate
   a. The representativeness of the sample
   b. The randomness of the division into experimental and control groups

3. Explain how well the experimental results support the proposed theory or hypothesis.

Counseling May Diminish Chance of Heart Attack   A study released last week indicates that Type A individuals, who are characteristically impatient, competitive, insecure, and short-tempered, can halve their chances of having a heart attack by changing their behavior with the help of psychological counseling.

In 1978, scientists at Mt. Zion Hospital and Medical Center in San Francisco and Stanford University School of Education began their study of 862 predominantly male heart attack victims. Of this number, 592 received group counseling to ease their Type A behavior and improve their self-esteem. After three years, only 7 percent had another heart attack, compared with 13 percent of a matched group of 270 subjects who received only cardiological advice. Among 328 men who continued with the counseling for the full three years, 79 percent reduced their Type A behavior. About half of the comparison group was similarly able to slow down and cope better with stress.

Mortality Shown to Center Around Birthdays   A new study, based on 2,745,149 deaths from natural causes, has found that men tend to die just before their birthdays, while women tend to die just after their birthdays. Thus an approaching birthday seems to prolong the life of women and precipitate death in men. The study, published in the journal *Psychosomatic Medicine*, found 3 percent more deaths than expected among women in the week after a birthday and a slight decline the week before. For men, deaths peaked just before birthdays and showed no rise above normal afterward.

Few People Get Sufficient Sleep   Experts in sleep behavior and sleep disorders have found that a majority of people are sleeping at least an hour to 90 minutes less each night than they should, based on a series of studies of several hundred college and graduate students between the ages of 18 and 30. In one representative experiment with young adults who were generally healthy and got an average of seven to eight hours sleep a night, sleep researchers discovered that 20 percent of these apparently normal students could fall asleep almost instantaneously throughout the day if allowed to lie down in a darkened room, evidence that they were sleep deprived. Researchers further discovered that even the students who seemed alert and did not quickly fall asleep under test conditions could benefit from more sleep. If they spent one week getting to bed an hour to 90 minutes earlier than usual, the students improved their performance markedly on psychological and cognitive tests.

A Shorter Life for Lefties   A survey of 5,000 people by Stanley Coren found that while 15 percent of the population at age 10 was left-handed, there was a pronounced drop-off as people grew older, leaving 5 percent among 50-year-olds and less than 1 percent for those aged 80 and above. Where have all the lefties gone? They seem to have died. Lefties have a shorter life expectancy than righties, by an average of 9 years in the general population, apparently due to the ills and accidents they are more likely to suffer by having to live in a "right-handed world."

Nuns Offer Clues to Alzheimer's and Aging   The famous "Nun Study" is considered by experts on aging to be one of the most innovative efforts to answer questions about who gets Alzheimer's disease and why. Studying 678 nuns at seven convents has shown that folic acid may help stave off Alzheimer's disease, and that early language ability may be linked to lower risk of Alzheimer's because nuns who packed more ideas into the sentences of their early autobiographies were less likely to get Alzheimer's disease six decades later. Also, nuns who expressed more positive emotions in their autobiographies lived significantly longer — in some cases 10 years longer — than those expressing fewer positive emotions.

On the Tongue, Fat Passes Taste Test   Researchers are proposing a new entry to the list of tastes, like sweet and salty, that the tongue can discern. It's called fat, and it appears to have a flavor of its own. The researchers did an experiment in which subjects were allowed to taste fat or smell it, or both, but not eat it. The subjects were given crackers with cream cheese to smell or chew, but not swallow. Some who chewed also wore nose plugs, so that they could not smell the food. Just having cream cheese in the mouth, whether subjects could smell it or not, led to increased levels of blood fat. Merely smelling the cheese did not. The only explanation left, researchers say, is that the tongue can perceive a flavor in fat.

◎ Causal Fallacies

Because causality plays such a dominant role in the way we make sense of the world, it is not surprising that people make many mistakes and errors in judgment in trying to determine causal relationships. The following are some of the most common fallacies associated with causality:

- Questionable cause
- Misidentification of the cause
- *Post hoc ergo propter hoc*
- Slippery slope

Questionable Cause

The fallacy of *questionable cause* occurs when someone presents a causal relationship for which no real evidence exists. Superstitious beliefs, such as "If you break a mirror, you will have seven years of bad luck," usually fall into this category. Some people feel that astrology, a system of beliefs tying one's personality and fortunes in life to the position of the planets at the moment of birth, also falls into this category.

Consider the following passage from St. Augustine's *Confessions*. Does it seem to support or deny the causal assertions of astrology? Why or why not?

Firminus had heard from his father that when his mother had been pregnant with him, a slave belonging to a friend of his father's was also about to bear. It happened that since the two women had their babies at the same instant, the men were forced to cast exactly the same horoscope for each newborn child down to the last detail, one for his son, the other for the little slave. Yet Firminus, born to wealth in his parents' house, had one of the more illustrious careers in life whereas the slave had no alleviation of his life's burden.

Other examples of this fallacy include explanations like those given by four-teenth-century sufferers of the bubonic plague who claimed that "the Jews are poisoning the Christians' wells." This was particularly nonsensical since an equal percentage of Jews were dying of the plague as well. The evidence did not support the explanation.

Misidentification of the Cause

In causal situations we are not always certain about what is causing what — in other words, what is the cause and what is the effect. *Misidentifying the cause* is easy to do. For example, which are the causes and which are the effects in the following pairs of items? Why?

- Poverty and alcoholism

- Headaches and tension

- Failure in school and personal problems

- Shyness and lack of confidence

- Drug dependency and emotional difficulties

Of course, sometimes a third factor is responsible for both of the effects we are examining. For example, the headaches and tension we are experiencing may both be the result of a third element — such as some new medication we are taking. When this occurs, we are said to commit the fallacy of *ignoring a common cause*. There also exists the fallacy of *assuming a common cause* — for example, assuming that both a sore toe and an earache stem from the same cause.

Post Hoc Ergo Propter Hoc

The translation of the Latin phrase *post hoc ergo propter hoc* is "After it, there-fore because of it." It refers to those situations in which, because two things occur close together in time, we assume that one caused the other. For exam-ple, if your team wins the game each time you wear your favorite shirt, you might be tempted to conclude that the one event (wearing your favorite shirt) has some influence on the other event (winning the game). As a result, you might continue to wear this shirt "for good luck." It is easy to see how this sort of mistaken thinking can lead to all sorts of superstitious beliefs.

Consider the causal conclusion arrived at by Mark Twain's fictional charac-ter Huckleberry Finn in the following passage. How would you analyze the conclusion that he comes to?

I've always reckoned that looking at the new moon over your left shoulder is one of the carelessest and foolishest things a body can do. Old Hank Bunker done it once, and bragged about it; and in less than two years he got drunk and fell off a shot tower and spread himself out so that he was just a kind of layer. . . . But anyway, it all come of looking at the moon that way, like a fool.

Can you identify any of your own superstitious beliefs or practices that might have been the result of *post hoc* thinking?

Slippery Slope

The causal fallacy of *slippery slope* is illustrated in the following advice:

Don't miss that first deadline, because if you do, it won't be long before you're missing all your deadlines. This will spread to the rest of your life, as you will be late for every appointment. This terminal procrastination will ruin your career, and friends and relatives will abandon you. You will end up a lonely failure who is unable to ever do anything on time.

Slippery slope thinking asserts that one undesirable action will inevitably lead to a worse action, which will necessarily lead to a worse one still, all the way down the "slippery slope" to some terrible disaster at the bottom. Although this progression may indeed happen, there is certainly no causal guarantee that it will. Create slippery slope scenarios for one of the following warnings:

- If you get behind on one credit card payment . . .

- If you fail that first test . . .

- If you eat that first fudge square . . .

Review the causal fallacies just described and then identify and explain the reasoning pitfalls illustrated in the following examples:

- The person who won the lottery says that she dreamed the winning numbers. I'm going to start writing down the numbers in my dreams.

- Yesterday I forgot to take my vitamins, and I immediately got sick. That mistake won't happen again!

- I'm warning you — if you start missing classes, it won't be long before you flunk out of school and ruin your future.

VISUAL THINKING

Slipping and Sliding

● The fallacy of slippery slope suggests that one undesirable action will inevitably lead to others, taking you down the "slippery slope" to some unavoidable terrible disaster at the bottom. Can you think of an example in which you have used this kind of thinking ("If you continue to _____, then things will get progressively worse until you ultimately find yourself _____")? What are some strategies for clarifying this sort of fallacious thinking?

- I always take the first seat in the bus. Today I took another seat, and the bus broke down. And you accuse me of being superstitious!

- I think the reason I'm not doing well in school is that I'm just not interested. Also, I simply don't have enough time to study.

Many people want us to see the cause and effect relationships that they believe exist, and they often utilize questionable or outright fallacious reasoning. Consider the following examples:

- Politicians assure us that a vote for them will result in "a chicken in every pot and a car in every garage."

- Advertisers tell us that using this detergent will leave our wash "cleaner than clean, whiter than white."
- Doctors tell us that eating a balanced diet will result in better health.
- Educators tell us that a college degree is worth an average of $1,140,000 additional income over an individual's life.
- Scientists inform us that nuclear energy will result in a better life for all.

In an effort to persuade us to adopt a certain point of view, each of these examples makes certain causal claims about how the world operates. As critical thinkers, it is our duty to evaluate these various causal claims in an effort to figure out whether they are sensible ways of organizing the world.

Explain how you might go about evaluating whether each of the following causal claims makes sense:

Example: *Taking the right vitamins will improve health.*

Evaluation: *Review the medical research that examines the effect of taking vitamins on health; speak to a nutritionist; speak to a doctor.*

- Sweet Smell deodorant will keep you drier all day long.
- Allure perfume will cause people to be attracted to you.
- Natural childbirth will result in a more fulfilling birth experience.
- Aspirin Plus will give you faster, longer-lasting relief from headaches.
- Listening to loud music will damage your hearing.

◎ Fallacies of Relevance

Many fallacious arguments appeal for support to factors that have little or nothing to do with the argument being offered. In these cases, false appeals substitute for sound reasoning and a critical examination of the issues. Such appeals, known as *fallacies of relevance*, include the following kinds of fallacious thinking, which are grouped by similarity into "fallacy families":

- Appeal to authority
- Appeal to tradition
- Bandwagon

- Appeal to pity
- Appeal to fear
- Appeal to flattery
- Special pleading

- Appeal to ignorance
- Begging the question
- Straw man
- Red herring
- Appeal to personal attack
- Two wrongs make a right

Appeal to Authority

In Chapter 4, "Perceiving, Believing, and Knowing," we explored the ways in which we sometimes *appeal to authorities* to establish our beliefs or prove our points. At that time, we noted that to serve as a basis for beliefs, authorities must have legitimate expertise in the area in which they are advising — like an experienced mechanic diagnosing a problem with your car. People, however, often appeal to authorities who are not qualified to give an expert opinion. Consider the reasoning in the following advertisements. Do you think the arguments are sound? Why or why not?

> Hi. You've probably seen me out on the football field. After a hard day's work crushing halfbacks and sacking quarterbacks, I like to settle down with a cold, smooth Maltz beer.

> SONY. Ask anyone.

> Over 11 million women will read this ad. Only 16 will own the coat.

Each of these arguments is intended to persuade us of the value of a product through appeal to various authorities. In the first case, the authority is a well-known sports figure; in the second, the authority is large numbers of people; and in the third, the authority is a select few, appealing to our desire to be exclusive ("snob appeal"). Unfortunately, none of these authorities offer legitimate expertise about the product. Football players are not beer experts; large numbers of people are often misled; exclusive groups of people are frequently mistaken in their beliefs. To evaluate authorities properly, we have to ask:

- What are the professional credentials on which the authorities' expertise is based?

- Is their expertise in the area they are commenting on?

Appeal to Tradition

A member of the same fallacy family as appeal to authority, *appeal to tradition* argues that a practice or way of thinking is "better" or "right" simply because it is older, it is traditional, or it has "always been done that way." Although traditional beliefs often express some truth or wisdom — for example, "Good nutrition, exercise, and regular medical check-ups are the foundation of good health" — traditional beliefs are often misguided or outright false. Consider, for example, the belief that "intentional bleeding is a source of good health because it lets loose evil vapors in the body" or traditional practices like Victorian rib-crushing corsets or Chinese footbinding. How do we tell which traditional beliefs or practices have merit? We need to think critically, evaluating the value based on informed reasons and compelling evidence. Critically evaluate the following traditional beliefs:

- Spare the rod and spoil the child.

- Children should be seen and not heard.

- Never take "no" for an answer.

- I was always taught that a woman's place was in the home, so pursuing a career is out of the question for me.

- Real men don't cry — that's the way I was brought up.

Bandwagon

Joining the illogical appeals to authority and tradition, the fallacy *bandwagon* relies on the uncritical acceptance of others' opinions, in this case because "everyone believes it." People experience this all the time through "peer pressure," when an unpopular view is squelched and modified by the group opinion. For example, you may change your opinion when confronted with the threat of ridicule or rejection from your friends. Or you may modify your point of view at work or in your religious organization in order to conform to the prevailing opinion. In all of these cases your views are being influenced by a desire to "jump on the bandwagon" and avoid getting left by yourself on the side of the road. The bandwagon mentality also extends to media appeals based on views of select groups such as celebrities or public opinion polls. Again, critical thinking is the tool that you have to distinguish an informed belief from a popular but uninformed belief. Critically evaluate the following bandwagon appeals:

- I used to think that _____ was my favorite kind of music. But my friends convinced me that only losers enjoy this music. So I've stopped listening to it.

- Hollywood celebrities and supermodels agree: Tattoos in unusual places are very cool. That's good enough for me!

- In the latest Gallup poll 86 percent of those polled believe that economic recovery will happen in the next six months, so I must be wrong.

Appeal to Pity

Consider the reasoning in the following arguments. Do you think that the arguments are sound? Why or why not?

I know that I haven't completed my term paper, but I really think that I should be excused. This has been a very difficult semester for me. I caught every kind of flu that came around. In addition, my brother has a drinking problem, and this has been very upsetting to me. Also, my dog died.

I admit that my client embezzled money from the company, your honor. However, I would like to bring several facts to your attention. He is a family man, with a wonderful wife and two terrific children. He is an important member of the community. He is active in the church, coaches a little league baseball team, and has worked very hard to be a good person who cares about people. I think that you should take these things into consideration in handing down your sentence.

In each of these *appeal to pity* arguments, the reasons offered to support the conclusions may indeed be true. They are not, however, relevant to the conclusion. Instead of providing evidence that supports the conclusion, the reasons are designed to make us feel sorry for the person involved and therefore agree with the conclusion out of sympathy. Although these appeals are often effective, the arguments are not sound. The probability of a conclusion can be established only by reasons that support and are relevant to the conclusion.

Of course, not every appeal to pity is fallacious. There *are* instances in which pity may be deserved, relevant, and decisive. For example, if you are soliciting a charitable donation, or asking a friend for a favor, an honest and straightforward appeal to pity may be appropriate.

Appeal to Fear

Consider the reasoning in the following arguments. Do you think that the arguments are sound? Why or why not?

> I'm afraid I don't think you deserve a raise. After all, there are many people who would be happy to have your job at the salary you are currently receiving. I would be happy to interview some of these people if you really think that you are underpaid.

> If you continue to disagree with my interpretation of *The Catcher in the Rye*, I'm afraid you won't get a very good grade on your term paper.

In both of these arguments, the conclusions being suggested are supported by an *appeal to fear*, not by reasons that provide evidence for the conclusions. In the first case, the threat is that if you do not forgo your salary demands, your job may be in jeopardy. In the second case, the threat is that if you do not agree with the teacher's interpretation, you will fail the course. In neither instance are the real issues — Is a salary increase deserved? Is the student's interpretation legitimate? — being discussed. People who appeal to fear to support their conclusions are interested only in prevailing, regardless of which position might be more justified.

Appeal to Flattery

Flattery joins the emotions of pity and fear as a popular source of fallacious reasoning. This kind of "apple polishing" is designed to influence the thinking of others by appealing to their vanity as a substitute for providing relevant evidence to support your point of view. Of course, flattery is often a harmless lubricant for social relationships, and it can also be used in conjunction with compelling reasoning. But *appeal to flattery* enters the territory of fallacy when it is the main or sole support of your claim, such as "This is absolutely the best course I've ever taken. And I'm really hoping for an A to serve as an emblem of your excellent teaching." Think critically about the following examples:

- You have a great sense of humor, boss, and I'm particularly fond of your racial and homosexual jokes. They crack me up! And while we're talking, I'd like to remind you how much I'm hoping for the opportu work with you if I receive the promotion that you're plannin one of us.

- You are a beautiful human being, inside and out. Why don't you stay the night?

- You are *so* smart. I wish I had a brain like yours. Can you give me any hints about the chemistry test you took today? I'm taking it tomorrow.

Special Pleading

This fallacy occurs when someone makes themselves a special exception, *without sound justification*, to the reasonable application of standards, principles, or expectations. For example, consider the following exchange:

"Hey, hon, could you get me a beer? I'm pooped from work today."
"Well, I'm exhausted from working all day, too! Why don't you get it yourself?"
"I need you to get it because I'm really thirsty."

As we saw in Chapter 4, "Perceiving, Believing, and Knowing" we view the world through our own lenses, and these lenses tend to see the world as tilted toward our interests. That's why *special pleading* is such a popular fallacy: We're used to treating our circumstances as unique and deserving of special consideration when compared to the circumstances of others. Of course, other people tend to see things from a very different perspective. Critically evaluate the following examples.

- I know that the deadline for the paper was announced several weeks ago and that you made clear there would be no exceptions, but I'm asking you to make an exception because I experienced some very bad breaks.

- I really don't like it when you check out other men and comment on their physiques. I know that I do that toward other women, but it's a "guy thing."

- Yes, I would like to play basketball with you guys, but I want to warn you: As a woman, I don't like getting bumped around, so keep your distance.

- I probably shouldn't have used funds from the treasury for my own personal use, but after all I *am* the president of the organization.

Appeal to Ignorance

Consider the reasoning in the following arguments. Do you think that the arguments are sound? Why or why not?

VISUAL THINKING

Fallacies in Action

- What fallacies do you think are being put forward by the two debaters in this illustration? How persuasive have you found those techniques to be in your own life, from your perspectives as both a speaker and a listener?

You say that you don't believe in God. But can you prove that He doesn't exist? If not, then you have to accept the conclusion that He does in fact exist.

Greco Tires are the best. No others have been proved better.

With me, abortion is not a problem of religion. It's a problem of the Constitution. I believe that until and unless someone can establish that the unborn child is not a living human being, then that child is already protected by the Constitution, which guarantees life, liberty, and the pursuit of happiness to all of us.

When the *appeal to ignorance* argument form is used, the person offering the conclusion is asking his or her opponent to *disprove* the conclusion. If the opponent is unable to do so, then the conclusion is asserted to be true. This argument form is not valid because it is the job of the person proposing the argument to prove the conclusion. Simply because an opponent cannot *disprove* the conclusion offers no evidence that the conclusion is in fact justified. In the first example, for instance, the fact that someone cannot prove that God does not exist provides no persuasive reason for believing that He does.

Begging the Question

This fallacy is also known as circular reasoning because the premises of the argument assume or include the claim that the conclusion is true. For example:

"How do I know that I can trust you?"

"Just ask Adrian; she'll tell you."

"How do I know that I can trust Adrian?"

"Don't worry; I'll vouch for her."

Begging the question is often found in self-contained systems of belief, such as politics or religion. For example:

"My religion worships the one true God."

"How can you be so sure?"

"Because our Holy Book says so."

"Why should I believe this Holy Book?"

"Because it was written by the one true God."

In other words, the problem with this sort of reasoning is that instead of providing relevant evidence in support of a conclusion, it simply "goes in a circle" by assuming the truth of what it is supposedly proving. Critically evaluate the following examples:

- Smoking marijuana has got to be illegal. Otherwise, it wouldn't be against the law.

- Of course, I'm telling you the truth. Otherwise, I'd be lying.

Straw Man

This fallacy is best understood by visualizing its name: You attack someone's point of view by creating an exaggerated *straw man* version of the position, and then you knock down the straw man you just created. For example, consider the following exchange:

"I'm opposed to the missile defense shield because I think it's a waste of money."

"So you want to undermine the security of our nation and leave the country defenseless. Are you serious?"

The best way to combat this fallacy is to point out that the straw man does not reflect an accurate representation of your position. For instance:

"On the contrary, I'm very concerned about national security. The money that would be spent on a nearly useless defense shield can be used to combat terrorist threats, a much more credible threat than a missile attack. Take your straw man somewhere else!"

How would you respond to the following arguments?

- You're saying that the budget for our university has to be reduced by 15 percent to meet state guidelines. That means reducing the size of the faculty and student population by 15 percent, and that's crazy.

- "I think we should work at keeping the apartment clean; it's a mess."

  "So you're suggesting that we discontinue our lives and become full-time maids so that we can live in a pristine, spotless, antiseptic apartment. That's no way to live!"

Red Herring

Also known as "smoke screen" and "wild goose chase," the *red herring* fallacy is committed by introducing an irrelevant topic in order to divert attention from the original issue being discussed. So, for example:

I'm definitely in favor of the death penalty. After all, overpopulation is a big problem in our world today.

Although this is certainly a novel approach to addressing the problem of over-population, it's not really relevant to the issue of capital punishment. Critically evaluate the following examples:

- I think all references to sex should be eliminated from films and music. Premarital sex and out-of-wedlock childbirths are creating moral decay in our society.

- I really don't believe that grade inflation is a significant problem in higher education. Everybody wants to be liked, and teachers are just trying to get students to like them.

Appeal to Personal Attack

Consider the reasoning in the following arguments. Do you think that the arguments are valid? Why or why not?

Your opinion on this issue is false. It's impossible to believe anything you say.

How can you have an intelligent opinion about abortion? You're not a woman, so this is a decision that you'll never have to make.

Appeal to personal attack has been one of the most frequently used fallacies through the ages. Its effectiveness results from ignoring the issues of the argument and focusing instead on the personal qualities of the person making the argument. By trying to discredit the other person, this argument form tries to discredit the argument — no matter what reasons are offered. This fallacy is also referred to as the *"ad hominem"* argument, which means "to the man" rather than to the issue, and *"poisoning the well,"* because we are trying to ensure that any water drawn from our opponent's well will be treated as undrinkable.

The effort to discredit can take two forms, as illustrated in the preceding examples. The fallacy can be *abusive* in the sense that we are directly attacking the credibility of our opponent (as in the first example). The fallacy can be *circumstantial* in the sense that we are claiming that the person's circumstances, not character, render his or her opinion so biased or uninformed that it cannot be treated seriously (as in the second example). Other examples of the circumstantial form of the fallacy would include disregarding the views on nuclear plant safety given by an owner of one of the plants or ignoring the views of a company comparing a product it manufactures with competing products.

Two Wrongs Make a Right

This fallacy attempts to justify a morally questionable action by arguing that it is a response to another wrong action, either real or imagined, in fact, that *two wrongs make a right.* For example, someone undercharged at a store might justify keeping the extra money by reasoning that "I've probably been overcharged many times in the past, and this simply equals things out." Or he or she might even speculate, "I am likely to be overcharged in the future, so I'm keeping this in anticipation of being cheated." This is a fallacious way of thinking because each action is independent and must be evaluated on its own merits. If you're overcharged and knowingly keep the money, that's stealing. If the store knowingly overcharges you, that's stealing as well. If the store inadvertently overcharges you, that's a mistake. Or as expressed in a common saying, "Two wrongs *don't* make a right." Critically evaluate the following examples:

- Terrorists are justified in killing innocent people because they and their people have been the victims of political repression and discriminatory policies.

- Capital punishment is wrong because killing murderers is just as bad as the killings they committed.

THINKING ACTIVITY 7.5

Identifying Fallacies

Locate (or develop) an example of each of the following kinds of false appeals. For each example, explain why you think that the appeal is not warranted.

1. Appeal to authority
2. Appeal to pity
3. Appeal to fear
4. Appeal to ignorance
5. Appeal to personal attack

The Critical Thinker's Guide to Reasoning

This book has provided you with the opportunity to explore and develop many of your critical thinking and reasoning abilities. As you have seen, these abilities are complex and difficult to master. The process of becoming an accomplished critical thinker and effective reasoner is a challenging quest that requires ongoing practice and reflection. This section will present a critical thinking/reasoning model that will help you pull together the important themes of this book into an integrated perspective. This model is illustrated on page 261. In order to become familiar with the model, you will be thinking through an important issue that confronts every human being: Are people capable of choosing freely?

What Is My Initial Point of View?

Reasoning always begins with a point of view. As a critical thinker, it is important for you to take thoughtful positions and express your views with confidence. Using this statement as a starting point, respond as specifically as you can:

- *I believe (or don't believe) that people can choose freely because . . .*

Here is a sample response:

> *I believe that people are capable of choosing freely because when I am faced with choosing among a number of possibilities, I really have the feeling that it is up to me to make the choice that I want to.*

How Can I Define My Point of View More Clearly?

After you state your initial point of view, the next step is to define the issues more clearly and specifically. As you have seen, the language that we use has multiple levels of meaning, and it is often not clear precisely what meaning(s) people are expressing. To avoid misunderstandings and sharpen your own thinking, it is essential that you clarify the key concepts as early as possible. In this case the central concept is "choosing freely." Respond by beginning with the following statement:

- *From my point of view, the concept of "choosing freely" means . . .*

Here is a sample response:

From my point of view, the concept of "choosing freely" means that when you are faced with a number of alternatives, you are able to make your selection based solely on what you decide, not on force applied by other influences.

What Is an Example of My Point of View?

Once your point of view is clarified, it's useful to provide an example that illustrates your meaning. The process of forming and defining concepts involves the process of generalizing (identifying general qualities) and the process of interpreting (locating specific examples). Respond to the issue we have been considering by beginning with the following statement:

- *An example of a free choice I made (or was unable to make) is . . .*

Here is a sample response:

An example of a free choice I made was deciding what area to major in. There are a number of career directions I could have chosen to go with, but I chose my major entirely on my own, without being forced by other influences.

What Is the Origin of My Point of View?

To fully understand and critically evaluate your point of view, it's important to review its history. How did this point of view develop? Have you always held this view, or did it develop over time? This sort of analysis will help you understand how your perceiving lenses regarding this issue were formed. Respond to the issue of free choice by beginning with the following statement:

- *I formed my belief regarding free choice . . .*

Here is a sample response:

I formed my belief regarding free choice when I was in high school. I used to believe that everything happened because it had to, because it was determined. Then when I was in high school, I got involved with the "wrong crowd" and developed some bad habits. I stopped doing schoolwork and even stopped attending most classes. I was on the brink of failing when I suddenly came to my senses and said to myself, "This isn't what I want for my life." Through sheer willpower, I turned everything around. I changed my friends, improved my habits, and ultimately graduated with flying colors. From that time on I knew that I had the power of free choice and that it was up to me to make the right choices.

What Are My Assumptions?

Assumptions are beliefs, often unstated, that underlie your point of view. Many disputes occur and remain unresolved because the people involved do not recognize or express their assumptions. For example, in the very emotional debate over abortion, when people who are opposed to abortion call their opponents "murderers," they are assuming the fetus, at *any* stage of development from the fertilized egg onward, is a "human life," since murder refers to the taking of a human life. When people in favor of abortion call their opponents "moral fascists," they are assuming that antiabortionists are merely interested in imposing their narrow moral views on others.

Thus, it's important for all parties to identify clearly the assumptions that form the foundation of their points of view. They may still end up disagreeing, but at least they will know what they are arguing about. Thinking about the issue that we have been exploring, respond by beginning with the following statement:

- *When I say that I believe (or don't believe) in free choice, I am assuming . . .*

Here is a sample response:

> *When I say that I believe in free choice, I am assuming that people are often presented with different alternatives to choose from, and I am also assuming that they are able to select freely any of these alternatives independent of any influences.*

What Are the Reasons, Evidence, and Arguments That Support My Point of View?

Everybody has opinions. What distinguishes informed opinions from uninformed opinions is the quality of the reasons, evidence, and arguments that support the opinions. Respond to the issue of free choice by beginning with the following statement:

- *There are a variety of reasons, evidence, and arguments that support my belief (or disbelief) in free choice. First . . . Second . . . Third . . .*

Here is a sample response:

> *There are a variety of reasons, evidence, and arguments that support my belief in free choice. First, I have a very strong and convincing personal intuition when I am making choices that my choices are free. Second, freedom is tied to responsibility. If people make free choices, then they are responsible for the consequences*

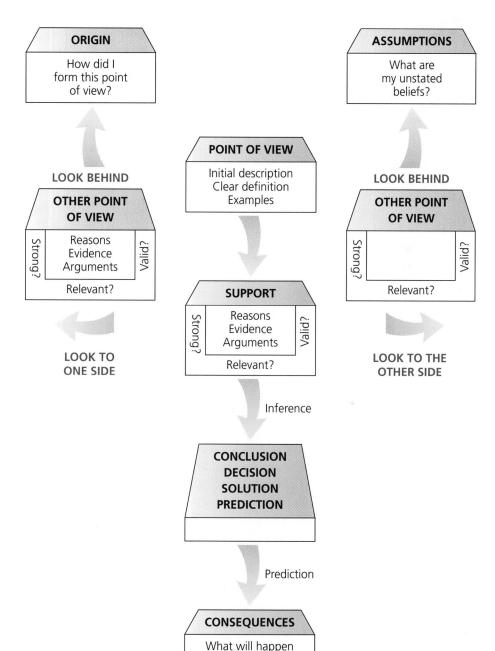

A modified version of a schema originally devised by Ralph H. Johnson; design and layout by J. A. Blair

of their choices. Since we often hold people responsible, that means that we believe that their choices are free. Third, if people are not free, and all of their choices are determined by external forces, then life would have little purpose and there would be no point in trying to improve ourselves. But we do believe that life has purpose and we do try to improve ourselves, suggesting that we also believe that our choices are free.

What Are Other Points of View on This Issue?

One of the hallmarks of critical thinkers is that they strive to view situations from perspectives other than their own, to "think empathically" within other viewpoints, particularly those of people who disagree with their own. If we stay entrenched in our own narrow ways of viewing the world, the development of our minds will be severely limited. This is the only way to achieve a deep and full understanding of life's complexities. In working to understand other points of view, we need to identify the reasons, evidence, and arguments that have brought people to these conclusions. Respond to the issue we have been analyzing by beginning with the following statement:

- *A second point of view on this issue might be . . . A third point of view on this issue might be . . .*

Here is a sample response:

A second point of view on this issue might be that many of our choices are conditioned by experiences that we have had in ways that we are not even aware of. For example, you might choose a career because of someone you admire or because of the expectations of others, although you may be unaware of these influences on your decision. Or you might choose to date someone because he or she reminds you of someone from your past, although you believe you are making a totally free decision. A third point of view on this issue might be that our choices are influenced by people around us, although we may not be fully aware of it. For example, we may go along with a group decision of our friends, mistakenly thinking that we are making an independent choice.

What Is My Conclusion, Decision, Solution, or Prediction?

The ultimate purpose of reasoning is to reach an informed and successful conclusion, decision, solution, or prediction. Chapters 1 and 3 described reasoning approaches for making decisions and solving problems; Chapters 2 and 4 analyzed reaching conclusions; Chapter 5 explored the inferences we use to make predictions. With respect to the sample issue we have been considering — determining whether we can make free choices — the goal is to achieve a thoughtful conclusion. This is a complex process of analysis and synthesis in which we consider all points of view; evaluate the supporting reasons, evidence, and arguments; and then construct our most informed conclusion. Respond to our sample issue by using the following statement as a starting point:

- *After examining different points of view and critically evaluating the reasons, evidence, and arguments that support the various perspectives, my conclusion about free choice is . . .*

Here is a sample response:

After examining different points of view and critically evaluating the reasons, evidence, and arguments that support the various perspectives, my conclusion about free choice is that we are capable of making free choices but that our freedom is sometimes limited. For example, many of our actions are conditioned by our past experience, and we are often influenced by other people without being aware of it. In order to make free choices, we need to become aware of these influences and then decide what course of action we want to choose. As long as we are unaware of these influences, they can limit our ability to make free, independent choices.

What Are the Consequences?

The final step in the reasoning process is to determine the *consequences* of our conclusion, decision, solution, or prediction. The consequences refer to what is likely to happen if our conclusion is adopted. Looking ahead in this fashion is helpful not simply for anticipating the future but also for evaluating the present. Identify the consequences of your conclusion regarding free choice by beginning with the following statement:

- *The consequences of believing (or disbelieving) in free choice are . . .*

Here is a sample response:

The consequences of believing in free choice are taking increasing personal responsibility and showing people how to increase their freedom. The first consequence is that if people are able to make free choices, then they are responsible for the results of their choices. They can't blame other people, bad luck, or events

"beyond their control." They have to accept responsibility. The second conse-
quence is that, although our freedom can be limited by influences of which we are
unaware, we can increase our freedom by becoming aware of these influences and
then deciding what we want to do. If people are not able to make free choices, then
they are not responsible for what they do, nor are they able to increase their free-
dom. This could lead people to adopt an attitude of resignation and apathy.

THINKING ACTIVITY 7.6

Applying the "Guide to Reasoning"

Identify an important issue in which you are interested, and apply **The Criti-**
cal Thinker's Guide to Reasoning to analyze it.

- What is my initial point of view?

- How can I define my point of view more clearly?

- What is an example of my point of view?

- What is the origin of my point of view?

- What are my assumptions?

- What are the reasons, evidence, and arguments that support my point
  of view?

- What are other points of view on this issue?

- What is my conclusion, decision, solution, or prediction?

- What are the consequences?

THINKING PASSAGE

Critical Thinking and Obedience to Authority

The following reading selection by John Sabini and Maury Silver demonstrates
graphically the destructive effects of *failing* to think critically and suggests
ways to avoid these failures. After reading this provocative selection, answer
the questions that follow.

CRITICAL THINKING AND OBEDIENCE TO AUTHORITY
by John Sabini and Maury Silver

In his 1974 book, *Obedience to Authority,* Stanley Milgram reports experiments on destructive obedience. In these experiments the subjects are faced with a dramatic choice, one apparently involving extreme pain and perhaps injury to someone else. When the subject arrives at the laboratory, the experimenter tells him (or her) and another subject — a pleasant, avuncular, middle-aged gentleman (actually an actor) — that the study concerns the effects of punishment on learning. Through a rigged drawing, the lucky subject wins the role of teacher and the experimenter's confederate becomes the "learner."

In the next stage of the experiment, the teacher and learner are taken to an adjacent room; the learner is strapped into a chair and electrodes are attached to his arm. It appears impossible for the learner to escape. While strapped in the chair, the learner diffidently mentions that he has a heart condition. The experimenter replies that while the shocks may be painful, they cause no permanent tissue damage. The teacher is instructed to read to the learner a list of word pairs, to test him on the list, and to administer punishment — an electric shock — whenever the learner errs. The teacher is given a sample shock of 45 volts (the only real shock administered in the course of the experiment). The experimenter instructs the teacher to increase the level of shock one step on the shock generator for each mistake. The generator has thirty switches labeled from 15 to 450 volts. Beneath these voltage readings are labels ranging from "SLIGHT SHOCK" to "DANGER: SEVERE SHOCK," and finally "XX."

The experiment starts routinely. At the fifth shock level, however, the confederate grunts in annoyance, and by the time the eighth shock level is reached, he shouts that the shocks are becoming painful. Upon reaching the tenth level (150 volts), he cries out, "Experimenter, get me out of here! I won't be in the experiment any more! I refuse to go on!" This response makes plain the intensity of the pain and underscores the learner's right to be released. At the 270-volt level, the learner's response becomes an agonized scream, and at 300 volts the learner refuses to answer further. When the voltage is increased from 300 volts to 330 volts, the confederate shrieks in pain at each shock and gives no answer. From 330 volts on, the learner is heard from no more, and the teacher has no way of knowing whether the learner is still conscious or, for that matter, alive (the teacher also knows that the experimenter cannot tell the con-

VISUAL THINKING

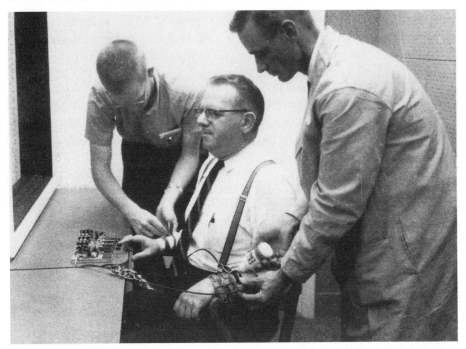

Milgram's Experiment

● In this actual photo from Milgram's obedience study, the man being strapped into the chair for the experiment is one of Milgram's research assistants and will receive no shock. What do you think the research assistant thought of the experiment? In his place, would you have been surprised by the findings?

dition of the victim since the experimenter is in the same room as the teacher).

Typically the teacher attempts to break off the experiment many times during the session. When he tries to do so, the experimenter instructs him to continue. If he refuses, the experimenter insists, finally telling him, "You must continue. You have no other choice." If the subject still refuses, the experimenter ends the experiment.

We would expect that at most only a small minority of the subjects, a cross section of New Haven residents, would continue to shock beyond the point where the victim screams in pain and demands to be released. We certainly would expect that very, very few people would continue to the point of administering shocks of 450 volts. Indeed, Milgram asked a sample of psychiatrists and a sample of adults with various occupations to predict whether they would obey the orders of the experimenter. All of the people asked claimed that they would disobey at some point. Aware that people would be unwilling to admit that they themselves would obey such an unreasonable and unconscionable order, Milgram asked another sample of middle-class adults to predict how far other people would go in such a procedure. The average prediction was that perhaps one person in a thousand would continue to the end. The prediction was wrong. In fact, 65 percent (26/40) of the subjects obeyed to the end.

It is clear to people who are not in the experiment what they should do. The question is, *What features of the experimental situation make this clear issue opaque to subjects?* Our aim is to suggest some reasons for such a failure of thinking and action and to suggest ways that people might be trained to avoid such failures — not only in the experiment, of course, but in our practical, moral lives as well. What are some of the sources of the failure?

The experimental conditions involve entrapment, and gradual entrapment affects critical thought. One important feature inducing obedience is the gradual escalation of the shock. Although subjects in the end administered 450-volt shocks, which is clearly beyond the limits of common morality and, indeed, common sense, they began by administering 15-volt shocks, which is neither. Not only did they begin with an innocuous shock, but it increased in innocuous steps of 15 volts. This gradualness clouds clear thinking: we are prepared by our moral training to expect moral problems to present themselves categorically, with good and evil clearly distinguished. But here they were not. By administering the first shock, subjects did two things at once — one salient, the other implicit. They administered a trivial shock, a morally untroublesome act, and they in that same act committed themselves to a policy and procedure which ended in clear evil.

Surely in everyday life, becoming entrapped by gradual increases in commitment is among the most common ways for us to find ourselves engaging in immoral acts, not to mention simple folly. The corrective cannot be, of course, refusing to begin on any path which *might* lead to immorality, but rather to foresee where paths are likely to lead, and to arrange for ourselves points beyond which we will not go. One suspects that had the subjects committed themselves—publicly—to some shock level they would not exceed, they would not have found themselves pushing the 450-volt lever. We cannot expect to lead, or expect our young to lead, lives without walking on slopes: our only hope is to reduce their slipperiness.

Distance makes obedience easier. Another force sustaining obedience was the *distance* between the victim and the subject. Indeed, in one condition of the experiment, subjects were moved physically closer to the victim; in one condition they had to hold his hand on the shock plate (through Mylar insulation to protect the teachers from shock). Here twelve out of forty subjects continued to the end, roughly half the number that did so when the subjects were farther from their victim.

Being closer to the victim did not have its effect by making subjects think more critically or by giving them more information. Rather it intensified their *discomfort* at the victim's pain. Still, being face to face with someone they were hurting probably caused them at least to focus on their victim, which might well be a first step in their taking seriously the pain they were causing him.

Both the experimenter's presence and the objective requirements of the situation influenced decisions to obey authority. The experimenter's *presence* is crucial to the subjects' obedience. In one version of the experiment he issued his commands at a distance, over the phone, and obedience was significantly reduced — to nine out of forty cases. The experimenter, then, exerts powerful *social influence* over the subjects.

One way to think about the experimenter's influence is to suppose that subjects uncritically cede control of their behavior to him. But this is too simple. We suggest that if the experimenter were to have told the subjects, for example, to shine his shoes, every subject would have refused. They would have refused because shining shoes is not a sensible command within the experimental context. Thus, the experimenter's ability to confuse and control subjects follows from his issuing commands which make sense given the ostensible purpose of the experiment; he was a guide, for them, to the experiment's objective requirements.

This interpretation of the experimenter's *role* is reinforced by details of his behavior. For example, his language and demeanor were cold — bureaucratic rather than emotional or personal. The subjects were led to see his commands to them as his dispassionate interpretations of something beyond them all: the requirements of the experiment.

Embarrassment plays a key role in decisions to obey authority. The experimenter entrapped subjects in another way. Subjects could not get out of the experiment without having to explain and justify their abandoning their duty to the experiment and to him. And how were they to do this?

Some subjects attempted to justify their leaving by claiming that they could not bear to go on, but such appeals to "personal reasons" were rebutted by the experimenter's reminding them of their duty to stay. If the subjects could not escape the experiment by such claims, then how could they escape? *They could fully escape his power only by confronting him on moral grounds.* It is worth noting that this is something that virtually none of the hundreds of subjects who took part in one condition or another fully did. Failing to address the experimenter in moral terms, even "disobedient" subjects just passively resisted; they stayed in their seats refusing to continue until the experimenter declared the experiment over. They did *not* do things we might expect them to: leave, tell the experimenter off, release the victim from his seat, and so on. Why did even the disobedient subjects not confront the experimenter?

One reason seems too trivial to mention: confronting the experimenter would be embarrassing. This trivial fact may have much to do with the subjects' obedience. To confront the experimenter directly, on moral grounds, would be to disrupt in a profound way implicit expectations that grounded this particular, and indeed most, social interaction: namely, that the subject and experimenter would behave as competent moral actors. Questioning these expectations is on some accounts, at least, the source of embarrassment. . . .

How can we train individuals to avoid destructive obedience? Our analysis leads to the view that obedience in the Milgram experiment is not primarily a result of a failure of knowledge, or at least knowledge of the crucial issue of what is right or wrong to do in this circumstance. People do not need to be told that torturing an innocent person is something they should not do — even in the context of the experiment. Indeed, when the experimenter turns his back, most subjects are able to apply their moral principles and disobey. The subjects' problem instead is not knowing how to break off, how to make the moral response without social stickiness. If the subjects' defect is not primarily one of thinking correctly, then how is education, even education in critical thinking, to repair the defect? We have three suggestions.

First, we must teach people how to confront authority. We should note as a corollary to this effort that teaching has a wide compass: we teach people how to ride bikes, how to play the piano, how to make a sauce. Some teaching of how to do things we call education: we teach students how to do long division, how to parse sentences, how to solve physics problems. We inculcate these skills in students not by, or not only by, giving them facts or even strategies to remember, but also by giving them certain sorts of experiences, by correcting them when they err, and so on. An analogy would be useful here. Subjects in the Milgram experiment suffered not so much from a failure to remember that as center fielders they should catch fly balls as they did from an inability to do so playing under lights at night, with a great deal of wind, and when there is ambiguity about whether time-out has been called. To improve the players' ability to shag fly balls, in game conditions, we recommend practice rather than lectures, and the closer the circumstances of practice to the conditions of the actual game, the more effective the practice is likely to be.

Good teachers from Socrates on have known that the intellect must be trained; one kind of training is in criticizing authority. We teachers are authorities and hence can provide practice. Of course, we can only do that if we *remain* authorities. Practice at criticizing us if we do not respect our own authority is of little use. We do not have a recipe for being an authority who at the same time encourages criticism, but we do know that is what is important. And sometimes we can tell when we are either not encouraging criticism or when we have ceased being an authority. Both are equally damaging.

Practice with the Milgram situation might help too; it might help for students to "role play" the subjects' plight. If nothing else, doing this might bring home in a forcible way the embarrassment that subjects faced in confronting authority. It might help them develop ways of dealing with this embarrassment. Certainly, it would at least teach them that doing the morally right thing does not always "feel" right, comfortable, natural. There is no evidence about whether such experiences generalize, but perhaps they do.

If they are to confront authority assertively, individuals must also be taught to use social pressure in the service of personal values. Much of current psychology and education sees thought, even critical thought, as something that goes on within individuals. But we know better than this. Whether it be in science, law, or the humanities, scholarship is and must be a public, social process. To train subjects to think critically is to train them to expose their thinking to others, to open *themselves* to criticism, from their peers as well as from authority. We insist on this in scholarship because we know that individual thinking, even the best of it, is prey to distortions of all kinds, from mere ignorance to "bad faith."

Further, the support of others is important in another way. We know that subjects who saw what they took to be two other naive subjects disobey, and thus implicitly criticize the action of continuing, were very likely to do so themselves. A subject's sense that the experimenter had the correct reading was undermined by the counter reading offered by the "other subjects." Public reinforcement of our beliefs can liberate us from illegitimate pressure. The reason for this is twofold.

Agreement with others clarifies the cognitive issue and helps us see the morally or empirically right answer to questions. But it also can have another effect — a nonrational one.

We have claimed that part of the pressure subjects faced in disobeying was produced by having to deal with the embarrassment that might emerge from confrontation. Social support provides a counter-pressure. Had the subjects committed themselves publicly to disobedience before entering the experiment then they could have countered pressures produced by disobedience (during the experiment) by considering the embarrassment of admitting to others (after the experiment) that they had obeyed. Various self-help groups like Alcoholics Anonymous and Weight Watchers teach individuals to manage social pressures to serve good ends.

Social pressures are forces in our lives whether we concede them or not. The rational person, the person who would keep his action in accord with his values, must learn to face or avoid those pressures when they act to degrade his action, but equally important he ought to learn to *employ* the pressure of public commitment, the pressure implicit in making clear to others what he values, in the service of his values.

Students should know about the social pressures that operate on them. They should also learn how to use those pressures to support their own values. One reason we teach people to think critically is so that they may take charge of their own creations. We do not withhold from engineers who would create buildings knowledge about gravity or vectors or stresses. Rather we teach them to enlist this knowledge in their support.

A second area requires our attention. We need to eliminate intellectual illusions fostering nonintellectual obedience. These are illusions about human nature which the Milgram experiment renders transparent. None of these illusions is newly discovered; others have noticed them before. But the Milgram experiment casts them in sharp relief.

The most pernicious of these illusions is the belief, perhaps implicit, that only evil people do evil things and that evil announces itself. This belief, in different guises, bewildered the subjects in several ways.

First, the experimenter looks and acts like the most reasonable and rational of people: a person of authority in an important institution. All of this is, of course, irrelevant to the question of whether his commands are evil, but it does not seem so to subjects. The experimenter had no personally corrupt motive in ordering subjects to continue, for he wanted nothing more of them than to fulfill the requirements of the experiment. So the experimenter was not seen as an evil man, as a man with corrupt desires. He was a man, like Karl Adolf Eichmann, who ordered them to do evil because he saw that evil as something required of him (and of them) by the requirements of the situation they faced together. Because we expect our morality plays to have temptation and illicit desire arrayed against conscience, our ability to criticize morally is subverted when we find evil instructions issued by someone moved by, of all things, duty. [For a fuller discussion of this point, see Hannah Arendt's *Eichmann in Jerusalem* (1965), where the issue is placed in the context of the Holocaust.]

And just as the experimenter escaped the subjects' moral criticism because he was innocent of evil desire, the subjects escaped their own moral criticism because *they too* were free of evil intent: they did not *want* to hurt the victim; they really did not. Further, some subjects, at least, took action to relieve the victim's plight — many protested the experimenter's commands, many tried to give the victim hints about the right answers — thus further dramatizing their purity of heart. And because they acted out of duty rather than desire, the force of their conscience against their own actions was reduced. But, of course, none of this matters in the face of the evil done.

The "good-heartedness" of people, their general moral quality, is something very important to us, something to which we, perhaps rightly, typically pay attention. But if we are to think critically about the morality of our own and others' acts, we must see through this general fact about people to assess the real moral quality of the acts they do or are considering doing.

A second illusion from which the subjects suffered was a confusion about the notion of responsibility. Some subjects asked the experimenter who was responsible for the victim's plight. And the experimenter replied that he was. We, and people asked to predict what they would do in the experiment, see that this is nonsense. We see that the experimenter cannot discharge the subjects' responsibility — no more than the leader of a bank-robbing gang can tell his cohorts, "Don't worry. If we're caught, I'll take full responsibility." We are all conspirators when we participate in planning and executing crimes.

Those in charge have the right to assign *technical* responsibility to others, responsibility for executing parts of a plan, but moral responsibility cannot be given, taken away, or transferred. Still, these words — mere words — on the part of the experimenter eased subjects' "sense of responsibility." So long as the institutions of which we are a part are moral, the need to distinguish technical from moral responsibility need not arise. When those institutions involve wanton torture, we are obliged to think critically about this distinction.

There is a third illusion illustrated in the Milgram experiment. When subjects threatened to disobey, the experimenter kept them in line with prods, the last of which was, "You have no choice; you must go on." Some subjects fell for this, believed that they had no choice. But this is also nonsense. There may be cases in life when we *feel* that we have no choice, but we know we always do. Often feeling we have no choice is really a matter of believing that the cost of moral action is greater than we are willing to bear — in the extreme we may not be willing to offer our lives, and sometimes properly so. Sometimes we use what others have done to support the claim that we have no choice; indeed, some students interpret the levels of obedience in the Milgram experiment as proof that the subjects had no choice. But we all know they did. Even in extreme situations, we have a choice, whether we choose to exercise it or not. The belief that our role, our desires, our past, or the actions of others preclude our acting morally is a convenient but illusory way of distancing ourselves from the evil that surrounds us. It is an illusion from which we should choose to disabuse our students.

Questions for Analysis

1. The authors of this article describe the reasons they believe that the majority of subjects in the Stanley Milgram experiment were willing to inflict apparent pain and injury on an innocent person. Explain what you believe were the most significant reasons for this disturbing absence of critical thinking and moral responsibility.

2. The authors argue that the ability to think critically must be developed within a social context, that we must expose our thinking to the criticism of others because "individual thinking, even the best of it, is prey to distortions of all kinds, from mere ignorance to 'bad faith.'" Evaluate this claim, supporting your answer with examples and reasons.

3. The authors contend that in order to act with critical thinking and moral courage, people must be taught to confront authority. Explain how you

think people could be taught and encouraged to confront authority in a constructive way.

4. "Even in extreme situations, we have a choice, whether we choose to exercise it or not. The belief that our role, our desires, our past, or the actions of others preclude our acting morally is a convenient but illusory way of distancing ourselves from the evil that surrounds us." Evaluate this claim and give examples and reasons to support your view.

8 Thinking Critically, Living Creatively

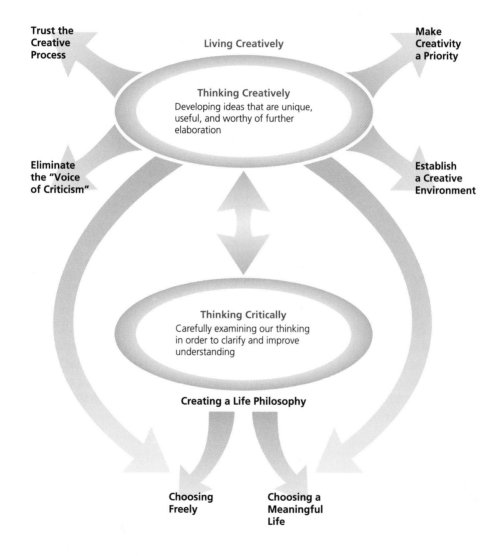

Living Creatively

Trust the Creative Process

Make Creativity a Priority

Thinking Creatively
Developing ideas that are unique, useful, and worthy of further elaboration

Eliminate the "Voice of Criticism"

Establish a Creative Environment

Thinking Critically
Carefully examining our thinking in order to clarify and improve understanding

Creating a Life Philosophy

Choosing Freely

Choosing a Meaningful Life

Thinking critically and thinking creatively are two essential and tightly inter-woven dimensions of the thinking process. These two forms of thinking work as partners to produce effective thinking, enabling us to make informed decisions and lead successful lives.

> **thinking creatively** *The cognitive process we use to develop ideas that are unique, useful, and worthy of further elaboration*

> **thinking critically** *The cognitive process we use to carefully examine our thinking (and the thinking of others) in order to clarify and improve our understanding*

For example, imagine that you are confronted with a problem to solve. Thinking critically enables you to identify and accept the problem. When you generate alternatives for solving the problem, you are using your *creative thinking* abilities, while when you evaluate the various alternatives and select one or more to pursue, you are *thinking critically.* Developing ideas for implementing your alternative(s) involves thinking creatively, while constructing a practical plan of action and evaluating the results depend on thinking critically.

It is apparent that thinking creatively and thinking critically interact in continual and complex relationships in the mind of an effective thinker. Although this text has emphasized critical thinking abilities, creative thinking has been involved in every part of our explorations of the mind. In this chapter, we will shift the emphasis to creative thinking, working to gain insight into this powerful and mysterious dimension of the thinking process.

◎ Living Creatively

You are an artist, creating your life portrait, and your paints and brush strokes are the choices you make each day of your life. This metaphor provides you with a way to think about your personal development and underscores your responsibility for making the most intelligent decisions possible.

Sometimes students become discouraged about their lives, concluding that their destinies are shaped by forces beyond their control. Although difficult circumstances *do* hamper our striving for success, this fatalistic sentiment can also reflect a passivity that is the opposite of thinking critically. As a critical thinker, you should be confident that you can shape the person that you want to become through insightful understanding and intelligent choices.

In working with this book, you have been developing the abilities and attitudes needed to become an educated thinker and a successful person. In this final chapter, we will integrate these goals into a larger context, exploring how to live a life that is creative, professionally successful, and personally fulfilling. By using both your creative and your critical thinking abilities, you can develop informed beliefs and an enlightened life philosophy. In the final analysis, the person who looks back at you in the mirror is the person you have created.

THINKING ACTIVITY 8.1

Describing Your Current and Future Self

1. Describe a portrait of yourself as a person. What sort of person are you? What are your strengths and weaknesses? In what areas do you feel you are creative?

2. Describe some of the ways you would like to change yourself.

"Can I Be Creative?"

The first day of my course "Creative Thinking: Theory and Practice," I always ask the students in the class if they think they are creative. Typically less than half of the class members raise their hands. One reason for this is that people often confuse being "creative" with being "artistic" — skilled at art, music, poetry, creative writing, drama, or dance. Although artistic people are certainly creative, there are an infinite number of ways to be creative that are *not* artistic. This is a mental trap that I fell into growing up. In school I always dreaded art class because I was so inept. My pathetic drawings and art projects were always good for a laugh for my friends, and I felt no overwhelming urges to write poetry, paint, or compose music. I was certain that I had simply been born "uncreative" and accepted this "fact" as my destiny. It wasn't until I graduated from college that I began to change this view of myself. I was working as a custom woodworker to support myself, designing and creating specialized furniture for people when it suddenly struck me: I was being creative! I then began to see other areas of my life in which I was creative: playing sports, decorating my apartment, even writing research papers. I finally understood that being creative was a state of mind and a way of life. As writer Eric Gill expresses it, "The artist is not a different kind of person, but each one of us is a different kind of artist."

Are you creative? Yes! Think of all of the activities that you enjoy doing: cooking, creating a wardrobe, raising children, playing sports, cutting or braiding hair, dancing, playing music. Whenever you are investing your own personal ideas, putting on your own personal stamp, you are being creative. For example, imagine that you are cooking your favorite dish. To the extent that you are expressing your unique ideas developed through inspiration and experimentation, you are being creative. Of course, if you are simply following someone else's recipe without significant modification, your dish may be tasty — but it is not creative. Similarly, if your moves on the dance floor or the basketball court express your distinctive personality, you are being creative, as you are when you stimulate the original thinking of your children or make your friends laugh with your unique brand of humor.

Living your life creatively means bringing your unique perspective and creative talents to all of the dimensions of your life. The following passages are written by students about creative areas in their lives. After reading the passages, complete Thinking Activity 8.2, which gives you the opportunity to describe a creative area from your own life.

One of the most creative aspects of my life is my diet. I have been a vegetarian for the past five years, while the rest of my family has continued to eat meat. I had to overcome many obstacles to make this lifestyle work for me, including family dissension. The solution was simple: I had to learn how to cook creatively. I have come to realize that my diet is an ongoing learning process. The more I learn about and experiment with different foods, the healthier and happier I become. I feel like an explorer setting out on my own to discover new things about food and nutrition. I slowly evolved from a person who could cook food only if it came from a can into someone who could make bread from scratch and grow yogurt cultures. I find learning new things about nutrition and cooking healthful foods very relaxing and rewarding. I like being alone in my house baking bread; there is something very comforting about the aroma. Most of all I like to experiment with different ways to prepare foods, because the ideas are my own. Even when an effort is less than successful, I find pleasure in the knowledge that I gained from the experience. I discovered recently, for example, that eggplant is

VISUAL THINKING

"Expect the Unexpected" — Heraclitus

● Can you think of a time when a creative inspiration enabled you to see a solution to a problem that no one else could see? What can we do to increase these creative breakthroughs in our lives? What strategies can we use to "expect the unexpected"?

terrible in soup! Making mistakes seems to be a natural way to increase creativity, and I now firmly believe that people who say that they do not like vegetables simply have not been properly introduced to them!

As a tropical fish hobbyist, I create an ecosystem most suited to the variety of fish I keep. My most recent choice of fish has been pacus, a close cousin of the Piranha native to South America and Africa. I then added two barracuda of the same approximate size. These two genera are nervous, aggressive fish not ordinarily found together in nature. As "dither fish," which are used as a distraction between two or more genera, I chose two Jack Dempseys, which are large, territorial cichlids. Since these fish require different habitats, it was necessary to create a blend of environments. The pacus need an area to be well planted, providing cover, which I placed in the corners of the aquarium. The Dempseys require rocks, caves, and tree branches to do their cavorting and establish their domain. The barracuda, being the most dominant and aggressive of the lot, got the center area of the tank to swim about freely. When raising fish, you become familiar with their distinct personalities, and you have to be both knowledgeable and creative to develop appropriate habitats for them.

As any parent knows, children have an abundance of energy to spend, and toys or television do not always meet their needs. In response, I create activities to stimulate their creativity and preserve my sanity. For example, I involve them in the process of cooking, giving them the skin from peeled vegetables and a pot so they make their own "soup." Using catalogs, we cut out pictures of furniture, rugs, and curtains, and they paste them onto cartons to create their own interior decors: vibrant living rooms, plush bedrooms, colorful family rooms. I make beautiful boats from aluminum foil, and my children spend hours in the bathtub playing with them. We "go bowling" with empty soda cans and a ball, and they star in "track meets" by running an obstacle course we set up. When it comes to raising children, creativity is a way of survival!

After quitting the government agency I was working at because of too much bureaucracy, I was hired as a carpenter at a construction site, although I had little knowledge of this profession. I learned to handle a hammer and other tools by watching other co-workers, and within a matter of weeks I was skilled enough to organize my own group of workers for projects. Most of my fellow workers used the old-fashioned method of construction carpentry, building panels with inefficient and poorly made bracings. I redesigned the panels in order to save construction time and materials. My supervisor and site engineer were thrilled with my creative ideas, and I was assigned progressively more challenging projects, including the construction of an office building that was completed in record time.

THINKING ACTIVITY 8.2

Describing a Creative Area

1. Describe a creative area of your life in which you are able to express your unique personality and talents. Be specific and give examples.
2. Analyze your creative area by answering the following questions:
   - Why do you feel that this activity is creative? Give examples.
   - How would you describe the experience of being engaged in this activity? Where do your creative ideas come from? How do they develop?
   - What strategies do you use to increase your creativity? What obstacles block your creative efforts? How do you try to overcome these blocks?

Becoming More Creative

Although we each have nearly limitless potential to live creatively, most people use only a small percentage of their creative gifts. In fact, there is research to suggest that people typically achieve their highest creative point as young children, after which there is a long, steady decline into uncreativity. Why? Well, to begin with, young children are immersed in the excitement of exploration and discovery. They are eager to try out new things, act on their impulses, and make unusual connections between disparate ideas. They are not afraid to take risks in trying out untested solutions, and they are not compelled to identify the socially acceptable "correct answer." Children are willing to play with ideas, creating improbable scenarios and imaginative ways of thinking without fear of being ridiculed.

All of this tends to change as we get older. The weight of "reality" begins to smother our imagination, and we increasingly focus our attention on the nuts and bolts of living rather than on playing with possibilities. The social pressure to conform to group expectations increases dramatically. Whether the group is our friends, schoolmates, or fellow employees, there are clearly defined "rules" for dressing, behaving, speaking, and thinking. When we deviate from these rules, we risk social disapproval, rejection, or ridicule. Most groups have little tolerance for individuals who want to think independently and creatively. As we become older, we also become more reluctant to pursue untested courses of action because we become increasingly afraid of failure. Pursuing creativity inevitably involves failure, because we are trying to break out of established ruts and go beyond traditional methods. For example, going beyond the safety of a proven recipe to create an innovative dish may involve some disasters, but it's the only way to create something genuinely unique. The history of creative discoveries is littered with failures, a fact we tend to forget when we are debating whether we should risk an untested idea. Those people who are courageous enough to risk failure while expressing their creative impulses are rewarded with unique achievements and an enriched life.

THINKING ACTIVITY 8.3

Identifying Creative Blocks

Reflect on your own creative development, and describe some of the fears and pressures that inhibit your own creativity. For example, have you ever been penalized for trying out a new idea that didn't work out? Have you ever suffered the wrath of the group for daring to be different and violating the group's unspoken rules? Do you feel that your life is so filled with responsibilities and the demands of reality that you don't have time to be creative?

Although the forces that discourage us from being creative are powerful, they can nevertheless be overcome with the right approaches. We are going to explore four productive strategies:

- Understand and trust the creative process.

- Eliminate the "Voice of Criticism."

- Establish a creative environment.

- Make creativity a priority.

Understand and Trust the Creative Process   Discovering your creative talents requires that you understand how the creative process operates and then have confidence in the results it produces. There are no fixed procedures or formulas for generating creative ideas because creative ideas *by definition* go beyond established ways of thinking to the unknown and the innovative. As the ancient Greek philosopher Heraclitus once said, "You must expect the unexpected, because it cannot be found by search or trail."

Although there is no fixed path to creative ideas, there are activities you can pursue that make the birth of creative ideas possible. In this respect, generating creative ideas is similar to gardening. You need to prepare the soil; plant the seeds; ensure proper water, light, and food; and then be patient until the ideas begin to sprout. Here are some steps for cultivating your creative garden:

- *Absorb yourself in the task:* Creative ideas don't occur in a vacuum. They emerge after a great deal of work, study, and practice. For example, if you want to come up with creative ideas in the kitchen, you need to become knowledgeable about the art of cooking. The more knowledgeable you are, the better prepared you are to create valuable and innovative dishes. Similarly, if you are trying to develop a creative perspective for a research paper in college, you need to immerse yourself in the subject, developing an in-depth understanding of the central concepts and issues. Absorbing yourself in the task "prepares the soil" for your creative ideas.

- *Allow time for ideas to incubate:* After absorbing yourself in the task or problem, the next stage in the creative process is to *stop* working on the task or problem. Even when your conscious mind has stopped actively working on the task, the unconscious dimension of your mind continues working — processing, organizing, and ultimately generating innovative ideas and solutions. This process is known as *incubation* because it mirrors the process in which baby chicks gradually evolve inside the egg until the moment comes when they break out through the shell. In the same way, your creative mind is at work while you are going about your business until the moment of *illumination,* when the incubating idea finally erupts to the surface of your conscious mind. People report that these illuminating moments — when their mental light bulbs go on — often occur when they are engaged in activities completely unrelated to the task. One of the most famous cases was that of the Greek thinker Archimedes, whose moment of illumination came while he was taking a bath, causing him to run naked through the streets of Athens shouting, "Eureka" ("I have found it").

- *Seize on the ideas when they emerge and follow them through:* Generating creative ideas is of little use unless you recognize them when they appear and then act on them. Too often people don't pay much attention to these ideas when they occur, or they dismiss them as too impractical. You must have confidence in the ideas you create, even if they seem wacky or far-out. Many of the most valuable inventions in our history started as improbable ideas, ridiculed by the popular wisdom. For example, the idea of Velcro started with burrs covering the pants of the inventor as he walked through a field, and Post-it Notes resulted from the accidental invention of an adhesive that was weaker than normal. In other words, thinking effectively means thinking creatively *and* thinking critically. After you use your creative thinking abilities to generate innovative ideas, you then must employ your critical thinking abilities to evaluate and refine the ideas and design a practical plan for implementing them.

Eliminate the "Voice of Criticism"   The biggest threat to our creativity lies within ourselves, the negative "Voice of Criticism" (VOC). This VOC can undermine your confidence in every area of your life, including your creative activities, with statements like:

This is a stupid idea and no one will like it.

Even if I could pull this idea off, it probably won't amount to much.

Although I was successful the last time I tried something like this, I was lucky and I won't be able to do it again.

These statements, and countless others like them, have the ongoing effect of making us doubt ourselves and the quality of our creative thinking. As we lose confidence, we become more timid, more reluctant to follow through on ideas and present them to others. After a while our cumulative insecurity discourages us from even generating ideas in the first place, and we end up simply conforming to established ways of thinking and the expectations of others. And in so doing we surrender an important part of ourselves, the vital and dynamic creative core of our personality that defines our unique perspective on the world.

Where do these negative voices come from? Often they originate in the negative judgments we experienced while growing up, destructive criticisms that become internalized as a part of ourselves. In the same way that praising children helps make them feel confident and secure, consistently criticizing them does the opposite. Although parents, teachers, and acquaintances often don't intend these negative consequences with their critical judgments and lack of positive praise, the unfortunate result is still the same: a Voice of Criticism that keeps hammering away at the value of ourselves, our ideas, and our creations. As a teacher, I see this VOC evident when students present their creative projects to the class with apologies like "This isn't very good and it probably doesn't make sense."

How do we eliminate this unwelcome and destructive voice within ourselves? There are a number of effective strategies you can use, although you should be aware that the fight, while worth the effort, will not be easy.

- *Become aware of the VOC:* You have probably been listening to the negative messages of the VOC for so long that you may not even be consciously aware of it. To conquer the VOC, you need to first recognize when it speaks. In addition, it is helpful to analyze the negative messages, try to figure out how and why they developed, and then create strategies to overcome them. A good strategy is to keep a VOC journal, described in Thinking Activity 8.4.

- *Restate the judgment in a more accurate or constructive way:* Sometimes there is an element of truth in our self-judgments, but we have blown the reality out of proportion. For example, if you fail a test, your VOC may translate this as "I'm a failure." Or if you ask someone for a date and get turned down, your VOC may conclude: "I'm a social misfit with emotional bad breath!" In these instances, you need to translate the reality accurately: "I failed this test — I wonder what went wrong and how I can improve my performance in the future," and "This person turned me down for a date — I guess I'm not his or her type, or maybe he or she just doesn't know me well enough."

- *Get tough with the VOC:* You can't be a wimp if you hope to overcome the VOC. Instead, you have to be strong and determined, telling yourself as soon as the VOC appears, "I'm throwing you out and not letting you back in!" This attack might feel peculiar at first, but it will soon become an automatic response when those negative judgments appear. Don't give in to the judgments, even a little bit, by saying, "Well, maybe I'm just a little bit of a jerk." Get rid of the VOC entirely, and good riddance to it!

- *Create positive voices and visualizations:* The best way to destroy the VOC for good is to replace it with positive encouragements. As soon as you have stomped on the judgment "I'm a jerk," you should replace it with "I'm an intelligent, valuable person with many positive qualities and talents." Similarly, you should make extensive use of positive visualization, as you "see" yourself performing well on your examinations, being entertaining and insightful with other people, and succeeding gloriously in the sport or dramatic production in which you are involved. If you make the effort to create these positive voices and images, they will eventually become a natural part of your thinking. And since positive thinking leads to positive results, your efforts will become self-fulfilling prophecies.

- *Use other people for independent confirmation:* The negative judgments coming from the VOC are usually irrational, but until they are dragged out into the light of day for examination, they can be very powerful. Sharing our VOC with others we trust is an effective strategy because they can provide an objective perspective that reveals to us the irrationality and destructiveness of these negative judgments. This sort of "reality testing" strips the judgments of their power, a process that is enhanced by the positive support of concerned friends with whom we have developed relationships over a period of time.

THINKING ACTIVITY 8.4

Combatting the "Voice of Criticism"

1. Take a small notebook or pad with you one day, and record every self-defeating criticism that you make about yourself. At the end of the day classify your self-criticisms by category. For example: negative self-criticism about your physical appearance, your popularity with others, your academic ability.

2. Analyze the self-criticisms in each of the categories and try to determine where they came from and how they developed.

3. Use the strategies described in this section, and others of your own creation, to start fighting these self-criticisms when they occur.

Establish a Creative Environment An important part of eliminating the negative voices in our minds is to establish environments in which our creative resources can flourish. This means finding or developing physical environments conducive to creative expression as well as supportive social environments. Sometimes working with other people is stimulating and energizing to our creative juices; at other times we require a private place where we can work without distraction. For example, I have a specific location in which I do much of my writing: sitting at my desk, with a calm, pleasing view, music on the stereo, a cold drink, and a supply of Tootsie Roll Pops. I'm ready for creativity to strike me, although I sometimes have to wait for some time! Different environments work for different people: You have to find the environment(s) best suited to your own creative process and then make a special effort to do your work there.

The people in our lives who form our social environment play an even more influential role in encouraging or inhibiting our creative process. When we are surrounded by people who are positive and supportive, this increases our confidence and encourages us to take the risk to express our creative vision. They can stimulate our creativity by providing us with fresh ideas and new perspectives. By engaging in *brainstorming* (described on page 92), they can work with us to generate ideas and then later help us figure out how to refine and implement the most valuable ones.

However, when the people around us tend to be negative, critical, or belittling, then the opposite happens: We lose confidence and are reluctant to express ourselves creatively. Eventually, we begin to internalize these negative criticisms, incorporating them into our own VOC. When this occurs, we have the choice of telling people that we will not tolerate this sort of destructive behavior or, if they can't improve their behavior, moving them out of our lives. Of course, sometimes this is difficult because we work with them or they are related to us. In this case we have to work at diminishing their negative influence and spending more time with those who support us.

Make Creativity a Priority   Having diminished the voice of negative judgment in your mind, established a creative environment, and committed yourself to trusting your creative gifts, you are now in a position to live more creatively. How do you actually do this? Start small. Identify some habitual patterns in your life and break out of them. Choose new experiences whenever possible — for example, ordering unfamiliar items on a menu or getting to know people outside your circle of friends — and strive to develop fresh perspectives on things in your life. Resist falling back into the ruts you were previously in by remembering that living things are supposed to be continually growing, changing, and evolving, not acting in repetitive patterns like machines. The following student essay summarizes many of the reasons that choosing to live creatively may be one of the most fulfilling decisions that you ever make.

VISUAL THINKING

Are Carrots Really Good for You?

● What human behaviors are depicted in this illustration? Do you feel that the artist presents an accurate view of human behavior? Explain your answer.

CREATIVITY
by Michelle Austin

Creativity is an energizing force: powerful, generative, productive. Sadly, for the most part, its potential remains unused, as men and women circle the periphery of its domain. The author Kahlil Gibran writes: "For the self is a sea, boundless and measureless," and for many of us that sea remains largely undiscovered. Creativity is a treasure that if nurtured can become a harvest of possibilities and riches. Why is creativity important? Very simply, creativity brings fulfillment and enrichment to every dimension of our lives. A creative disposition sees difficulties not as problems but as challenges to be met. The intuitive thinker draws upon the combined resources of insight, illumination, imagination and an inner strength. He puts ideas and strategies into effect, while developing a sense of competency and control over his environment. Creativity fosters limitless opportunities because it draws upon the power of discovery and invention.

Creativity's realm is in the vast uncharted portions of the mind. What we call full consciousness is a very narrow thing, and creativity springs from the unknown and unconscious depths of our being. In the words of Gibran: "Vague and nebulous is the beginning of all things." Creativity always begins with a question and we must abandon preconceived ideas and expectations. But while the phenomenon of creativity involves innovating, developing, playing, and speculating, there must ultimately be a point of synthesis. Ideas in flight are of little use; a convergence and application gives substance to our visions. Fostering our creative gifts is a lifelong project. The Buddhists use the term "mindfulness" to describe the creative state of being. Mindfulness involves developing an openness to ideas, suggestions and even once discarded thoughts. The goal is to increase our sensitivity and awareness to the mystery and beauty of life. We must adopt a playful attitude, a willingness to fool around with ideas, with the understanding that many of these fanciful notions will not be relevant or practical. But some will, and these creative insights can lead to profound and wondrous discoveries. At the same time, cultivating a creative attitude stretches our imaginations and makes our lives vibrant and unique.

Worry and mental striving create anxiety that clogs rather than stimulates the flow of ideas. It is impossible to impose one's will with brute force on the chaos. We must be gentle with ourselves, harmonize rather than try to conquer, and, in the words of Albert Einstein, "The solution will present itself quietly and say 'Here I am.'" And while we need critical evaluation to provide direction and focus for our creative efforts, a premature and excessive critical judgment suppresses, overpowers, and smothers creative spontaneity. This "Voice of Criticism" shrinks our creative reservoir and undermines our courage to take creative risks. The author Napoleon Hill has stated, "Whatever the mind can conceive and believe, it can achieve." Similarly, if we approach our lives with a mindful sense of discovery and invention, we can continually create ourselves in ways that we can only imagine. In such lives, there are no predetermined outcomes, only creativity searching for seeds of progress.

THINKING ACTIVITY 8.5

Becoming More Creative

Select an area of your life in which you would like to be more creative. It can be in school, on your job, an activity you enjoy, or in your relationship with someone. Make a special effort to inject a fresh perspective and new ideas into this area, and keep a journal recording your efforts and their result. Be sure to allow yourself sufficient time to break out of your ruts and establish new patterns of thinking, feeling, and behaving. Focus on your creative antennae as you "expect the unexpected," and pounce on new ideas when they emerge from the depths of your creative resource.

Living a Life Philosophy

As the artist of your own life, your brush strokes express your philosophy of life, a vision that incorporates your most deeply held values, aspirations, and convictions. The challenge you face is to create a coherent view of the world that expresses who you are as well as the person you want to become. It should be a vision that not only guides your actions but also enables you to understand the value of your experiences, the significance of your relationships, and the meaning of your life.

The quality of your life philosophy is a direct result of your abilities to think critically and think creatively, abilities that you have been developing while working on activities presented throughout this book. But a life philosophy is incomplete until it is acted upon through the decisions you make, decisions made possible by your ability to choose freely. These are the three life principles of human transformation upon which this book is based. These three principles are interlocking pieces of the puzzle of your life. Working together as a unified force, these principles can illuminate your existence: answering questions, clarifying confusion, creating meaning, and providing fulfillment.

- *Think critically:* When used properly, your thinking process acts like a powerful beacon of light, illuminating the depths of your personality and the breadth of your experience. Clear thinking is a tool that helps you disentangle the often-confused jumble of thoughts and feelings that compose much of your waking consciousness. By becoming a more powerful critical thinker, you are acquiring the abilities you need to achieve your goals, solve problems, and make intelligent decisions. Critical thinkers are people who have developed thoughtful and well-founded beliefs to guide their choices in every area of their lives. In order to develop the strongest and most accurate beliefs possible, you need to become aware of your own biases, explore situations from many different perspectives, and develop sound reasons to support your points of view.

- *Live creatively:* Creativity is a powerful life force that can infuse your existence with meaning. Working in partnership with critical thinking, creative thinking helps you transform your life into a rich tapestry of productivity and success. When you approach your life with a mindful sense of discovery and invention, you can continually create yourself in ways limited only by your imagination. A creative lens changes everything for the better: Problems become opportunities for growth, mundane routines become challenges for inventive approaches, relationships become intriguing adventures. When you give free rein to your creative impulses, every aspect of your life takes on a special glow. You are able to break out of unthinking habitual responses and live fully in every minute, responding naturally and spontaneously. It sounds magical, and it is.

- *Choose freely:* People can transform themselves only if they choose to take different paths in their lives — and only if their choices are truly free. To exercise genuine freedom, you must have the insight to understand all of your options and the wisdom to make informed choices. When you fully accept your freedom, you redefine your daily life and view your future in a new light. By working to neutralize the constraints on your autonomy and guide your life in positive directions, you see alternatives that were not previously visible, having been concealed by the limitations of your previous vision. Your future becomes open, a field of rich possibilities that you can explore and choose among. A life that is free is one that is vital and exciting, suffused with unexpected opportunities and the personal fulfillment that comes from a life well lived.

Your "self" is, in its essence, a dynamic life force that is capable of thinking critically, creating, and choosing freely. These three essential dimensions of your self exist optimally when they work together in harmonious unity. When working together, these three basic elements create a person who is intelligent, creative, and determined — the ingredients for success in any endeavor. But consider the disastrous consequences of subtracting any of these elements from the dynamic equation. If you lack the ability to think critically, you won't be able to function very well in most challenging careers because you will have difficulty thinking clearly, solving complex problems, and making intelligent decisions. What's more, whatever creative ideas you come up with will be rootless, lacking an intelligible framework or practical strategies for implementing them. You will be an impractical dreamer, condemned to a life of frustrated underachieving. Without insight into yourself, your freedom will be imprisoned since you won't be able to see your choices clearly or to liberate yourself from the influences that are constraining you.

If you lack the ability to think creatively, then your thinking abilities may enable you to perform in a solid, workmanlike fashion, but your work will lack imagination, you will be afraid to try original approaches because of the risk of failure, and your personality will be lacking the spontaneous sparkle that people admire and are drawn to. You will in time become a competent but unimaginative "worker-bee," performing your duties with predictable adequacy but never rising to the lofty heights that you are capable of attaining. Your choices will be as limited as your imagination, and your habitual choices of safe and secure paths will eventually create a very small canvas for your personal portrait.

If you lack the ability to choose freely, then your abilities to think critically or creatively cannot save you from a life of disappointment. Though you may be able to clearly analyze and understand, you will lack the will to make the difficult choices and stay the course when you encounter obstacles and adversities. And though you may develop unique and valuable ideas, your inability to focus your energies and make things happen will doom these ideas to anonymity. Because you lack the will to create yourself as a strong individual of character and integrity, the people you encounter will come to view you as a shallow-rooted reed that bends with the wind of superficial trends, not as someone deserving of authority and responsibility.

Think of what you aspire to have: a life of purpose and meaning, the respect and devotion of those around you, success and fulfillment in your chosen endeavors, and a secure sense of who you are, a person with the courage and vision to accomplish great things. These aspirations are within your grasp, but only if you develop all of these fundamental dimensions of your self to their fullest potential: the abilities to think critically, think creatively, and choose freely.

Choosing Freely

You have the power to create yourself through the choices that you make, but only if your choices are truly free. To exercise genuine freedom, you must possess the insight to understand all of your options and the wisdom to make informed choices. In many instances passive, illogical, and superficial thinking inhibits people's abilities to make intelligent choices and erodes their motivation to persevere when obstacles are encountered. You can learn to redefine your daily life in a new light and enhance its value through free choices derived from thinking critically and creatively. The problem is that we get so caught up in routine, so mired in the day-to-day demands of reality and the pressures of conformity, that we don't even *see* alternatives to our condition, much less act on them. Our complaints often far outnumber our shining moments, as we tend to focus on the forces and people who have thwarted our intentions:

> If only that person hadn't sabotaged my career, I would have . . .
> If only I had had a chance to meet the right person . . .
> If only I had gotten the breaks now and then . . .
> If only I could get rid of my habitual tendency to ———, I would . . .
> If only other people were as dependable and caring as I am . . .
> If only I had been given the advantages of a different background . . .
> If only the world had not become so competitive . . .
> If only I had been given the opportunity to show what I could do . . .

These complaints, and the millions of others like them, bitterly betray W. E. Henley's notion that *"I am the master of my fate, I am the captain of my soul."* It is much more common for people to believe that fate mastered them and that they never had sufficient opportunity to live life "their way." Instead of feeling free, we often feel beleaguered, trying desperately to prevent our small dinghy from getting swamped in life's giant swells, rather than serenely charting a straight course in our sleek sailboat.

The end result is that when people think of "being free," they often conjure up a romantic notion of "getting away" from their concerns and responsibilities, imagining a world where anything is possible and there is plenty of money to pay for it. However appealing this fantasy may be, it is a misconceived and unrealistic notion of freedom. Genuine freedom consists of making thoughtful choices from among the available options, choices that reflect your genuine desires and deepest values, and resisting the pressures to surrender your autonomy to external pressures *or* internal forces. How can you accomplish this?

To begin with, you need to *make freedom a priority* in your life. Achieving greater freedom for yourself is based on placing a high value on personal freedom. If you are primarily focused on meeting your needs within the existing structure of your life, then maximizing your choices and enlarging the scope of your life may not be a top priority. However, if you feel dissatisfied with the status quo and long to increase your options and your ability to choose them, increasing your personal freedom will be a very important goal.

> ***Strategy:*** *Complete a brief inventory of your life, identifying some of the areas you would like to change, as well as those you are basically satisfied with but would like to enrich. Think about the ways in which increasing your personal freedom and making different choices could help you achieve these life goals.*

A second strategy for increasing your personal freedom is to *willingly accept your freedom and responsibility.* The most important and disturbing element of personal freedom is that it necessarily involves personal responsibility. And personal responsibility is the main reason that people are so reluctant to embrace their freedom and, in fact, actively seek to "escape" from it. If you acknowledge that your choices are free, then you must accept that you are responsible for the outcomes resulting from your choices. When people are successful, it is easy for them to take full responsibility for their accomplishments. But when failure occurs, people tend to dive for cover, blaming others or forces beyond their control. This is exactly what's going on in all the "if only" statements listed previously and any others like them: They each express the belief that if only some outside force had not intervened, the person would have achieved the goal she or he had set. However, in many instances, these explanations are bogus, and these efforts to escape from freedom are illegitimate. They represent weak and inauthentic attempts to deny freedom *and* responsibility.

Your reaction to responsibility is an effective barometer of your attitude toward freedom. If you are comfortable with your personal responsibility, able openly to admit your mistakes as well as to take pleasure in your successes, this attitude is an indication that you accept your freedom. Similarly, if you take pride in your independence, welcoming the opportunity to make choices for which you are solely responsible, this attitude also reveals a willing embracing of your freedom.

> *Strategy: Create a "responsibility chart" that evaluates your acceptance of responsibility (and freedom) in various areas of your life. On one side of the page, describe common activities in which you are engaged ("Decisions at work," "Conflicts with my partner"), and on the other side, list typical judgments that you make ("I am solely responsible for that mistaken analysis"; "You made me do that embarrassing thing, and I can't forgive you"). After several days of record-keeping and reflection, you should begin to get an increasingly clear picture of the extent to which you accept (or reject) your personal freedom.*

A third way to increase your freedom is to *emphasize your ability to create yourself.* Although you may not be fully aware of it, you have your own psychological theory of human nature, which is expressed in how you view yourself and deal with other people. Do you believe that your personality is determined by your genetic history or by the environmental circumstances that have shaped you? Or do you believe that people are able to transcend their histories and choose freely?

> *Strategy: Instead of explaining your (and others') behavior entirely in terms of genes and environmental conditioning, develop the habit of analyzing your behavior in terms of the choices you make. Many people triumph over daunting odds, while others fail miserably, despite having every advantage in life. What are the key ingredients of such triumphs? They are an unshakable belief in the ability to choose one's destiny and the determination to do so.*

Increasing your freedom necessarily involves a fourth strategy, *becoming aware of constraints on your freedom and willing yourself to break free from them.* Freedom consists of making thoughtful choices that reflect your authentic self, your genuine desires and deepest values. But there are many forces that threaten to limit your freedom and even repress it altogether. The limits to your freedom can either come from outside yourself (*external constraints*) or they can come from within yourself (*internal constraints*). While external factors may limit your freedom — for example, being incarcerated or working at a dead-end job — the more challenging limits are imposed by yourself through internal constraints. For instance, people don't generally procrastinate, smoke, suffer anxiety attacks, feel depressed, or engage in destructive relationships because someone is coercing them to do so. Instead, they are victimizing themselves in ways that they are often unaware of. How can you tell if your choice originates from your genuine self or from an internal constraint? There is no simple answer. You have to think critically about your situation in order to understand it fully, but here are some questions to guide your reflective inquiry:

- Do you feel that you are making a free, unconstrained choice and that you could easily "do otherwise" if you wanted to? Or do you feel that your choice is in some sense beyond your conscious control, that you are in the grip of a force that does not reflect your genuine self, a compulsion that has in some way "taken possession" of you?

- Does your choice add positive qualities to your life: richness of experience, success, happiness? Or does your choice have negative results that undermine many of the positive goals that you are striving for?

- If you are asked why you are making a certain choice, are you able to provide a persuasive, rational explanation? Or are you at a loss to explain why you are behaving this way, other than to say, "I can't help myself."

In order to remove constraints, you first have to become aware that they exist. For example, if someone is manipulating you to think or feel a certain way, you can't begin to deal with the manipulation until you first become aware of it. Similarly, you can't solve a personal problem, such as insecurity or emotional immaturity, without first acknowledging that it *is* a problem and then developing insight into the internal forces that are driving your behavior. Once you have achieved this deeper level of understanding, you are then in a position to choose a different path for yourself, using appropriate decision-making and problem-solving approaches such as those that we have been developing and addressing throughout this book.

> **Strategy:** *Identify the external limitations (people or circumstances) on your freedom, and think about ways to remove these constraints. Then identify — as best you can — the internal compulsions that are influencing you to act in ways at variance with your genuine desires. Use the critical and creative thinking abilities you have been developing to diminish or eliminate their influence.*

Finally, maximizing your freedom involves *creating new options to choose from* instead of passively accepting the choices that are initially presented to you. The most vigorous exercise of freedom involves actively creating alternatives that may not be on the original menu of options. This talent involves both thinking critically by taking active initiatives and thinking creatively by generating unique possibilities. For example, if you are presented with a project at work, you should not restrict yourself to considering the conventional alternatives for meeting the goals; instead actively seek improved possibilities. If you are enmeshed in a problem situation with someone else, you should not permit the person to establish the alternatives from which to choose; instead work to formulate new or modified ways of solving the problem. Too often people are content to sit back and let the situation define their choices instead of taking the initiative to shape the situation in their own way. Critical and creative thinkers view the world as a malleable environment that they have a responsibility to form and shape. This perspective liberates them to exercise their freedom of choice to the fullest extent possible.

Active thinking, like passive thinking, is habit forming. But once you develop the habit of looking beyond the information given — to transcend consistently the framework within which you are operating — you will be increasingly unwilling to be limited by the alternatives determined by others. Instead, you will seek to create new possibilities and actively shape situations to fit your needs.

> *Strategy:* When you find yourself in situations with different choices, make a conscious effort to identify alternatives that are different from those explicitly presented. You don't necessarily have to choose the new options you have created if they are not superior to the others, but you do want to start developing the habit of using your imagination to look beyond the circumstances as presented.

Choosing "the Good Life"

What is the ultimate purpose of your life? What is "the good life" that you are trying to achieve?

Psychologist Carl Rogers, who has given a great deal of thought to these issues, has concluded that the good life is

- *not* a fixed state like virtue, contentment, nirvana, or happiness

- *not* a condition like being adjusted, fulfilled, or actualized

- *not* a psychological state like drive or tension reduction

Instead, the good life is a *process* rather than a state of being, a *direction* rather than a destination. But what direction? According to Rogers, "The direction which constitutes the Good Life is that which is selected by the total organism when there is psychological freedom to move in any direction." In other words, the heart of the good life is creating yourself through genuinely free choices once you have liberated yourself from external and internal constraints. When you are living such a life, you are able to fulfill your true potential in every area of your existence. You are able to be completely open to your experience, becoming better able to listen to yourself, to experience what is going on within yourself. You are more aware and accepting of feelings of fear, discouragement, and pain, but also more open to feelings of courage, tenderness, and awe. You are more able to live your experiences fully instead of shutting them out through defensiveness and denial.

How do you know what choices you should make, what choices will best create the self you want to be and help you achieve your good life? As you achieve psychological freedom, your *intuitions* become increasingly trustworthy since they reflect your deepest values, your genuine desires, your authentic self. It is when we are hobbled by constraints on ourselves that our intuitions are distorted and often self-destructive. As previously noted, you need to think clearly about yourself, to have an optimistic, self-explanatory style that enables you to approach life in the most productive way possible. When you have achieved this clarity of vision and harmony of spirit, what "feels right" — the testimony of your reflective consciousness and common sense — will serve as a competent and trustworthy guide to the choices you ought to make. The choices that emerge from this enlightened state will help you create a life that is enriching, exciting, challenging, stimulating, meaningful, and fulfilling. It will enable you to stretch and grow, to become more and to attain more of your potentialities. As author Albert Camus noted, "Freedom is nothing else but a chance to be better, whereas enslavement is a certainty of the worst."

The good life is different for each person, and there is no single path or formula for achieving it. It is the daily process of creating yourself in ways that express your deepest desires and highest values — your authentic self. Thinking critically and thinking creatively provide you with the insight to clearly see the person you want to become, while choosing freely gives you the power actually to create the person you have envisioned.

> **Strategy:** *Describe your ideal "good life." Make full use of your imagination, and be specific regarding the details of the life you are envisioning for yourself. Compare this imagined good life with the life you have now. What different choices do you have to make in order to achieve your good life?*

The Meaning of Your Life

According to psychiatrist and concentration camp survivor Victor Frankl, "Man's search for meaning is the primary motivation in his life." A well-known Viennese psychiatrist in the 1930s, Dr. Frankl and his family were arrested by the Nazis, and he spent three years in the Auschwitz concentration camp. Every member of his family, including his parents, siblings, and pregnant wife, were killed. He himself miraculously survived, enduring the most unimaginably abusive and degrading conditions. Following his liberation by the Allied troops, he wrote *Man's Search for Meaning*, an enduring and influential work, which he began on scraps of paper during his internment. Since its publication in 1945, it has become an extraordinary best-seller, read by millions of people and translated into twenty languages. Its success reflects the profound hunger for meaning that people have continually been experiencing, trying to answer a question that, in the author's words, "burns under their fingernails." This hunger expresses the pervasive *meaninglessness* of our age, the "existential vacuum" in which many people exist.

Dr. Frankl discovered that even under the most inhumane conditions, it is possible to live a life of purpose and meaning. But for the majority of prisoners at Auschwitz, a meaningful life did not seem possible. Immersed in a world that no longer recognized the value of human life and human dignity, that robbed prisoners of their will and made them objects to be exterminated, most people suffered a loss of their values. If a prisoner did not struggle against this spiritual destruction with a determined effort to save his or her self-respect, the person lost the feeling of being an individual, a being with a mind, with inner freedom and personal value. The prisoner's existence descended to the level of animal life, plunging him or her into a depression so deep that he or she became incapable of action. No entreaties, no blows, no threats would have any effect on the person's apathetic paralysis, and he or she soon died, underscoring Russian novelist Fyodor Dostoyevsky's observation, "Without a firm idea of himself and the purpose of life, man cannot live, and would sooner destroy himself than remain on earth, even if he was surrounded with bread."

Dr. Frankl found that the meaning of his life in this situation was to try to help his fellow prisoners restore their psychological health. He had to find ways for them to look forward to the future: a loved one waiting for the person's return, a talent to be used, or perhaps work yet to be completed. These were the threads he tried to weave back into the patterns of meaning in these devastated lives. His efforts led him to the following insight:

> We had to learn ourselves, and furthermore we had to teach the despairing men, that it did not matter what we expected from life, but rather *what life expected from us.* We needed to stop asking about the meaning of life but instead to think of ourselves as those who were being questioned by life, daily and hourly. Our answer must consist not in talk and meditation, but in right action and in right conduct. Life ultimately means taking the

responsibility to find the right answer to its problems and to fulfill the tasks which it constantly sets for each individual.

We each long for a life of significance, to feel that in some important way our life has made a unique contribution to the world and to the lives of others. We each strive to create our self as a person of unique quality, someone who is admired by others as extraordinary. We hope for lives characterized by unique accomplishments and lasting relationships that will distinguish us as memorable individuals both during and after our time on earth.

The purpose of this book has been to help provide you with the thinking abilities you will need to guide you on your personal journey of self-discovery and self-transformation. Its intention has been *not* to provide you with answers but to equip you with the thinking abilities, conceptual tools, and personal insights to find your own answers. Each chapter has addressed an essential dimension of the thinking process, and the issues raised form a comprehensive blueprint for your life, a life that you wish to be clear in purpose and rich in meaning.

In order for you to discover the meaning of your life, you need to seek meaning actively, to commit yourself to meaningful projects, to meet with courage and dignity the challenges that life throws at you. You will have little chance of achieving meaning in your life if you simply *wait* for meaning to present itself to you or if you persist in viewing yourself as a *victim* of life. If you squander your personal resources by remaining trapped in unproductive patterns, then there will be no room left in your life for genuine meaning. Reversing this negative orientation requires a radical shift of perspective from complaining about what life "owes" you to accepting the responsibility of meeting life's expectations, whether they be rewarding or cruel. Even in the dire conditions of the concentration camp, there were men like Victor Frankl who chose to act heroically, devoting themselves to comforting others or giving away their last piece of bread. They were living testament to the truth that even though life may take everything away from a person, it cannot take away "the last of the human freedoms — to choose one's attitude in any given set of circumstances, to choose one's own way."

Though you may have to endure hardship and personal tragedy, you still have the opportunity to invest your life with meaning by the way that you choose to respond to your suffering: whether you let it defeat you or whether you are able to rise above it triumphantly. Your ultimate and irreducible freedom to freely choose your responses to life's situations defines you as a person and determines the meaningfulness of your existence.

But how do you determine the "right" way to respond, select the path that will infuse your life with meaning and fulfillment? You need to think critically, think creatively, and make enlightened choices — all of the thinking abilities and life attitudes that you have been cultivating throughout your work with this book. They will provide you with the clear vision and strength of character that will enable you to create yourself as a worthy individual living a life of purpose and meaning. Your explorations of issues presented throughout this book have given you the opportunity to become acquainted with yourself and with the potential that resides within you: your unique intellectual gifts, imaginative dreams, and creative talents. As psychologist Abraham Maslow notes, you are so constructed that you naturally press toward fuller and fuller being, realizing your potentialities, becoming fully human, everything that you can become. But you alone can determine what choices you will make among all of the possibilities: which will be condemned to nonbeing and which will be actualized, creating your immortal portrait, the monument to your existence.

Clearly, the ultimate meaning of your life can never be fully realized within the confines of your own self. Meaning is encountered and created through your efforts to *go beyond* yourself. In the same way that "happiness" and "success" are the outgrowths of purposeful and productive living rather than ends in themselves, so your life's meaning is a natural by-product of reaching beyond yourself to touch the lives of others. This self-transcendence may take the form of a creative work or a heroic action that you display to the human community. It may also be expressed through your loving and intimate relationships with other people, your contribution to individual members of your human community.

What is the meaning of your life? It is the truth that you will discover as you strive, through your daily choices, to create yourself as an authentic individual, committed to enhancing the lives of others, fulfilling your own unique potential, and attuning yourself to your spiritual nature and the mysteries of the universe. It is the reality you will find as you choose to respond to both the blessings and the suffering in your life with courage and dignity. Joy and suffering, fulfillment and despair, birth and death — these are the raw materials that life provides you. Your challenge and responsibility are to shape these experiences into a meaningful whole — guided by a philosophy of life that you have constructed with your abilities to think critically, think creatively, and choose freely. This is the path you must take in order to live a life that is rich with meaning, lived by a person who is noble and heroic — a life led as an enlightened thinker.

THINKING PASSAGE

Original Spin

The process of creating yourself through your choices is a lifelong one that involves all the creative and critical thinking abilities that we have been exploring in this book. The processes of creative thinking and critical thinking are related to one another in complex, interactive ways. We use the creative thinking process to develop ideas that are unique, useful, and worthy of further elaboration, and we use the critical thinking process to analyze, evaluate, and refine these ideas. Creative thinking and critical thinking work as partners, enabling us to lead fulfilling lives. The following article, "Original Spin" by Lesley Dormen and Peter Edidin, provides a useful introduction to creative thinking and suggests strategies for increasing your creative abilities. After reading the article and reflecting on its ideas, answer the questions that follow.

ORIGINAL SPIN*
by Lesley Dormen and Peter Edidin

Creativity, somebody once wrote, is the search for the elusive "Aha," that moment of insight when one sees the world, or a problem, or an idea, in a new way. Traditionally, whether the discovery results in a cubist painting or an improved carburetor, we have viewed the creative instant as serendipitous and rare — the product of genius, the property of the elect.

Unfortunately, this attitude has had a number of adverse consequences. It encourages us to accept the myth that the creative energy society requires to address its own problems will never be present in sufficient supply. Beyond that, we have come to believe that "ordinary" people like ourselves can never be truly creative. As John Briggs, author of *Fire in the Crucible: The Alchemy of Creative Genius,* said, "The way we talk about creativity tends to reinforce the notion that it is some kind of arbitrary gift. It's amazing the way 'not having it' becomes wedded to people's self-image. They invariably work up a whole series of rationalizations about why they 'aren't creative,' as if they were damaged goods of some kind." Today, however, researchers are looking at creativity, not as an advantage of the human elite, but as a basic human endowment. As Ruth Richards, a psychiatrist and creativity researcher at

---

* "Original Spin" by Lesley Dormen and Peter Edidin, *Psychology Today,* July/August 1989. Reprinted with permission from *Psychology Today* magazine. Copyright © 1989 (Sussex Publishers, Inc.).

McLean Hospital in Belmont, MA, says, "You were being creative when you learned how to walk. And if you are looking for something in the fridge, you're being creative because you have to figure out for yourself where it is." Creativity, in Richards' view, is simply fundamental to getting about in the world. It is "our ability to adapt to change. It is the very essence of human survival."

In an age of rampant social and technological change, such an adaptive capability becomes yet more crucial to the individual's effort to maintain balance in a constantly shifting environment. "People need to recognize that what Alvin Toffler called future shock is our daily reality," says Ellen McGrath, a clinical psychologist who teaches creativity courses at New York University. "Instability is an intrinsic part of our lives, and to deal with it every one of us will need to find new, creative solutions to the challenges of everyday life." . . .

But can you really become more creative? If the word *creative* smacks too much of Picasso at his canvas, then rephrase the question in a less intimidating way: Do you believe you could deal with the challenges of life in a more effective, inventive, and fulfilling manner? If the answer is yes, then the question becomes, "What's stopping you?"

Defining Yourself as a Creative Person

People often hesitate to recognize the breakthroughs in their own lives as creative. But who has not felt the elation and surprise that come with the sudden, seemingly inexplicable discovery of a solution to a stubborn problem? In that instant, in "going beyond the information given," as psychologist Jerome Bruner has said, to a solution that was the product of your own mind, you were expressing your creativity.

This impulse to "go beyond" to a new idea is not the preserve of genius, stresses David Henry Feldman, a developmental psychologist at Tufts University and the author of *Nature's Gambit*, a study of child prodigies. "Not everybody can be Beethoven," he says, "but it is true that all humans, by virtue of being dreamers and fantasizers, have a tendency to take liberties with the world as it exists. Humans are always transforming their inner and outer worlds. It's what I call the 'transformational imperative.'"

The desire to play with reality, however, is highly responsive to social control, and many of us are taught early on to repress the impulse. As Mark Runco, associate professor of psychology at California State University at Fullerton and the founder of the new *Creativity Research Journal*, says, "We put children in groups and make them sit in desks and raise

VISUAL THINKING

"Express Yourself!"

● Our creative talents can be expressed in virtually every area of our lives. How is the woman in the photo expressing herself creatively? What are some of your favorite activities in which you are able to express your unique personality in innovative ways?

their hands before they talk. We put all the emphasis on conformity and order, then we wonder why they aren't being spontaneous and creative."

Adults too are expected to conform in any number of ways and in a variety of settings. Conformity, after all, creates a sense of order and offers the reassurance of the familiar. But to free one's natural creative impulses, it is necessary, to some extent, to resist the pressure to march in step with the world. Begin small, suggests Richards. "Virtually nothing you do can't be done in a slightly different, slightly better way. This has nothing to do with so-called creative pursuits but simply with breaking with your own mindsets and trying an original way of doing some habitual task. Simply defer judgment on yourself for a little while and try something new. Remember, the essence of life is not getting things right, but taking risks, making mistakes, getting things *wrong*."

But it also must be recognized that the creative life is to some degree, and on some occasions, a solitary one. Psycholinguist Vera John-Steiner, author of *Notebooks of the Mind: Explorations of Thinking*, is one of many creativity researchers who believe that a prerequisite for creative success is "intensity of preoccupation, being pulled into your activity to such an extent that you forget it's dinnertime." Such concentration, John-Steiner believes, is part of our "natural creative bent," but we learn to ignore it because of a fear that it will isolate us from others. To John-Steiner, however, this fear is misplaced. Creative thought, she has written, is a "search for meaning," a way to connect our inner sense of being with some aspect of the world that preoccupies us. And she believes that only by linking these two aspects of reality — the inner and the outer — can we gain "some sense of being in control of life."

Avoiding the Myths

David Perkins, co-director of Project Zero at the Harvard Graduate School of Education, asks in *The Mind's Best Work*, "When you have it — creativity, that is — what do you have?" The very impalpability of the subject means that often creativity can be known only by its products. Indeed, the most common way the researchers define creativity is by saying it is whatever produces something that is: a. original; b. adaptive (i.e., useful); c. meaningful to others. But because we don't understand its genesis, we're often blocked or intimidated by the myths that surround and distort this mercurial subject.

One of these myths is, in Perkins's words, that creativity is "a kind of 'stuff' that the creative person has and uses to do creative things, never mind other factors." This bit of folk wisdom, that creativity is a sort of intangible psychic organ — happily present in some and absent in others — so annoys Perkins that he would like to abolish the word itself.

Another prevalent myth about creativity is that it is restricted to those who are "geniuses" — that is, people with inordinately high IQs. Ironically, this has been discredited by a study begun by Stanford psychologist Lewis Terman, the man who adapted the original French IQ test for America. In the early 1920s, Terman had California schoolteachers choose 1,528 "genius" schoolchildren (those with an IQ above 135), whose lives were then tracked year after year. After six decades, researchers found that the putative geniuses, by and large, did well in life. They entered the professions in large numbers and led stable, prosperous lives. But very few made notable creative contributions to society, and none did extraordinary creative work.

According to Dean Simonton, professor of psychology at the University of California at Davis and the author of *Genius, Creativity, and Leadership* and *Scientific Genius,* "There just isn't any correlation between creativity and IQ. The average college graduate has an IQ of about 120, and this is high enough to write novels, do scientific research, or any other kind of creative work."

A third myth, voiced eons ago by Socrates, lifts creativity out of our own lives altogether into a mystical realm that makes it all but unapproachable. In this view, the creative individual is a kind of oracle, the passive conduit or channel chosen by God, or the tribal ancestors, or the muse, to communicate sacred knowledge.

Although there *are* extraordinary examples of creativity, for which the only explanation seems to be supernatural intervention (Mozart, the story goes, wrote the overture to *Don Giovanni* in only a few hours, after a virtually sleepless night and without revision), by and large, creativity begins with a long and intensive apprenticeship.

Psychologist Howard Gruber believes that it takes at least 10 years of immersion in a given domain before an eminent creator is likely to be able to make a distinctive mark. Einstein, for example, who is popularly thought to have doodled out the theory of relativity at age 26 in his spare time, was in fact compulsively engaged in thinking about the problem at least from the age of 16.

Finally, many who despair of ever being creative do so because they tried once and failed, as though the truly creative always succeed. In fact, just the opposite is true, says Dean Simonton. He sees genius, in a sense, as inseparable from failure. "Great geniuses make tons of mistakes," he says. "They generate lots of ideas and they accept being wrong. They have a kind of internal fortress that allows them to fail and just keep going. Look at Edison. He held over 1,000 patents, but most of them are not only forgotten, they weren't worth much to begin with."

Mindlessness Versus Mindfulness

"Each of us desires to share with others our vision of the world, only most of us have been taught that it's wrong to do things differently or look at things differently," says John Briggs. "We lose confidence in ourselves and begin to look at reality only in terms of the categories by which society orders it."

This is the state of routinized conformity and passive learning that Harvard professor of psychology Ellen Langer calls, appropriately enough, mindlessness. For it is the state of denying the perceptions and promptings of our own minds, our individual selves. Langer and her colleagues' extensive research over the past 15 years has shown that when we act mindlessly, we behave automatically and limit our capacity for creative response. Mired down in a numbing daily routine, we may virtually relinquish our capacity for independent thought and action.

By contrast, Langer refers to a life in which we use our affective, responsive, perceptive faculties as "mindful." When we are mindful, her research has shown, we avoid rigid, reflexive behavior in favor of a more improvisational and intuitive response to life. We notice and feel the world around us and then act in accordance with our feelings. "Many, if not all, of the qualities that make up a mindful attitude are characteristic of creative people," Langer writes in her new book, *Mindfulness*. "Those who can free themselves of mindsets, open themselves to new information and surprise, play with perspective and context, and focus on process rather than outcome are likely to be creative, whether they are scientists, artists, or cooks."

Much of Langer's research has demonstrated the vital relationship between creativity and uncertainty, or conditionality. For instance, in one experiment, Langer and Alison Piper introduced a collection of objects to one group of people by saying, "This is a hair dryer," and "This is a dog's chew toy," and so on. Another group was told "This *could be* a hair dryer," and "This *could be* a dog's chew toy." Later, the experimenters for both groups invented a need for an eraser, but only those people who had been conditionally introduced to the objects thought to use the dog's toy in this new way.

The intuitive understanding that a single thing is, or could be, many things, depending on how you look at it, is at the heart of the attitude

Langer calls mindfulness. But can such an amorphous state be cultivated? Langer believes that it can, by consciously discarding the idea that any given moment of your day is fixed in its form. "I teach people to 'componentize' their lives into smaller pieces," she says. "In the morning, instead of mindlessly downing your orange juice, *taste it*. Is it what you want? Try something else if it isn't. When you walk to work, turn left instead of right. You'll notice the street you're on, the buildings and the weather. Mindfulness, like creativity, is nothing more than a return to who you are. By minding your responses to the world, you will come to know yourself again. How you feel. What you want. What you want to do."

Creating the Right Atmosphere

Understanding the genesis of creativity, going beyond the myths to understand your creative potential, and recognizing your ability to break free of old ways of thinking are the three initial steps to a more creative life. The fourth is finding ways to work that encourage personal commitment and expressiveness.

Letting employees learn what they want to do has never been a very high priority in the workplace. There, the dominant regulation has always been, "Do what you are told."

Today, however, economic realities are providing a new impetus for change. The pressure on American businesses to become more productive and innovative has made creative thinking a hot commodity in the business community. But innovation, business is now learning, is likely to be found wherever bright and eager people *think* they can find it. And some people are looking in curious places.

Financier Wayne Silby, for example, founded the Calvert Group of funds, which today manages billions of dollars in assets. Silby, whose business card at one point read Chief Daydreamer, occasionally retreats for inspiration to a sensory deprivation tank, where he floats in warm water sealed off from light and sound. "I went into the tank during a time when the government was changing money-market deposit regulations, and I needed to think how to compete with banks. Floating in the tank I got the idea of joining them instead. We wound up creating an $800-million program. Often we already have answers to our problems, but we don't quiet ourselves enough to see the solutions bubbling just below the surface." Those solutions will stay submerged, he says, "unless you create a culture that encourages creative approaches, where it's OK to have bad ideas."

Toward this goal, many companies have turned to creativity consultants, like Synectics, Inc., in Cambridge, MA. Half the battle, according to Synectics facilitator Jeff Mauzy, is to get the clients to relax and accept that they are in a safe place where the cutthroat rules of the workplace don't apply, so they can allow themselves to exercise their creative potential in group idea sessions.

Pamela Webb Moore, director of naming services (she helps companies figure out good names for their products) at Synectics, agrees. One technique she uses to limber up the minds of tightly focused corporate managers is "sleight of head." While working on a particular problem, she'll ask clients to pretend to work on something else. In one real-life example, a Synectics-trained facilitator took a group of product-development and marketing managers from the Etonic shoe corporation on an "excursion," a conscious walk away from the problem — in this case, to come up with a new kind of tennis shoe.

The facilitator asked the Etonic people to imagine they were at their favorite vacation spot. "One guy," Moore says, "was on a tropical island, walking on the beach in his bare feet. He described how wonderful the water and sand felt on his feet, and he said, 'I wish we could play tennis barefoot.' The whole thing would have stopped right there if somebody had complained that while his colleague was wandering around barefoot, they were supposed to come up with a *shoe*. Instead, one of the marketing people there was intrigued, and the whole group decided to go off to play tennis barefoot on a rented court at 10 at night."

While the Etonic people played tennis, the facilitator listed everything they said about how it felt. The next morning, the group looked at her assembled list of comments, and they realized that what they liked about playing barefoot was the lightness of being without shoes, and the ability to pivot easily on both the ball of the foot and the heel. Nine months later, the company produced an extremely light shoe called the Catalyst, which featured an innovative two-piece sole that made it easier for players to pivot.

The Payoff

In *The Courage to Create*, Rollo May wrote that for much of [the twentieth] century, researchers had avoided the subject of creativity because they perceived it as "unscientific, mysterious, disturbing and too corruptive of the scientific training of graduate students." But today researchers are coming to see that creativity, at once fugitive and ubiquitous, is the mark of human nature itself.

Whether in business or the arts, politics or personal relationships, creativity involves "going beyond the information given" to create or reveal something new in the world. And almost invariably, when the mind exercises its creative muscle, it also generates a sense of pleasure. The feeling may be powerfully mystical, as it is for New York artist Rhonda Zwillinger, whose embellished artwork appeared in the film *Slaves of New York*. Zwillinger reports, "There are times when I'm working and it is almost as though I'm a vessel and there is a force operating through me. It is the closest I come to having a religious experience." The creative experience may also be quiet and full of wonder, as it was for Isaac Newton, who compared his lifetime of creative effort to "a boy playing on the seashore and diverting himself and then finding a smoother pebble or prettier shell than ordinary, while the greater ocean of truth lay all undiscovered before me."

But whatever the specific sensation, creativity always carries with it a powerful sense of the mind working at the peak of its ability. Creativity truly is, as David Perkins calls it, the mind's best work, its finest effort. We may never know exactly how the brain does it, but we can feel that it is exactly what the brain was meant to do.

Aha!

Questions for Analysis

1. According to the authors, "Creativity . . . is the search for the elusive 'Aha,' that moment of insight when one sees the world, or a problem, or an idea, in a new way." Describe an "aha" moment that you have had recently, detailing the origin of your innovative idea and how you implemented it.

2. Identify some of the influences in your life that have inhibited your creative development, including the "myths" about creativity that are described in the article.

3. Using the ideas contained in this chapter and in this article, identify some of the strategies that you intend to use in order to become more creative in your life: for example, becoming more "mindful," destroying the "voice of criticism," and creating an atmosphere more conducive to creativity.

GLOSSARY

accomplishment Something completed successfully; an achievement. Also, an acquired skill or expertise.

accurate Conforming exactly to fact; errorless; deviating only slightly or within acceptable limits from a standard.

active learner One who takes initiative in exploring one's world, thinks independently and creatively, and takes responsibility for the consequences of one's decisions.

active participant One who is always trying to understand the sensations one encounters instead of being a passive receiver of information, a "container" into which sense experience is poured.

alternative A choice between two mutually exclusive possibilities, a situation presenting such a choice, or either of these possibilities.

altruistic Showing unselfish concern for the welfare of others.

ambiguous Open to more than one interpretation; doubtful or uncertain.

analogical relationships Relationships which relate things belonging to different categories in terms of each other.

analogy A comparison between things that are basically dissimilar made for the purpose of illuminating our understanding of the things being compared.

analysis The study of the parts of an intellectual or material whole and their interrelationships in making up a whole.

appeal to authority A type of fallacious thinking in which the argument is intended to persuade through the appeal to various authorities with legitimate expertise in the area in which they are advising.

appeal to fear An argument in which the conclusion being suggested is supported by a reason invoking fear and not by a reason that provides evidence for the conclusion.

appeal to flattery A source of fallacious reasoning designed to influence the thinking of others by appealing to their vanity as a substitute for providing relevant evidence to support a point of view.

appeal to ignorance An argument in which the person offering the conclusion calls upon his or her opponent to disprove the conclusion. If the opponent is unable to do so, then the conclusion is asserted to be true.

appeal to personal attack A fallacy that occurs when the issues of the argument are ignored and focus is instead directed to the personal qualities of the person making the argument in an attempt to discredit the argument. Also referred to as the "*ad hominem*" argument ("to the man" rather than to the issue) or "poisoning the well."

appeal to pity An argument in which the reasons offered to support the conclusions are designed to invoke sympathy toward the person involved.

appeal to tradition A misguided way of reasoning that argues that a practice or way of thinking is "better" or

---

* Glossary definitions have been adapted and reproduced by permission of *The American Heritage Dictionary of the English Language,* Fourth Edition. Copyright © 2000 by Houghton Mifflin Company.

"right" simply because it is older, traditional, or has "always been done that way."

application The act of putting something to a special use or purpose.

argument A form of thinking in which certain statements (reasons) are offered in support of another statement (a conclusion).

assumption Something taken for granted or accepted as true without proof.

authoritarian moral theory A moral theory in which there are clear values of "right" and "wrong," with authorities determining what these are.

authority An accepted source of expert information or advice.

bandwagon A fallacy that relies on the uncritical acceptance of others' opinions because "everyone believes it."

begging the question A circular fallacy that assumes in the premises of the argument that the conclusion about to be made is already true. Also known as "circular reasoning."

beliefs Interpretations, evaluations, conclusions, or predictions about the world that we endorse as true.

bias A preference or an inclination, especially one that inhibits impartial judgment.

blueprint A detailed plan of action, model, or prototype.

brainstorming A method of shared problem solving in which all members of a group spontaneously contribute ideas.

causal chain A situation in which one thing leads to another, which then leads to another, and so on.

causal fallacies Mistakes and errors made in judgment in trying to determine causal relationships.

causal reasoning A form of inductive reasoning in which it is claimed that an event (or events) is the result of the occurrence of another event (or events).

causal relationship A relationship that involves relating events in terms of the influence or effect they have on one another.

cause Anything that is responsible for bringing about something else — usually termed the *effect*.

cause-to-effect experiment (with intervention) A form of controlled experiment in which the conditions of one designated "experimental group" are altered while those of a distinct "control group" (both within a target population) remain constant.

cause-to-effect experiment (without intervention) A form of experimental design, similar to cause-to-effect experiment (with intervention), except that the experimenter does not intervene to expose the experimental group to a proposed cause.

certain Established beyond doubt or question; indisputable.

challenge A test of one's abilities or resources in a demanding but stimulating undertaking.

choose freely To choose to take different paths in life by exercising genuine freedom.

chronological Arranged in order of time of occurrence.

chronological relationship A relationship that relates events in time sequence.

circumstantial Of, relating to, or dependent on the conditions or details accompanying or surrounding an event.

classify To arrange or organize according to class or category.

cognition The thinking process of constructing beliefs that forms the basis of one's understanding of the world.

commit To pledge or obligate one's own self.

comparative relationship A relationship which relates things in the same general category in terms of similarities and dissimilarities.

compared subject In an analogy, the object or idea that the original subject is being likened to.

comparing Evaluating similarities and differences.

concepts General ideas that we use to identify and organize our experience.

conclusion A statement that explains, asserts, or predicts on the basis of statements (known as reasons) that are offered as evidence for it. The result or outcome of an act or process.

conflict To be in or come into opposition; differ.

consequence Something that logically or naturally follows from an action or condition.

constructive criticism Analysis that serves to develop a better understanding of what is going on.

context The circumstances in which an event occurs; a setting.

contradict To be contrary to; be inconsistent with.

contribute To give or supply in common with others; give to a common fund or for a common purpose.

controlled experiment A powerful reasoning strategy used by scientists.

creative Able to break out of established patterns of thinking and approach situations from innovative directions.

creative thinking The act or habit of using our thinking process to develop ideas that are unique, useful, and worthy of further elaboration.

criteria A set of standards, rules, or tests on which a judgment or decision can be based.

critical analysis Analysis characterized by careful, exact evaluation and judgment.

critical thinking The act or habit of carefully exploring the thinking process, in order to clarify our understanding and make more intelligent decisions.

cue words Key words that signal that a reason is being offered in support of a conclusion or that a conclusion is being announced on the basis of certain reasons.

curious Willing to explore situations with probing questions which penetrate beneath the surface of issues, instead of being satisfied with superficial explanations.

deductive argument An argument form in which one reasons from premises that are known or assumed to be true to a conclusion that follows necessarily from these premises.

define To describe the nature or basic qualities of; explain.

desirability The degree to which something is worth having, seeking, doing, or achieving, as by being useful, advantageous, or pleasing.

dialogue A systematic exchange of ideas or opinions.

dilemma A situation that requires a choice between options that are or seem equally unfavorable or mutually exclusive.

disadvantage Something that places one in an unfavorable condition or circumstance.

disjunctive Presenting several alternatives.

disprove To prove to be false, invalid, or in error; refute.

distinguish To perceive as being different or distinct.

effect Something brought about by a cause or agent; a result.

effectiveness The degree to which something produces an intended or expected effect.

effect-to-cause experiment A form of reasoning employing the controlled experimental design in which the experimenter works backward from an existing effect to a suspected cause.

e-mail A system for sending and receiving messages electronically over a computer network, as between personal computers.

empirical generalization A form of inductive reasoning in which a general statement is made about an entire group (the "target population") based on observing some members of the group (the "sample population").

endorsement The act of giving approval or support.

evaluate To examine and judge carefully, based on specified criteria.

evidence A thing or things helpful in forming a conclusion or judgment.

external constraints Limits to one's freedom that come from outside oneself.

fact Knowledge or information based on real-world occurrences.

factual beliefs Beliefs based on observations.

factual evidence Evidence derived from a concrete, reliable source or foundation.

fallacies Unsound arguments that are often persuasive and can appear to be logical because they usually appeal to our emotions and prejudices, and because they often support conclusions that we want to believe are accurate.

fallacy of relevance A fallacious argument which appeals for support to factors that have little or nothing to do with the argument being offered.

false dilemma A fallacy that occurs when we are asked to choose between two extreme alternatives without being able to consider additional options. Also known as the "either/or fallacy" or the "black-or-white fallacy."

falsifiable beliefs Beliefs that pass a set of tests or stated conditions formulated to test the beliefs.

fictional Relating to or characterized by an imaginative creation or a pretense that does not represent actuality but has been invented.

flexible Responsive to change; adaptable.

form To develop in the mind; conceive.

generalize To focus on the common properties shared by a group of things.

genuine Honestly felt or experienced.

hasty generalization A general conclusion reached that is based on a very small sample.

hedonism A moral theory which advises people to do whatever brings them pleasure.

hypothesis A possible explanation that is introduced to account for a set of facts and that can be used as a basis for further investigation.

identify To ascertain the origin, nature, or definitive characteristics.

illumination Spiritual or intellectual enlightenment; clarification; elucidation.

incomplete comparison A comparison in which focus is placed on too few points of comparison.

independent thinkers Those who are not afraid to disagree with the group opinion. They develop well-supported beliefs through thoughtful analysis, instead of uncritically "borrowing" the beliefs of others.

inductive reasoning An argument form in which one reasons from premises that are known or assumed to be true to a conclusion that is supported by the premises but does not necessarily follow from them.

infer To conclude from evidence or premises.

inference The act or process of deriving logical conclusions from premises known or assumed to be true; the act of reasoning from factual knowledge or evidence.

inferential beliefs Beliefs that are based on inferences, that go beyond what can be directly observed.

inferring Going beyond factual information to describe what is not known.

informed Well acquainted with knowledge of a subject.

insightful Displaying an incisive understanding of a complex event.

interactive Acting or capable of acting on each other.

internal constraints Limits to one's freedom that come from within oneself.

Internet An interconnected system of networks that connects computers around the world via the TCP/IP protocol.

interpret To explain the meaning of; to conceive the significance of; construe.

interpretation The result of conceiving or explaining the meaning of.

intuition A sense of something not evident or deducible; an impression.

invalid argument An argument in which the reasons do not support the conclusion so that the conclusion does not follow from the reasons offered.

jargon A style of language made up of words, expressions, and technical terms that are intelligible to professional circles or interest groups but not to the general public.

judging Expressing an evaluation based on certain criteria.

justification The act of demonstrating or proving to be just, right, or valid.

key questions Questions that can be used to explore situations and issues systematically.

knowledge Familiarity, awareness, or understanding gained through experience or study. Information doesn't become knowledge until it has been thought about critically.

knowledgeable Perceptive or well-informed.

language A system of symbols for thinking and communicating.

link A segment of text or a graphical item that serves as a cross-reference between parts of a hypertext document or between files or hypertext documents. Also called hotlink, hyperlink. By clicking on a link, one might more directly access a web site or homepage.

live creatively To approach life with a mindful sense of discovery and invention, enabling one to continually create oneself in ways limited only by the imagination.

mentally active Those who take initiative and actively use intelligence to confront problems and meet challenges, instead of responding passively to events.

metaphor An implied comparison between basically dissimilar things made for the purpose of illuminating our understanding of the things being compared.

mindful Making use of our responsive, perceptive faculties, thus avoiding rigid, reflexive behavior in favor of a more improvisational and intuitive response to life.

mind map A visual presentation of the ways concepts can be related to one another.

misidentification of the cause An error that occurs in causal situations when identification of the cause and the effect are unclear.

modus ponens "Affirming the antecedent"; a valid deductive form commonly used in our logical thinking.

modus tollens "Denying the consequence"; a commonly used valid deductive form.

moral Of or concerned with the judgment of the goodness or badness of human action and character.

moral agnosticism A theory of morality that holds there is no way to determine clearly what is "right" or "wrong" in moral situations.

narrative A way of thinking and communicating in which someone tells a story about experiences he or she has had.

necessary Needed to achieve a certain result or effect; requisite.

open-minded Listening carefully to every viewpoint, evaluating each perspective carefully and fairly.

organize To put together into an orderly, functional, structured whole.

original subject In an analogy, the primary object or idea being described or compared.

paradox A seemingly contradictory statement that may nonetheless be true.

passionate Having a passion for understanding; always striving to see issues and problems with more clarity.

perceiving Actively selecting, organizing, and interpreting what is experienced by your senses.

perceptual meaning   A component of a word's total meaning that expresses the relationship between a linguistic event and an individual's consciousness.

personal experience   Examples from one's own life; one of the four categories of evidence.

perspective   Point of view or vista.

post hoc ergo propter hoc   "After it, therefore because if it"; refers to situations in which, because two things occur close together in time, an assumption is made that one causes the other.

pragmatic   Dealing or concerned with facts or actual occurrences; practical.

pragmatic meaning   A component of a word's total meaning that involves the person who is speaking and the situation in which the word is spoken. Also known as situational meaning.

precision   The state or quality of being specific, detailed, and exact.

prediction   The act of stating, telling about, or making known in advance, especially on the basis of special knowledge.

premise   A proposition upon which an argument is based or from which a conclusion is drawn.

principle   A plausible or coherent scenario that has yet to be applied to experience.

prioritize   To organize things in order of importance.

process analysis   A method of analysis involving two steps: (1) to divide the process or activity being analyzed into parts or stages, (2) to explain the movement of the process through these parts or stages from beginning to end.

process relationships   Relationships based on the relation of aspects of the growth or development of an event or object.

procrastinate   To put off doing something, especially out of habitual carelessness or laziness; to postpone or delay needlessly.

properties   Qualities or features that all things named by a word or sign share in common.

psychological   Of, relating to, or arising from the mind or emotions.

quality   An inherent or distinguishing characteristic; property; essential character or nature.

questionable cause   A causal fallacy that occurs when someone presents a causal relationship for which no real evidence exists.

random selection   A selection strategy in which every member of the target population has an equal chance of being included in the sample.

reasoning   The type of thinking that uses argument — reasons in support of conclusions.

reasons   Statements that support another statement (known as a conclusion), justify it, or make it more probable.

red herring   A fallacy that is committed by introducing an irrelevant topic in order to divert attention from the original issue being discussed. Also known as "smoke screen" and "wild goose chase."

referents   All the various examples of

a concept.

relate   To bring into or link in logical or natural association; to establish or demonstrate a connection between.

relativism   A view according to the tradition of philosophy that says that the truth is relative to any individual or situation, that there is no standard we can use to decide which beliefs make most sense.

relevant   Having a bearing on or connection with the matter at hand.

reliable   Offering dependable information.

reporting   Describing information in ways that can be verified through investigation.

representative   In statistical sampling, when the sample is considered to accurately reflect the larger whole, or target population, from which the sample is taken.

revise   To reconsider and change or modify.

role   The characteristic and expected social behavior of an individual.

sample   A portion, piece, or segment that is intended to be representative of a whole.

scientific method   An organized approach devised by scientists for discovering causal relationships and testing the accuracy of conclusions.

selective comparisons   A problem that occurs in making comparisons when a one-sided view of a comparative situation is taken.

self-aware   Those who are aware of their own biases and are quick to point them out and take them into consideration when analyzing a situation.

semantic meaning   A component of a word's total meaning of a word that expresses the relationship between a linguistic event and a nonlinguistic event.

senses   Sight, hearing, smell, touch, and taste; means through which you experience your world, aware of what occurs outside you.

sign   The word or symbol used to name or designate a concept.

simile   An explicit comparison between basically dissimilar things made for the purpose of illuminating our understanding of the things being compared.

skilled discussants   Those who are able to discuss ideas in an organized and intelligent way. Even when the issues are controversial, they listen carefully to opposing viewpoints and respond thoughtfully.

slang   A kind of language occurring chiefly in casual and playful speech, made up typically of short-lived coinages and figures of speech that are deliberately used in place of standard terms for added raciness, humor, irreverence, or other effect.

slippery slope   A causal fallacy that asserts that one undesirable action will inevitably lead to a worse action, which will necessarily lead to a worse one still, all the way down the "slippery slope" to some terrible disaster at the bottom.

solution   The answer to or disposition of a problem.

sound argument   A deductive argument in which the premises are true and the logical structure is valid.

source   A person or document that supplies information needed.

special pleading   A fallacy that occurs

when someone makes themselves a special exception, without sound justification, to the reasonable application of standards, principles, or expectations.

standards Degrees or levels of requirement, excellence, or attainment.

stereotype A conventional, formulaic, and oversimplified conception, opinion, or image.

stimulus Something causing or regarded as causing a response.

straw man A fallacy in which a point of view is attacked by first creating a "straw man" version of the position and then "knocking down" the straw man created. The fallacy lies in that the straw man does not reflect an accurate representation of the position being challenged.

sweeping generalization A general conclusion reached that overlooks exceptions to the generalizations because of special features that the exceptions possess.

syllogism A form of deductive reasoning consisting of a major premise, a minor premise, and a conclusion.

symbolize To represent something else.

syntactic meaning A component of a word's total meaning which defines its relation to other words in the sentence.

synthesis The combining of separate elements or substances to form a coherent whole.

target population The entire group regarding which conclusions are drawn through statistical sampling and inductive reasoning.

testimony A declaration by a witness under oath, as that given before a court or deliberative body.

theist moral theory A theory of morality that holds that "right" and "wrong" are determined by a supernatural Supreme Being ("God").

theory A plausible or coherent scenario that has yet to be applied to experience. A set of statements or principles devised to explain a group of facts or phenomena, normally involving a number of interconnected hypotheses.

thesis A proposition that is maintained by argument; the issue on which an argument takes position.

thinking A purposeful, organized cognitive process that we use to understand the world and make informed decisions.

thinking creatively Using our thinking process to develop ideas that are unique, useful, and worthy of further elaboration.

thinking critically The cognitive process we use to carefully examine our thinking (and the thinking of others) in order to clarify and improve our understanding.

total meaning The meaning of a word believed by linguists to be composed of the semantic meaning, perceptual meaning, syntactic meaning, and pragmatic meaning.

two wrongs make a right A fallacy that attempts to justify a morally questionable action by arguing that it is a response to another wrong action, either real or imagined.

uninformed decision A decision that is the product of inaccurate information or inadequate experience.

unsound argument A deductive argument in which the premises are false, the logical structure is invalid, or both.

valid argument An argument in which the reasons support the conclusion so that the conclusion follows from the reasons offered.

values Beliefs regarding what is most important to us.

written references Evidence derived from the written opinions of another person; one of the four categories of evidence.

ACKNOWLEDGMENTS

(continued from page iv)

ILLUSTRATION ACKNOWLEDGMENTS

p. 3: Illustration by Warren Gebert

p. 5: Illustration by Warren Gebert

p. 12: Illustration by Warren Gebert

p. 21: Illustration by Warren Gebert

p. 30: Bob Daemmrich/Stock Boston

p. 39: Michael Newman/PhotoEdit

p. 43: J. Nourok/PhotoEdit

p. 53: Illustration by Warren Gebert

p. 58: Bob Daemmrich/Stock Boston

p. 68: Illustration by Warren Gebert

p. 73: Photo by Toshiyuki Aizawa, Reuters

p. 84: Illustration by Warren Gebert

p. 93: Illustration by Warren Gebert

p. 97: Illustration by Warren Gebert

p. 114: The Investigation © John Jonik. Reproduced with permission. This cartoon first appeared in *Psychology Today*, February 1984.

p. 116: George Mars Cassidy/The Picture Cube

p. 124: Jose Jimenez/Primera Hora/Getty Images

p. 135: Illustration by Warren Gebert

p. 151: Miro Vintoniv/Stock Boston

p. 159: Courtesy of Frankel Gallery, San Francisco and © The Estate of Gary Winogrand

p. 162: Illustration by Warren Gebert

p. 165: Illustration by Warren Gebert

p. 178: David McNew/Newsmaker

p. 192: Mark Mellett/Stock Boston

p. 204: Illustration by Warren Gebert

p. 238: Ernesto Bazan/Getty Images

p. 238: Alyssa Banta/Getty Images

p. 245: Illustration by Warren Gebert

p. 253: Illustration by Warren Gebert

p. 266: Stanley Milgram, 1972, by permission of Alexandra Milgram

p. 279: Illustration by Warren Gebert

p. 288: Illustration by Warren Gebert

p. 304: David Young Wolff/PhotoEdit

TEXT ACKNOWLEDGMENTS

Page 11: From *My American Journey* by Colin Powell with Joseph E. Persico, copyright © 1995 by Colin L. Powell. Used by permission of Random House, Inc.

Page 57: Thinking Activity 2.6, "Writing from Interactive Perspectives," by Frank Juszczyk of Western New Mexico University. Reprinted by permission of the author.

Page 72: "Liberty v. Security" from *The Economist*, September 29, 2001. Copyright © 2001 The Economist Newspaper Group, Inc. Reprinted with permission. Further reproduction prohibited. *www.economist.com*

Page 105: Lisa Haarlander, "Racism Creeps into Campus Lives," *The Digital Collegian*, January 30, 1996. Published independently by students at Penn State. Reprinted by permission.

Page 121: From *The New York Post*, February 22, 1965. Reprinted by permission.

Page 122: From *The Amsterdam News*, February 27, 1965. Reprinted by permission of N.Y. Amsterdam News.

Page 125: Hamburger Morgenpost, "The Cowardly Attack on the Heart of America." Reprinted by permission.

Page 127: From "America Awakes to Terrorism by Timetable and the Darkest National Catastrophe" by Michael Gove, *The Times*, London, 12th September 2001. © Times Newspapers Limited, 2001.

Page 184: Robert Coles, "The Disparity Between Intellect and Character," *The Chronicle of Higher Education*, September 22, 1995, p. A68.

Page 265: From "Critical Thinking and Obedience to Authority" by John Sabini and Maury Silver, reprinted from *National Forum: The Phi Kappa Phi Journal*, Winter 1985, pp. 13–17, by permission.

INDEX